Creating, Using and Linking of Parliamentary Corpora with Other Types of Political Discourse (ParlaCLARIN II)

Marseille, France
11-16 May 2020

Editors:

Darja Fišer
Maria Eskevich
Franciska de Jong

ISBN: 978-1-7138-1273-9

LREC 2020 Workshop
Language Resources and Evaluation Conference
11–16 May 2020

Creating, Using and Linking of Parliamentary Corpora with Other Types of Political Discourse (ParlaCLARIN II)

PROCEEDINGS

Editors: Darja Fišer, Maria Eskevich, Franciska de Jong

Proceedings of the LREC 2020 Workshop on Creating, Using and Linking of Parliamentary Corpora with Other Types of Political Discourse (ParlaCLARIN II)

Edited by: Darja Fišer, Maria Eskevich, Franciska de Jong

Acknowledgement: Organisation of the workshop is supported by CLARIN ERIC.
Workshop web site: https://www.clarin.eu/ParlaCLARIN-II

For more information:
European Language Resources Association (ELRA)
9 rue des Cordelières
75013, Paris
France
http://www.elra.info
Email: lrec@elda.org

Introduction

Parliamentary data is a major source of scholarly and socially relevant content. In line with the trend towards open access to digitised sources of materials from the public domain, parliamentary records are available in ever larger quantities and the number of languages for which such records are made public is also increasing. The materials are accompanied by rich metadata, and in addition there is the characteristic that the original spoken word sources, traditionally archived in transcribed form only, are now increasingly released also in audio and video formats. In linguistically and culturally diverse regions such as Europe there is harmonization of the data curation practices can advance the field significantly. As a result there is immense potential for developing models for collaborative work, comparative perspectives and multidisciplinary research, and we envision that the ParlaCLARIN II workshop will contribute to the further articulation of this agenda.

An inspiring and highly successful first edition of the ParlaCLARIN scientific workshop[1] was held at LREC 2018 and a follow-up developmental workshop was organized by CLARIN ERIC in 2019 under the name ParlaFormat[2]. These events led to a comprehensive overview[3] of a multitude of existing parliamentary resources worldwide as well as tangible first steps towards better harmonization, interoperability and comparability of the resources and tools relevant for the study of parliamentary discussions and decisions.

The second ParlaCLARIN workshop aims to broaden the scope of research questions that is enabled thanks to proposed data harmonisation approach, as well as to continue the effort of building a multidisciplinary community around parliamentary data by bringing together developers, curators and researchers of regional, national and international parliamentary debates that are suitable for research in disciplines in the Humanities and Social Sciences. We invited unpublished original work focusing on the compilation, annotation, visualisation and utilisation of parliamentary records as well as linking or comparing parliamentary records with other datasets of political discourse such as party manifestos, political speeches, political campaign debates, social media posts, etc. Apart from dissemination of the results, the workshop also addresses the identified obstacles, discusses open issues and coordinates future efforts in this increasingly trans-national and cross-disciplinary community.

The accepted papers address the following topics:

- Creation and annotation of parliamentary data in textual and spoken format

- Enrichment of parliamentary data with semantic and name entity tagging

- Querying and visualisation of parliamentary data

- Text mining over parliamentary and other political language data

- Comparative studies of parliamentary corpora

- Diachronic studies based on parliamentary corpora

The workshop programme is composed of a keynote talk by Pola Lehmann and Bernhard Weßels and 13 peer-reviewed papers by 30 authors from 10 countries.

---

[1] https://www.clarin.eu/ParlaCLARIN
[2] https://www.clarin.eu/event/2019/parlaformat-workshop
[3] https://www.clarin.eu/resource-families/parliamentary-corpora

We would like to thank the reviewers for their careful and constructive reviews which have contributed
to the quality of the event.

Due to the COVID-19 pandemic, the main conference is postponed, for this reason, there will be only a
virtual ParlaCLARIN II meeting in May 2020.

D. Fišer, M. Eskevich, F. de Jong   May 2020

Organizers:

Darja Fišer, University of Ljubljana and Jožef Stefan Institute, Slovenia
Franciska de Jong, CLARIN ERIC, The Netherlands
Maria Eskevich, CLARIN ERIC, The Netherlands

Program Committee:

Kaspar Beelen, The Alan Turing Institute, UK
Andreas Blätte, The University of Duisburg-Essen, Germany
Tomaž Erjavec, Jožef Stefan Institute, Slovenia
Francesca Frontini, Université Paul Valéry - Montpellier, France
Maria Gavriilidou, ILSP/Athena RC, Greece
Henk van den Heuvel, Radboud University, The Netherlands
Klaus Illmayer, Austrian Academy of Sciences, Austria
Bente Maegaard, CLARIN ERIC, The Netherlands
Monica Monachini, National Research Council of Italy, Italy
Laura Morales, Sciences Po, France
Jan Odijk, Utrecht University, The Netherlands
Maciej Ogrodniczuk, Institute of Computer Science, Polish Academy of Sciences, Poland
Petya Osenova, IICT-BAS and Sofia University "St. Kl. Ohridski", Bulgaria
Stelios Piperidis, ILSP/Athena RC, Greece
Maria Pontiki, ILSP/Athena RC, Greece
Simone Paolo Ponzetto, University of Mannheim, Germany
Sara Tonelli, Fondazione Bruno Kessler, Italy
Tamás Váradi, Hungarian Academy of Sciences, Hungary
Tanja Wissik, Austrian Academy of Sciences, Austria

Invited Speaker:

Pola Lehmann and Bernhard Weßels, Berlin Social Science Center (WZB), Germany

Workshop Program

Creation of parliamentary corpora

New Developments in the Polish Parliamentary Corpus
Maciej Ogrodniczuk and Bartłomiej Nitoń 1

Anföranden: Annotated and Augmented Parliamentary Debates from Sweden
Stian Rødven Eide 5

IGC-Parl: Icelandic Corpus of Parliamentary Proceedings
Steinþór Steingrímsson, Starkaður Barkarson and Gunnar Thor Örnólfsson 11

Compiling Czech Parliamentary Stenographic Protocols into a Corpus
Barbora Hladka, Matyáš Kopp and Pavel Straňák 18

Unfinished Business: Construction and Maintenance of a Semantically Tagged Historical Parliamentary Corpus, UK Hansard from 1803 to the present day
Matthew Coole, Paul Rayson and John Mariani 23

The siParl corpus of Slovene parliamentary proceedings
Andrej Pancur and Tomaž Erjavec 28

Tools for parliamentary corpora

Who mentions whom? Recognizing political actors in proceedings
Lennart Kerkvliet, Jaap Kamps and Maarten Marx 35

Challenges of Applying Automatic Speech Recognition for Transcribing EU Parliament Committee Meetings: A Pilot Study
Hugo de Vos and Suzan Verberne 40

Parsing Icelandic Alþingi Transcripts: Parliamentary Speeches as a Genre
Kristján Rúnarsson and Einar Freyr Sigurðsson 44

Investigations of parliamentary corpora

Identifying Parties in Manifestos and Parliament Speeches
Costanza Navarretta and Dorte Haltrup Hansen 51

Comparing Lexical Usage in Political Discourse across Diachronic Corpora
Klaus Hofmann, Anna Marakasova, Andreas Baumann, Julia Neidhardt and Tanja
Wissik 58

*The Europeanization of Parliamentary Debates on Migration in Austria, France,
Germany, and the Netherlands*
Andreas Blaette, Simon Gehlhar and Christoph Leonhardt 66

Querying a large annotated corpus of parliamentary debates
Sascha Diwersy and Giancarlo Luxardo 75

Proceedings of ParlaCLARIN II Workshop, pages 1–4
Language Resources and Evaluation Conference (LREC 2020), Marseille, 11–16 May 2020
© European Language Resources Association (ELRA), licensed under CC-BY-NC

New Developments in the Polish Parliamentary Corpus

Maciej Ogrodniczuk, Bartłomiej Nitoń

Institute of Computer Science, Polish Academy of Sciences
Warsaw, Poland
maciej.ogrodniczuk@ipipan.waw.pl, bartek.niton@gmail.com

Abstract

This short paper presents the current (as of February 2020) state of preparation of the Polish Parliamentary Corpus (PPC) — an extensive collection of transcripts of Polish parliamentary proceedings dating from 1919 to present. The most evident developments as compared to the 2018 version is harmonization of metadata, standardization of document identifiers, uploading contents of all documents and metadata to the database (to enable easier modification, maintenance and future development of the corpus), linking utterances to the political ontology, linking corpus texts to source data and processing historical documents.

Keywords: written corpora, quasi-spoken data, parliament transcripts, Polish

1. Introduction

The Polish Parliamentary Corpus[1] (Ogrodniczuk, 2018) is a collection of proceedings of Polish parliament dating from 1919 to present. It includes transcripts of Sejm sittings (including Legislative Sejm and State National Council), Sejm committee sittings from 1993, Sejm interpellations and questions from 1997, Senate sittings from 1922–1939 and 1989 to present[2] and Senate committee sittings from 2015. The collection is consequently updated with the most current data acquired from the Sejm and the Senate web portals. Currently the size of the textual data in the corpus amounts to over 340 thousand documents and almost 750 million tokens.

The data features annotation following the National Corpus of Polish (Przepiórkowski et al., 2012, NKJP)[3] (Przepiórkowski et al., 2012) TEI P5 XML format and conventions. Paragraph-, sentence- and token-level segmentation, lemmatization and morphosyntactic description was automatically produced with Morfeusz2 (Kieraś and Woliński, 2017) and disambiguated with Concraft2 (Waszczuk et al., 2018). The named entity layer was produced with Liner2 (Marcińczuk et al., 2013) and the dependency annotation layer with COMBO (Rybak and Wróblewska, 2018).

2. Corpus improvements

Apart from the main improvement consisting in adding new data (see Table 1 for detailed statistics) several improvements have been made in the corpus.

Harmonization of metadata The basic list of metadata for all document types (plenary sittings, committee sittings and questions) was set to comprise document title, publisher (Sejm or Senate), political system (Second Polish Republic — 1918–1939, Polish People's Republic — 1945–1989, the transition period with the Contract Sejm — 1989–1991 and the current Third Republic — from 1991 to present day), chamber (Sejm, Senate or the National Council), term of office, document type and the major date of the source.

Assignment of historical documents to the term of office was also adjusted, the information on the regime and chamber has been added, document names have been standardized and several naming errors corrected. Missing information on speakers has been filled in and the corpus header has been updated.

Standardization of document identifiers The corpus has been divided into 27 periods corresponding to the terms of office of chambers in three different political systems of Poland in the last 100 years (see rows of Table 1).

All identifiers of documents have been standardized reflecting the logical structure of the system:

```
191922- sjm -ppxxx- 00002 - 01
         ↓     ↓       ↓      ↓       ↓
      period chamber  type sitting/number day/part
```

Database development The contents of all documents and metadata have been uploaded to a specifically developed database to enable easier modification, maintenance and future development of the corpus.

The current size of the corpus amounts to 749M segments with detailed distribution over houses, periods, and document types presented in Table 1. Apart from the stenographic records of plenary sittings (261M segments) and committee sittings (288M segments), the corpus contains 199M segments of interpellations and questions.

Linking utterances to the political ontology The Polish Political Ontology[4] (PPO) is an RDF resource created in 2015 and modelling the Polish political scene of the period 1989–2014. It includes significant actors based in Polish political and other public institutions, including members

---

[1]Pol. Korpus Dyskursu Parlamentarnego, see `clip.ipipan.waw.pl/PPC`.

[2]The gap results from the fact that the Senate was abolished by the authorities of the Polish People's Republic and re-established after the reinstatement of democracy after the collapse of the communist government.

[3]Pol. Narodowy Korpus Języka Polskiego, see `http://nkjp.pl`.

[4]`http://zil.ipipan.waw.pl/PolishPoliticalOntology`

System	Years	Period	Sittings		Committees		Interpellations	
			docs	segments	docs	segments	docs	segments
Second Polish Republic	1919–1922	Legislative Sejm	312	6 945 162	–	–	–	–
	1922–1927	1st term of office	277	7 338 355	–	–	–	–
	1928–1930	2nd	58	2 139 835	–	–	–	–
	1930–1935	3rd	72	2 404 267	–	–	–	–
	1935–1938	4th	73	2 133 181	–	–	–	–
	1938–1939	5th	23	610 455	–	–	–	–
	1943–1947	State National Council	6	234 441	–	–	–	–
People's Poland	1947–1952	Legislative Sejm	107	2 575 136	–	–	–	–
	1952–1956	1st term of office	39	1 172 333	–	–	–	–
	1957–1961	2nd	59	2 502 936	–	–	–	–
	1961–1965	3rd	32	1 388 862	–	–	–	–
	1965–1969	4th	23	1 163 336	–	–	–	–
	1969–1972	5th	17	526 277	–	–	–	–
	1972–1976	6th	32	1 176 712	–	–	–	–
	1976–1980	7th	29	918 993	–	–	–	–
	1980–1985	8th	70	3 377 139	–	–	–	–
	1985–1989	9th	45	2 641 788	–	–	–	–
Third Polish Republic	1989–1991	10th	77	6 674 111	–	–	–	–
	1991–1993	1st term of office	142	7 739 147	–	–	–	–
	1993–1997	2nd	317	22 134 682	3 858	41 756 476	–	–
	1997–2001	3rd	320	24 138 142	4 691	42 510 604	23 507	12 101 453
	2001–2005	4th	337	28 743 846	4 945	49 302 521	30 986	17 519 177
	2005–2007	5th	148	11 737 186	2 359	18 970 036	26 689	14 777 377
	2007–2011	6th	298	22 415 708	5 565	44 363 063	59 353	36 412 001
	2011–2015	7th	292	20 765 505	5 126	38 541 083	85 679	61 565 989
	2015–2019	8th	239	19 131 000	4 561	36 708 873	79 194	56 720 590

System	Years	Period	Sittings		Committees	
			documents	segments	documents	segments
Second Polish Republic	1922–1927	1st term	96	1 979 541	–	–
	1928–1930	2nd	3	171 345	–	–
	1930–1935	3rd	64	1 804 635	–	–
	1935–1938	4th	29	724 687	–	–
	1938–1939	5th	20	347 430	–	–
Third Polish Republic	1989–1991	1st term	60	3 170 293	–	–
	1991–1993	2nd	48	1 459 440	–	–
	1993–1997	3rd	125	5 051 677	–	–
	1997–2001	4th	187	8 255 897	–	–
	2001–2005	5th	175	6 485 347	–	–
	2005–2007	6th	74	3 571 293	–	–
	2007–2011	7th	167	8 819 116	–	–
	2011–2015	8th	159	7 100 841	–	–
	2015–2019	9th	204	9 554 544	2 156	15 645 801
	2019–	10th	9	412 279	82	505 991

Table 1: Statistics of the Polish Parliamentary Corpus (2020)

of government and the parliament. Specifically, it contains information about the MPs (their gender, functions, terms of office, political affiliation) and political parties.

The corpus data, previously marked with speaker names only, was linked to the PPO by extending the `particDesc` section in TEI header files (`header.xml`) of individual documents of the corpus. Links were represented as pointers (`ptr` elements) to functions in PPO (see Fig. 2.).

Linking corpus texts to source data Corpus data have been updated with links to the original materials which were used as source of text, i.e.:

- websites from which the text of individual documents has been extracted

- websites from which the metadata for the document concerned has been extracted

- records of meetings in PDF format.

In order to prevent a possible loss of access to the source files (e.g. due to changes in parliamentary services) the source files were additionally downloaded to store their copies locally.

The process has been completed with a number of Internet robots browsing respective websites, separately for docu-

```
<teiHeader ...>
  ...
  <profileDesc>
    <particDesc>
      ...
      <person xml:id="PrezesRadyMinistrowDonaldTusk" role="speaker">
        <persName>The Prime Minister Donald Tusk</persName>
        <linkGrp type="function">
          <ptr target="http://legis.nlp.ipipan.waw.pl/onto/ppo.owl
                    #Donald_Franciszek_Tusk__Sejm6"/>
          <ptr target="http://legis.nlp.ipipan.waw.pl/onto/ppo.owl
                    #Donald_Tusk_2051"/>
          <ptr target="http://legis.nlp.ipipan.waw.pl/onto/ppo.owl
                    #Donald_Tusk_280"/>
        </linkGrp>
      </person>
    </particDesc>
  </profileDesc>
</teiHeader>
```

Figure 1: Representation of pointers to Polish Political Ontology in TEI header

ments between 1919 and 1997 as well as terms of office 2–6, 7–8 and 9 (due to changes in IT systems used in these periods). The processing consisted of keeping the URL address of the document source, the URL address of a file containing the content of the document, usually in PDF format and the address of the page containing document metadata.

Processing historical documents Due to changes in Polish ortography in 1936 modern tools are not always very successful with processing older data. To overcome this problem, a transcriber for historical documents and a customized version of morphological analyzer have been included in the process of linguistic analysis of 1027 documents between 1919 and 1939.

The processing pipeline consists of:

1. a rule transcriber[5] with a set of rules for nineteenth-century language[6] (Kieraś et al., 2017) (the original text is preserved in the database)

2. Morfeusz2 morphological analyzer using SGJP dictionary extended with vocabulary of the 19th century (Kieraś and Woliński, 2018) but with a set of tags consistent with contemporary vocabulary

3. Concraft2 tagger (no additional modifications)

4. Liner2 (no additional modifications);

5. COMBO (no additional modifications).

3.   MTAS-based search engine

The previous searchable version of the corpus was made available as Poliqarp (Janus and Przepiórkowski, 2006) search engine binary (to be run on user's computer) and a Poliqarp-powered simple online search engine was available to facilitate search in a familiar NKJP-like interface. Still, one of the major faults of Poliqarp was inability to combine search over different annotation layers.

To overcome this flaw, a new framework for building search engines was created based on MTAS (Brouwer et al., 2017), a stable and reliable solution for multi-layered linguistic search, currently also used for other corpora of Polish[7]. MTAS offers rich search functions, using regular expressions, filtering results using metadata or merging of analytical layers.

Figure 3. presents a sample search result linking the morphological analysis layer with named entity layer: proper names identical with common names can be easily filtered.

4.   Current and future work

The processing of the corpus is ongoing on many levels, starting with adding new historical data (transcripts of committee meetings before 1989).

Several 'administrative' tasks are also envisaged, starting from processing of corpus data with new versions of linguistic tools made available in the recent months. They are e.g. newest version of Morfeusz2, Concraft2 or COMBO parser, providing dependency trees.

Even though the manual correction of OCR-ed data has been successful, there are still numerous typos in this data, mostly due to poor quality of originals before 1989. To overcome this problem, new methods for automated discovery of errors in the texts will be developed, such as investigation of words unrecognized by the morphological analyser or detection of non-standard character ngrams. Related to this task is implementation of mechanisms that trigger linguistic analysis and re-indexation of corrected data after changes have been approved by an authorized user.

---

[5]`https://bitbucket.org/jsbien/pol`
[6]`http://chronofleks.nlp.ipipan.waw.pl/
static/files/reguly_xixw.zip`

[7]See e.g. the 1 million subcorpus of NKJP (`http://nkjp.
nlp.ipipan.waw.pl/`), the Electronic Corpus of 17th and 18th century Polish Texts (`http://korba.edu.pl/`) Corpus of 19th Century Polish (`http://korpus19.nlp.ipipan.
waw.pl/`) or the Polish Coreference Corpus `http://pcc.
nlp.ipipan.waw.pl/`

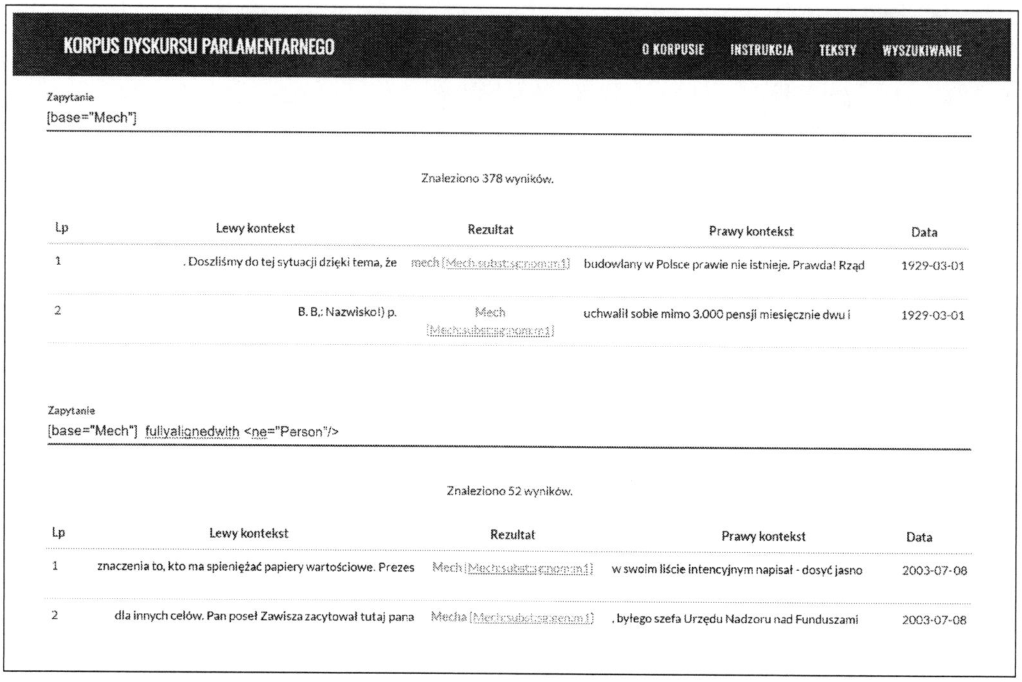

Figure 2: Sample search result in the corpus

Acknowledgements

The work reported here was financed as part of the investment in the CLARIN-PL research infrastructure funded by the Polish Ministry of Science and Higher Education.

Bibliographical references

Brouwer, M., Brugman, H., and Kemps-Snijders, M. (2017). MTAS: A Solr/Lucene based Multi Tier Annotation Search solution. In *Selected papers from the CLARIN Annual Conference 2016. Linköping Electronic Conference Proceedings 136*, pages 19–37. Linköping University Electronic Press.

Janus, D. and Przepiórkowski, A. (2006). Poliqarp 1.0: Some technical aspects of a linguistic search engine for large corpora. In Jacek Waliński, et al., editors, *Proceedings of Practical Applications of Linguistic Corpora 2005 conference*, Frankfurt am Main. Peter Lang.

Kieraś, W. and Woliński, M. (2017). Morfeusz 2 – analizator i generator fleksyjny dla języka polskiego. *Język Polski*, XCVII(1):75–83.

Kieraś, W. and Woliński, M. (2018). Manually annotated corpus of Polish texts published between 1830 and 1918. In Nicoletta Calzolari, et al., editors, *Proceedings of the Eleventh International Conference on Language Resources and Evaluation (LREC 2018)*, pages 3854–3859, Paris, France. European Language Resources Association (ELRA).

Kieraś, W., Komosińska, D., Modrzejewski, E., and Woliński, M. (2017). Morphosyntactic annotation of historical texts. The making of the baroque corpus of Polish. In Kamil Ekštein et al., editors, *Text, Speech, and Dialogue 20th International Conference, TSD 2017, Prague, Czech Republic, August 27-31, 2017, Proceedings*, number 10415 in Lecture Notes in Computer Science, pages 308–316. Springer International Publishing.

Marcińczuk, M., Kocoń, J., and Janicki, M. (2013). Liner2 — A Customizable Framework for Proper Names Recognition for Polish. In Robert Bembenik, et al., editors, *Intelligent Tools for Building a Scientific Information Platform*, volume 467 of *Studies in Computational Intelligence*, pages 231–253. Springer-Verlag, Cham, Heidelberg, New York, Dordrecht, London.

Ogrodniczuk, M. (2018). Polish Parliamentary Corpus. In Darja Fišer, et al., editors, *Proceedings of the LREC 2018 Workshop* ParlaCLARIN: Creating and Using Parliamentary Corpora, pages 15–19, Paris, France. European Language Resources Association (ELRA).

Przepiórkowski, A., Bańko, M., Górski, R. L., and Lewandowska-Tomaszczyk, B. (2012). *Narodowy Korpus Języka Polskiego*. Wydawnictwo Naukowe PWN, Warszawa.

Rybak, P. and Wróblewska, A. (2018). Semi-supervised Neural System for Tagging, Parsing and Lematization. In *Proceedings of the CoNLL 2018 Shared Task: Multilingual Parsing from Raw Text to Universal Dependencies*, pages 45–54, Brussels, Belgium, October. Association for Computational Linguistics.

Waszczuk, J., Kieraś, W., and Woliński, M. (2018). Morphosyntactic disambiguation and segmentation for historical Polish with graph-based conditional random fields. In Petr Sojka, et al., editors, *Text, Speech, and Dialogue: 21st International Conference, TSD 2018, Brno, Czech Republic, September 11-14, 2018, Proceedings*, number 11107 in Lecture Notes in Artificial Intelligence, pages 188–196. Springer-Verlag.

Proceedings of ParlaCLARIN II Workshop, pages 5–10
Language Resources and Evaluation Conference (LREC 2020), Marseille, 11–16 May 2020
© European Language Resources Association (ELRA), licensed under CC-BY-NC

Anföranden: Annotated and Augmented Parliamentary Debates from Sweden

Stian Rødven Eide
Språkbanken Text, Department of Swedish
University of Gothenburg
stian.rodven.eide@svenska.gu.se

Abstract

The Swedish parliamentary debates have been available since 2010 through the parliament's open data web site *Riksdagens öppna data*. While fairly comprehensive, the structure of the data can be hard to understand and its content is somewhat noisy for use as a quality language resource. In order to make it easier to use and process – in particular for language technology research, but also for political science and other fields with an interest in parliamentary data – we have published a large selection of the debates in a cleaned and structured format, annotated with linguistic information and augmented with semantic links. Especially prevalent in the parliament's data were end-line hyphenations – something that tokenisers generally are not equipped for – and a lot of the effort went into resolving these. In this paper, we provide detailed descriptions of the structure and contents of the resource, and explain how it differs from the parliament's own version.

Keywords: parliamentary data, Swedish, NLP, speech, politics, language resource

1. Introduction

Since the freedom of information acts started becoming implemented in various countries, we have seen a plethora of parliamentary corpora being released and enhanced, by governments as well as researchers. Significant corpora have been published e.g. from the parliaments of Norway (Lapponi et al., 2018), Slovenia (Pančur et al., 2018) and the UK (Nanni et al., 2018), to name but a few.

This paper presents and describes a corpus of Swedish parliamentary debates that has been adapted from the parliament's data. In order to make it easier for further research on this data – the government's own version has also been somewhat underdocumented – we have devoted section 2 to a detailed description of the content and structure of the corpus and the accompanying metadata. In section 3 we present our improvements to the resource, in particular the handling of prevalent end-line hyphenations.

The word *anförande* (plural: *anföranden*) refers to any entry in the Swedish parliamentary debates. While the most reasonable translation into English is *speech*, an *anförande* in this context can also be a short reply to a previous speech. For the remainder of this article, however, we will use the term *speech* for all debate entries, and *anföranden* only when referring to the resource as a whole.

2. Content and structure of the corpus

The Swedish parliament has published minutes for all parliamentary debates from 1971 and onward.[1] These files are derived from scans of printed or typed documents and the large amount of HTML formatting present in the files are only for preserving layout; it does not generally segment the text in a way that helps with parsing. Metadata is restricted to document level information, and as such does not say anything about which speakers participate or which topics are being discussed.

However, all debates from 1993 and onward are also available in a separate dataset aptly named *anföranden*, where each speech is complemented with appropriate metadata such as speaker, party, topic and speech order.[2] This is the resource that we have enhanced.

2.1. Resource size and contents

After removing 20 empty documents from the parliament's data, we have 325,202 speeches, the speech texts of our cleaned version containing 122,079,937 tokens as measured with the Spacy tokeniser.[3] This gives an average of 375.4 tokens per speech.

To get a better sense of the contents of the resource, we refer to table 1. The property *kammaraktivitet* (chamber activity) in each document provides an indication to the context of the text. Unfortunately, this is not applied entirely consistently across all documents. For instance, questions to the prime minister can be found under both *statsministerns frågestund* and *frågestund med statsministern*. More importantly, however, most of the regular debates have no value for this property; they are in the table listed as *None*. On the other hand, some of them do have a label; most of the categories whose descriptions contain the word *debatt* are the types of regular debates that also dominate the category *None*. For any research pertaining strictly to the debates, our recommendation is therefore to exclude the categories we know are not debates rather than vice versa.

2.2. Document structure

In table 2, we show the complete structure of a typical speech document. In our version of the corpus, all properties except for *anförandetext* (speech text) are XML attributes of the speech as a whole. These attributes have been transferred directly from the parliament's data, with the exception of *dok_datum* which erroneously listed all parliamentary sessions as having taken place at midnight; for this reason, we removed the time stamp from the data, leaving only the dates, which are correct.

---

[1] http://data.riksdagen.se/data/dokument/

[2] http://data.riksdagen.se/data/anforanden/

[3] https://spacy.io/

Type	Amount
None	139,446
interpellationsdebatt *interpellation debate*	61,781
föredragning av utskottsärende *presentation of committee report*	58,381
frågestund *question time*	20,975
ärendedebatt *legislative debate*	16,947
allmänpolitisk debatt *general policy debate*	7,906
partiledardebatt *party leader debate*	3,616
frågestund med statsministern *Prime Minister's question time*	2,878
aktuell debatt *topcial debate*	2,601
information från regeringen *information from the government*	2,411
bordläggning *tabling*	1,441
val *election*	1,306
utrikespolitisk debatt *foreign policy debate*	1,241
statsministerns frågestund *Prime Minister's question time*	1,098
debatt vid allmän debattimme *hour of general debate*	858
särskild debatt *special debate*	536
avgörande av utskottsärende *decision on committee proposal*	512
budgetdebatt *budgetary debate*	401
meddelande *message*	323
hänvisning till utskott *referral to committee*	236
avlämnande av regeringsförklaring *submission of government declaration*	72
återupptagning av förhandlingarna *resumption of negotiations*	67
ceremoni *ceremony*	47
beslutsfattande om uppdrag *assignment decision*	46
återrapportering *report*	36
anmälan *notification*	31
riksmötets öppnande *parliamentary opening*	6
regeringsförklaring *declaration of government*	2
hälsningsanförande *welcoming speech*	1

Table 1: Types of parliamentary activity.

Property	Description
dok_hangar_id	Internal document ID
dok_id	Meeting + speech no.
dok_titel	Protocol title
dok_rm	Parliamentary year
dok_nummer	Number of meeting
dok_datum	Date of speech
avsnittsrubrik	Topic title
kammaraktivitet	Type of debate
anforande_id	Unique speech ID
anforande_nummer	Speech number in debate
talare	Speaker name
parti	Speaker party
anforandetext	Full speech text
intressent_id	Speaker's ID
rel_dok_id	Document being debated
replik	Speech type
systemdatum	Date of publishing

Table 2: A typical speech document.

- **dok_hangar_id** is a unique and strictly numerical ID which is assigned to every document in the parliament's database. It is not referenced in other documents, however, and can normally be safely ignored.

- **dok_id** is a unique ID (different from dok_hangar_id) assigned to every document in the parliament's database. In contrast to the above, dok_id is alphanumeric and referenced by other documents. Its form is derived from a set of codes that signify the time and type of the document. The two first characters refer to the parliamentary period in which the document was created, the third and fourth characters refer to the type category to which the document belongs, while the remaining characters signify a category subtype and/or number within its category. In this dataset, the category is consistently 09, meaning *minutes from the chamber*, with the subsequent digits representing the chronological number of the meeting within the parliamentary year, corresponding to dok_nummer below. A more detailed description of the dok_id format is available on the Swedish parliament website.[4]

- **dok_titel** is a human readable label that for this dataset consistently states that it is the minutes from a given parliamentary session. While it does contain an hour / minute time reference, this refers to the time of the session and not of individual speeches during the session.

- **dok_rm** refers to the parliamentary period. Since the autumn of 1975, a parliamentary period lasts from the beginning of an autumn until the end of spring the following year. The format used here is e.g. 2015/16.

- **dok_nummer** is the chronological number of the parliamentary session within a parliamentary year.

---

[4]http://data.riksdagen.se/dokumentation/
sa-funkar-dokument-id/

- **dok_datum** refers to the date of the parliamentary session, using the format YYYY-MM-DD.

- **avsnittsrubrik** is a text label that for debates generally is informative, describing what is being debated. During a parliamentary session, it is common that several topics are debated, each usually from the premise of a proposal pertaining to legal or budgetary matters. The exact proposal being discussed is referenced by rel_dok_id below, while this label ranges from general topics such as 'climate politics' to rather specific ones such as 'increased possibilities of travelling within the European Union using national identity cards'. Not all categories of parliamentary activity feature an informative label, however; e.g. question time or debates between party leaders are only labelled with their respective categories as listed in table 1.

- **kammaraktivitet** refers to the type of parliamentary activity, as we described above in section 2.1 and listed in table 1.

- **anforande_id** is another unique alphanumeric ID assigned to each speech. As with dok_hangar_id, this is currently not referenced by other documents in the parliamentary database.

- **talare** is a string containing the name and party affiliation of the current speaker. For acting ministers, their title is usually also included, e.g. 'Finansministern Magdalena Andersson (S)'

- **parti** is a string containing only the party affiliation of the current speaker. This is listed using the common abbreviations for Swedish political parties, all currently with one or two letters.

- **anforandetext** is the transcribed speech.

- **intressent_id** is a unique ID number for the speaker. Each member of parliament since 1990 (as well as some before that) is assigned an ID of this type. This can be used to cross-reference with other data sources, as we will demonstrate later.

- **rel_dok_id** is a reference to the dok_id of whatever document is being discussed. Usually, what is being debated is some kind of proposal, from the parliament, the government, or from a commission. The formal document detailing this proposal features the dok_id referenced here. As such, it can be cross-referenced with a database containing proposals. Also, for many purposes of linguistic mining or classification, it can be more reliable as a topic than the avsnittsrubrik mentioned above.

- **replik** is a binary string, 'Y' if the speech is of the type *replik* (reply), 'N' if not. While many of the speeches not marked as *replik* may also contain or be regarded as replies to previous speeches, a *replik* is subject to slightly different rules than other speeches, the most significant being that they are much shorter.

- **systemdatum** refers to the date and time when the document was published to the parliament's database.

3. Processing the corpus

In this section, we detail our effort to improve the resource.

3.1. Cleaning

Although the digitisation of the Swedish parliamentary debates has involved optical character recognition (OCR) as part of the process, our relatively thorough manual investigation found that the result is, for the most part, excellent. There are very few typos or other indications of OCR errors. However, one particularly visible result of this process is the abundant prevalence of end-line hyphenations.

Generally, end-line hyphenation has been ignored by tokenisers, as they do not know whether to join the tokens together as a single word, join them as a hyphenated compound, or leave it as a hanging hyphen (used in elliptical constructions of a conjunction of several terms) (Grefenstette and Tapanainen, 1994; Frunza, 2008).

The commonly used tokenisers, most notably the widely used Stanford tokeniser, ignore this problem (Manning et al., 2014), and while projects such as Dridan and Oepen (2012) and Graën et al. (2018) suggest useful improvements in the area, the focus is on multi-lingual approaches which would have a hard time capturing the variety of Swedish compounds.

Due to Swedish compounding rules, where basically any number of nouns can be joined together, a pure dictionary approach is insufficient, and parliamentary debates in particular do contain a lot of hanging hyphens. This means that from the outset, a rule based approach to fixing end-line hyphenation needs to account for language specific features and preferably be complemented by manual corrections in order to reach a high accuracy.

One solution is of course to ignore them and treat them as noise, which often makes sense for large corpora where the amount of end-line hyphenation is negligible. For our anföranden, however, we found that not only were they especially prevalent, but that it often is longer low-frequency words that have been split. Such words can make a significant difference in several methods for information retrieval, text mining, and user modelling, which often use term frequency–inverse document frequency (tf-idf) or similar term weighting systems (Beel et al., 2016).

We therefore devised a rule-based method, which combined corpus look-up with hand-crafted rules and an interactive query allowing for simple manual correction of those cases that could not be resolved automatically. The procedure was as follows:

1. Generate a word frequency list from the resource. This will be used to decide whether line-end hyphenations should be kept or joined, with or without a hyphen.

2. Remove all line breaks. The reason for doing this instead of keeping the line break as a signifying feature is that there were several cases of end-line hyphenation in-line, indicating either OCR errors or several layers of OCR processing having been done.

3. Filter out all cases where the word after the hyphen is a conjunction. These cases are almost certainly part of an elliptical construction and should be kept as is.

Conjunction	English	Amount
och	and	90,025
eller	or	3,225
som	as	1,848
men	but	1,379
samt	and	744
till	to	186
respektive	respectively	172
än	yet	35
utan	without	6
såväl	as well as	7
og	and (Norwegian)	4
und	and (German)	4
kontra	versus	3
framför	before	2
liksom	as	2
snart	soon	1
inklusive	inclusive	1
o	and (shortened)	1
SUM		97,645

Table 3: Conjunctions in elliptical componds.

An overview of the frequency of the different conjunctions in elliptical compounds of several terms in the resource can be found in table 3.

4. Use regular expression matching to identify structures that almost certainly should be hyphenated compounds. These are:

   (a) All characters before the hyphen are upper-case and all characters after the hyphen are lower-case. This indicates an acronym used as a semantic qualifier.

   (b) The words before and after the hyphen are both capitalised. This indicates a proper name, which for some people and organisations is hyphenated in Swedish.

   (c) All characters before the hyphen are numerals, while the characters after the hyphen are not. This is common in Swedish, e.g. for time references such as *1990-talet*, 'the 1990s'.

   (d) The word *icke*, 'not', is particular to Swedish for requiring a hyphen when used as a prefix.

An overview of these can be seen in table 4.

5. Generate two word forms comprising all characters before and after the hyphen, one joined with hyphen and one joined without. Check whether any or both of these are present in the word frequency list. If only one is present, choose that. If both are present, choose the one that is most frequent. If both are either missing or equally frequent, ask the user what to do.

6. Whenever a selection has been made, either by the heuristics or the user, save that selection and apply it to subsequent identical cases.

Regular expression	Unique	Total
(a) [A-ZÅÄÖ]+- [a-zåäö]+	2,527	7,740
(b) [A-ZÅÄÖ][a-zåäö]+- [A-ZÅÄÖ][a-zåäö]+	338	1,560
(c) \d+- \w+	949	2,802
(d) icke- \w+	162	283
SUM	3,976	12,385

Table 4: Hyphenated compounds matched with regular expressions.

The overall statistics are presented in table 5. Please also note that we have no way of distinguishing between end-line hyphenations and elliptical compound constructions with a hanging hyphen prior to processing. The latter are therefore included in the number of end-line hyphenations in the table.

Property	Unique	Total
Files		325,202
Tokens (before processing)		123,261,960
Tokens (after processing)		122,079,937
Files with no ELH		180,350
Number of ELH		1,080,471
Ignored ELH due to conjunctions		97,645
H from regular expressions	3,976	12,385
Only J in WF	97,698	904,172
Only H in WF	519	1,091
J more frequent in WF	604	44,887
H more frequent in WF	124	971
J manually selected	8,509	8,908
H manually selected	397	433
Keep manually selected	111	116

Table 5: Statistics of the end-line hyphenation processing. For the purposes of fitting the table into one column we have abbreviated *end-line hyphenation* (ELH), *hyphenated compound* (H), *compound without hyphen* (J) and *word frequency list* (WF).

As we can see, even after subtracting the elliptical compound constructions, we end up with 982,826 end-line hyphenations, comprising 0.8% of the tokens. This puts them in line with frequent prepositions; the word *med*, 'with', occurs 1,090,275 times in the data. We can also see that the strategy of looking up in the word frequency list was very effective, capturing 96.77% of the remaining end-line hyphenations.

In order to test the accuracy of this process, we chose 1,000 random items from the set of selections that were made and assessed them manually. Of the 1,000 choices our system made, we only found a single error, indicating an accurracy of 99.9%.

Our de-hyphenator has been published on GitLab under the GNU GPLv3.[5]

---

[5] https://gitlab.com/Julipan/swedish-de-hyphenator

3.2. Annotating

After cleaning the end-line hyphenations, we imported the resulting files into Korp, via the Sparv pipeline. Korp is a tool for searching and exploring corpora (Borin et al., 2012), while Sparv is the annotation pipeline through which most of the corpora in Korp are processed (Borin et al., 2016). Both of the tools are developed and maintained by Språkbanken Text, a language technology research unit under the department of Swedish at the University of Gothenburg.[6]

The linguistic annotation provided by Sparv is thorough and multifaceted, ranging from part-of-speech and word sense to compound and dependency analyses. A complete list of the available annotations can be found on the Sparv web page and its user manual.[7][8] The annotated anföranden can be explored at `https://spraakbanken.gu.se/korp/?mode=default#?corpus=rd-anf` and XML files can be downloaded from `https://spraakbanken.gu.se/en/resources/rd-anf`.

3.3. Augmenting

For use with the annotated anföranden, we previously created the Swedish PoliGraph, a Prolog application designed for querying and exploring Swedish members of parliament, along with their roles and activity in parliament and government (Rødven Eide, 2019).

One of the use-cases we envision is to explore speeches based on speaker metadata. Combining anföranden with the Swedish PoliGraph, we can examine questions such as which linguistic features are more common among which speakers or parties, who speaks more or less on which topics, or how commission work affects the speeches of members of parliament.

Seeing as we have exact temporal metadata for both speakers and speeches, the corpus can also be examined diachronically. We can examine how speeches change over time, for instance in the context of an individual speaker from newly elected to established, of a party changing their rhetoric in response to external events or internal conditions, or of changing attitudes as the years go by.

For further augmentation, we have also matched the internal parliamentary ID for each politician with their respective Wiki-ID's in the Swedish PoliGraph. This enables exploration of connections from politicians and speeches with data that is not part of the parliament's database, but can be found on Wikipedia or Wikidata, or other resources that use the same references.

4. Conclusion and future work

Considering the importance and availability of parliamentary data in Swedish, as well as its practical advantages for natural language processing methods – in particular the standardised language and precise metadata – very little research has taken full advantage of these resources. We hope that the publication of *anföranden*, in a cleaned, annotated and augmented form, will be a step towards further investigation of parliamentary speech in Swedish.

As part of a Swe-Clarin project on named entity recognition (NER), our next step is to manually annotate named entities in speeches from the anföranden corpus. We will then apply and evaluate various algorithms to find the current state of NER on Swedish parliamentary debates, and see if we can improve the current state of the art further.

After that, we plan to perform named entity resolution to the recognised entities, automatically linking names of politicians found in the text to their respective ID in the Swedish PoliGraph. The aim is to be able to model a complete parliamentary debate; to understand and visualise who is replying to whom.

Following the 2019 ParlaFormat Workshop in Amersfoort,[9] we will also implement export to the Parla-CLARIN XML format from Korp, after a planned upgrade of the export pipeline of Språkbanken Text is in place.

As our de-hyphenator turned out to be successful, we also plan to incorporate it in Språkbanken Texts import pipeline as an optional pre-processing step.

5. Acknowledgements

The work presented here has been partly supported by an infrastructure grant to Språkbanken Text, University of Gothenburg, for contributing to building and operating a national e-infrastructure funded jointly by the Swedish Research Council (under contract no. 2017-00626) and the participating institutions.

We also give a heartfelt thanks to the reviewers, who provided us with a lot of constructive suggestions for improvement.

6. Bibliographical References

Beel, J., Gipp, B., Langer, S., and Breitinger, C. (2016). Research-paper recommender systems: a literature survey. *International Journal on Digital Libraries*, 17(4):305–338, Nov.

Borin, L., Forsberg, M., and Roxendal, J. (2012). Korp – the corpus infrastructure of Språkbanken. In *Proceedings of LREC 2012*, page 474–478, Istanbul, Turkey. ELRA.

Borin, L., Forsberg, M., Hammarstedt, M., Rosén, D., Schäfer, R., and Schumacher, A. (2016). Sparv: Språkbanken's corpus annotation pipeline infrastructure. In *SLTC 2016. The Sixth Swedish Language Technology Conference, Umeå University, 17-18 November, 2016*.

Dridan, R. and Oepen, S. (2012). Tokenization: Returning to a long solved problem — A survey, contrastive experiment, recommendations, and toolkit. In *Proceedings of the 50th Annual Meeting of the Association for Computational Linguistics (Volume 2: Short Papers)*, pages 378–382, Jeju Island, Korea. Association for Computational Linguistics.

Frunza, O. (2008). A trainable tokenizer, solution for multilingual texts and compound expression tokenization.

---

[6]`https://spraakbanken.gu.se/`

[7]`https://spraakbanken.gu.se/en/tools/sparv/annotations`

[8]`https://spraakbanken.gu.se/en/tools/sparv/usermanual`

[9]`https://www.clarin.eu/event/2019/parlaformat-workshop`

In *Proceedings of LREC 2008*, Marrakech, Morocco. ELRA. http://www.lrec-conf.org/proceedings/lrec2008/.

Graën, J., Bertamini, M., and Volk, M. (2018). Cutter – a universal multilingual tokenizer. In *Proceedings of the 3rd Swiss Text Analytics Conference – SwissText 2018*, pages 75–81, Winterthur, Switzerland.

Grefenstette, G. and Tapanainen, P. (1994). What is a word, what is a sentence? Problems of tokenization. In *The 3rd International Conference on Computational Lexicography*, pages 79–87, Budapest, Hungary.

Lapponi, E., Søyland, M. G., Velldal, E., and Oepen, S. (2018). The talk of Norway: a richly annotated corpus of the Norwegian parliament, 1998–2016. *Language Resources and Evaluation*, 52(3):873–893.

Manning, C. D., Surdeanu, M., Bauer, J., Finkel, J., Bethard, S. J., and McClosky, D. (2014). The Stanford CoreNLP natural language processing toolkit. In *Association for Computational Linguistics (ACL) System Demonstrations*, pages 55–60, Baltimore, Maryland. ACL.

Nanni, F., Osman, M., Cheng, Y.-R., Ponzetto, S. P., and Dietz, L. (2018). UKParl: A semantified and topically organized corpus of political speeches. In Darja Fišer, et al., editors, *Proceedings of LREC 2018*, Miyazaki, Japan. ELRA.

Pančur, A., Šorn, M., and Erjavec, T. (2018). SlovParl 2.0: The collection of Slovene parliamentary debates from the period of secession. In Darja Fišer, et al., editors, *Proceedings of LREC 2018*, Miyazaki, Japan. ELRA.

Rødven Eide, S. (2019). The Swedish PoliGraph. In *Proceedings of the 6th Workshop on Argument Mining*, Florence, Italy. Association for Computational Linguistics.

Proceedings of ParlaCLARIN II Workshop, pages 11–17
Language Resources and Evaluation Conference (LREC 2020), Marseille, 11–16 May 2020
© European Language Resources Association (ELRA), licensed under CC-BY-NC

IGC-Parl: Icelandic Corpus of Parliamentary Proceedings

Steinþór Steingrímsson, Starkaður Barkarson, Gunnar Thor Örnólfsson
The Árni Magnússon Institute for Icelandic Studies
Reykjavík, Iceland
steinthor.steingrimsson, starkadur.barkarson, gunnar.thor.ornolfsson@arnastofnun.is

Abstract

We describe the acquisition, annotation and encoding of the corpus of the Althingi parliamentary proceedings. The first version of the corpus includes speeches from 1911-2019. It comprises 404 thousand speeches and just under 219 million words. The corpus has been automatically part-of-speech tagged and lemmatised. It is annotated with extensive metadata about the speeches, speakers and political parties, including speech topic, whether the speaker is in the government coalition or opposition, age and gender of speaker at the time of delivery, references to sound and video recordings and more. The corpus is encoded in accordance with the Text Encoding Initiative (TEI) Guidelines and conforms to the Parla-CLARIN schema. We plan to update the corpus annually and its major versions will be archived in the CLARIN.IS repository. It is available for download and search using the KORP concordance tool. Furthermore, information on word frequency are accessible in a custom made web application and an n-gram viewer.

Keywords: corpora, parliamentary, Icelandic

1. Introduction

Parliamentary records, reports, written questions and inquiries, legal documents, and transcriptions of debates are a rich source of data for research in various disciplines. Not only do they enable new lines of research in fields as diverse as linguistics, political science, sociology, economic history, gender studies and information retrieval, they can also be an important source of data for natural language processing. This has led to a number of projects aiming to compile, analyze and enrich parliamentary records, some of which are listed in Section 2.

Transcriptions of speeches from debates in Althingi, the Icelandic parliament, have previously been made available as part of the Icelandic Gigaword Corpus (IGC) (Steingrímsson et al., 2018), but as parliamentary data differ in many ways from other data in the IGC we have compiled a special parliamentary corpus, IGC-Parl, enriched with meta-data pertaining to parliamentary corpora. This includes information about age, gender and role of the parliamentarian delivering the speech, when they were active in parliament, party affiliation, whether their political party was part of a ruling coalition or in opposition, topics of the speech and more. This project is the first step in compiling a number of different corpora with rich, relevant metadata, from the different text classes in the IGC. Others are for example: news media, books, adjudications, social media, etc. As with the IGC we plan to update the corpus annually and make it available through a variety of means as detailed in Section 5. In subsequent versions we also plan to add other parliamentary records, starting with inquiries, resolutions and bills as discussed in section 7.

In order for IGC-Parl to be in line with comparable corpora from other countries we aspire to adhere to the Parla-CLARIN scheme[1]. This is in accordance with the TEI-standard which is the standard the IGC follows. For further discussion on encoding and annotation of the corpus, refer to Section 4.

Icelandic parliamentary speeches have been used for linguistic research, most recently in (Stefánsdóttir and Ingason, 2019) where change in stylistic fronting in the speeches of one long-standing parliamentarian is used to support the hypothesis that a person's language can vary in accordance to change in social status.

By making parliamentary data available with rich metadata we facilitate replicability of results as well as further research in this field. In Section 6 we give a few examples of possible research directions the corpus data and accompanying metadata enable.

2. Related work

Parliamentary corpora have been available to NLP researchers for a long time. In the early days of statistical machine translation (SMT), the Canadian Hansard Corpus (Roukos and Melamed, 1995), consisting of debates from the Canadian Parliament parallel in English and Canadian French, was used by machine translation researchers to advance their field. Europarl (Koehn, 2005), a multilingual parallel corpus containing the proceedings of the European parliament has also proved to be useful for SMT, and the DCEP corpus (Hajlaoui et al., 2014) adds a variety of document types published by the European parliament, enabling new lines of research on the European parliament data.

Recently there has been increased interest in parliamentary corpora and compiling of corpora has been undertaken in a number of countries. Examples of monolingual corpora are the Hansard corpus, a collection of parliamentary records of the British Parliament from 1803-2005 (Alexander and Davies, 2015), the ParlAT beta corpus (Wissik and Pirker, 2018) containing Austrian parliamentary proceedings from 1996-2017, presented at the ParlaCLARIN workshop in 2018 (Fišer et al., 2018) along with a Slovenian Corpus (Andrej Pančur and Erjavec, 2018), a Polish one (Ogrodniczuk, 2018) and a corpus of the Grand National Assembly of Turkey (Onur Gungor and Çağıl Sönmez, 2018). As of February 2020, the CLARIN ERIC infrastructure offers access to 22 parliamentary corpora. This includes corpora in almost all of the languages spoken in CLARIN ERIC

---

[1] `https://clarin-eric.github.io/parla-clarin`

member and observer countries, including all the Nordic languages except Icelandic.[2]

As the number of parliamentary corpora increases, the need for a common format and interoperability grows accordingly. A common schema could facilitate comparison and analysis of topics across parliamentary data from different countries. A standard format for parliamentary data is being proposed by CLARIN. At a workshop in May 2019, Tomaž Erjavec & Andrej Pančur introduced the proposed scheme, Parla-CLARIN (Erjavec and Pančur, 2019).

3. Building the Corpus

The corpus covers speeches delivered from 1911 to mid 2019 in the Parliament of Iceland, Althingi, and are found on Althingi's website (www.althingi.is). Many of the older speeches are missing from the website despite still being listed, as discussed further in Section 6. Speeches predating 1991 are tagged only with a date, while those delivered after that time are tagged with a timestamp.

A short biography of each speaker is available on the website along with information about what political party and constituency they belonged to and what role they had in different periods.

Since 2001 debates concerning specific issues have been grouped by topic (e.g. Industries: Fisheries) so it is possible to link each speech to one or more topics.

A schedule of each session from 1995 onwards is available, but earlier speeches can only be grouped by date. This does not always cohere with sessions since one session can span more than one calendar day.

All the speeches on the website are available in HTML files. Older speeches, for which there are no available sound recordings, have been OCR-read from Alþingistíðindi, parliamentary records that have been published by the Icelandic Parliament since 1875. These speeches have been manually corrected. Refer to Section 6 for further discussion.

3.1. From IGC to IceCor-Parl

The first version of The Icelandic Gigaword Corpus (IGC) was published in 2018 and the second one in January 2020. It contains almost 1,400 million words from different sources, mainly official texts (e.g. parliamentary speeches as far back as 1911, law texts, adjudications) and texts from news media. By the end of 2021 we intend to split the corpus into various sub-corpora, contained in separate files, each with its own metadata structure. In the current version of the IGC each speech is contained in a separate file with information about the name of the speaker, date of delivery and the title. IGC-Parl contains much more detailed information about each speech and speaker.

We started by scraping the website and entering information about each speaker into a database: his or her id used on the website, full name, date of birth, and gender. For each period information was gathered about the person's status in the parliament, to which political party and constituency they belonged and if they held a position as a minister in the government. We also collected information about which political parties were in the government from 1944.

Information about all issues discussed, for each parliament, was inserted into the database and speeches linked to topics where possible.

4. Annotation

For annotation we opted for TEI rather than other XML schemas for encoding parliamentary proceedings, such as Political Mashups (Gielissen and Marx, 2009), Parliamentary Metadata Language (Gartner, 2014) or the Akoma Ntoso[3]. Iceland joined CLARIN ERIC in 2020 after having been an observer since 2018. CLARIN has advocated for the use of TEI and has published the Parla-CLARIN schema[4] for use for annotation of political proceedings. TEI has been used for annotation of other Icelandic corpora and the IGC is all annotated in TEI.

```
<teiCorpus>
  <teiHeader>
    <profileDesc>
      <particDesc>
        <listPerson>
          <!-- List of all speekers -->
        </listPerson>
        <listOrg>
          <!-- list of all political parties -->
        </listOrg>
      </particDesc>
    </profileDesc>
  </teiHeader>

  <TEI> <!-- TEI element for each day/session

    <teiHeader>
      <!-- information about time and setting -->
    </teiHeader>

    <TEI> <!-- TEI element for each speech
      <teiHeader>
        <sourceDesc>
          <biblStruct>
            <analytic>
              <title></title>
              <author>
                <!-- Information about the speaker -->
              </author>
              <date>
                <!-- date and time of delivery -->
              </date>
            </analytic>
            <ref> <!-- linkt to speech --> </ref>
          </biblStruct>
          <recordingStmt>
            <!-- information about and link to media files -->
          </recordingStmt>
        </sourceDesc>
        <profileDesc>
          <textClass>
            <catRef>
            <!-- list of topics -->
            <catRef>
          </textClass>
        </profileDesc>
      </teiHeader>
    </TEI>

  </TEI>

</teiCorpus>
```

Figure 1: The TEI encoding structure of IGC-Parl.

[2]https://www.clarin.eu/resource-families/parliamentary-corpora

[3]http://www.akomantoso.org
[4]https://clarin-eric.github.io/parla-clarin

4.1. Encoding into XML

We mostly follow the proposed schema, Parla-CLARIN. The root element <teiCorpus> contains a header with metadata for the entire corpus. The <particDesc> element contains a list of all the speakers in the <listPerson> element, their name, gender, date of birth, their party affiliation and roles in different periods. It also contains a list of all political parties, congresses, governments and constituencies in <listOrg> elements. The header is followed by teiCorpus-elements. Each teiCorpus-element contains data for one date (but not session due to lack of information as mentioned above) - a header with metadata and one TEI-element for each speech. Each TEI-element contains another header with metadata and the text element for each speech. The metadata contains detailed information about the speaker in the <author> element, where age, gender, party affiliation and role at the time of delivery are each in one <note> element. If the speaker belonged to the government when the speech was delivered another <note> will indicate that. The number and title of the issue discussed are in the <title> element, and date and time of delivery in the <date> element. Related topics and categories are listed in the <textClass> element in the <profileDesc> element while the link to the written speech on Althingi's website is located in a <ref> element nested in the <biblScope> element. Sound files for each speech have been available since 2006 and video files since 2009. Information and links to those files are in the <recordingStmt> element. The structure is shown in Figure 1.

The Parla-CLARIN schema proposes two layers, a <teiCorpus> containing a header and <TEI> elements that each contains one session, sitting or day. We have three layers since we keep all speeches in a separate TEI-element. The reason for this was twofold. Firstly we wanted to facilitate a search where a user of the corpus would for example only want to look at speeches by women or by a specific speaker. Secondly we want to keep a certain conformity between the sub-corpora of IGC and one of the general rules is that a text by one author/speaker is contained in one separate TEI-element.

Orðmynd	Greiningarstrengur	Fjöldi	Fjöldi texta	Sæti í tíðniröð	Sæti í tíðniröð án greinarmerkja
var	sfg3eþ	8834311	2336143	15	13
voru	sfg3fþ	2252238	1083273	55	50
sagði	sfg3eþ	1690576	841762	75	68
kom	sfg3eþ	1084631	705344	104	94
hafði	sfg3eþ	900518	514926	125	115
fór	sfg3eþ	642831	450943	173	161
varð	sfg3eþ	632753	420654	178	164
tók	sfg3eþ	488141	355812	236	223
átti	sfg3eþ	459798	312680	248	234
fékk	sfg3eþ	387899	285313	293	279

Figure 2: The word frequency database. An example of a search using wildcards. The search term *sf*þ* corresponds with verbs in the indicative mood and past tense. The columns of the results table are respectively: Word form, PoS-tag, Count, Number of texts containing word, Frequency ranking, Frequency ranking excluding punctuation tokens.

The speeches have been tokenised and both lemmas and PoS-tags are listed with each token. Sentences are marked up using the <s> element, words with the <w> element and punctuation symbols with the <c> element. The base form of words is given in the lemma attribute while the tag is given in the type attribute.

Alongside the main TEI-file another XML-file resides that contains a list of all the speakers and a link to all their speeches to facilitate search by speakers.

4.2. Tokenisation, POS-tagging and lemmatisation

All linguistic annotation is carried out automatically with no manual correction. *Tokenizer*, developed by Miðeind (Þorsteinsson, 2020) was used to divide the text into sentences and running words. Morphosyntactic tagging was performed with *ABLTagger* (Steingrímsson et al., 2019) and lemmatisation with the lemmatiser *Nefnir* (Ingólfsdóttir et al., 2019). These tools have been shown to achieve state-of-the-art results for Icelandic, with *ABLTagger* reaching over 95% accuracy on 10-fold validation using a gold standard corpus, and *Nefnir* has been shown to reach almost 97% accuracy when lemmatising words that have previously been tagged automatically. It should be noted that none of these tests have been carried out on texts from parliamentary speeches and thus the exact accuracy for this corpus is not known. The tagset used for tagging IGC is almost the same tagset that was developed for compiling the Icelandic Frequency Dictionary (IFD) (Pind et al., 1991), with only a few changes. A corpus made by concatenating the IFD corpus and the MIM-GOLD corpus (Loftsson et al., 2010) was used to train the tagger. Lexical data from The Database of Icelandic Inflections (DIM) (Bjarnadóttir et al., 2019) was used to augment the tagger for increased accuracy.

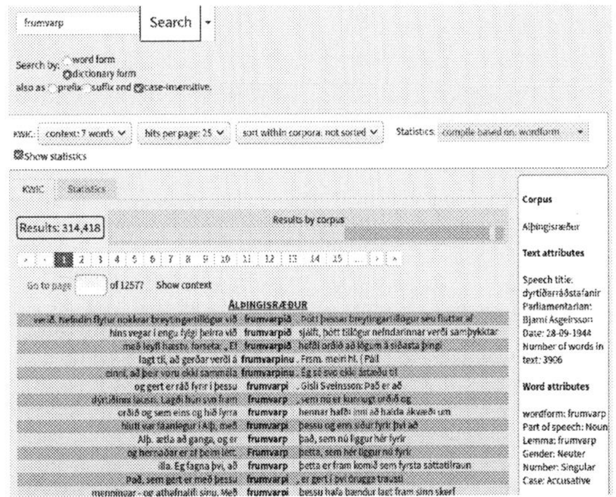

Figure 3: Search results as shown in the Korp-based concordance search tool. The text that matches the search term or pattern is shown in bold, with its context on either side displayed. The right-hand sidebar displays metadata about the text from which each result is sourced.

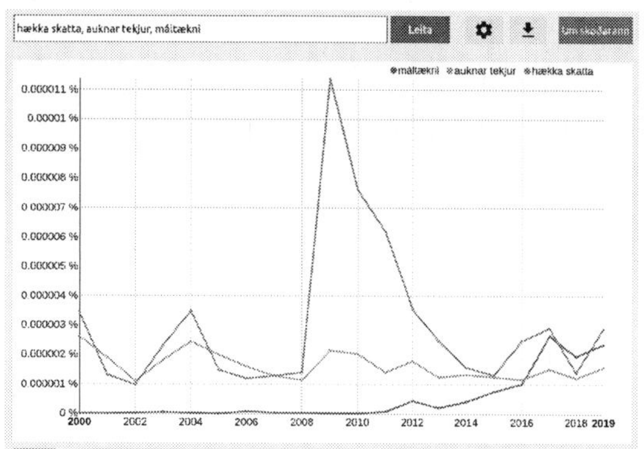

Figure 4: n-gram statistics displayed by the n-gram viewer. The search terms roughly correspond to "raise taxes", "increased income", and "language technology". The large spike is for "raise taxes" in 2009, in the wake of the financial collapse of 2008.

5. Availability and Maintenance

IGC-Parl is available for download on CLARIN.is, the official website of the Icelandic branch of CLARIN ERIC. It is published under a CC-BY 4.0 license and may therefore be used for both academic and industry purposes. We aim to publish a new version annually, adding more material and employing more sophisticated and accurate methods of tokenisation, PoS-tagging and lemmatisation as they become available. Furthermore, we will adapt existing Icelandic corpus tools to support IGC-Parl.

Various tools have recently been developed or adapted to make Icelandic text corpora more accessible to researchers and the general populace. These tools include a concordance search tool, a searchable word frequency database, and an n-gram viewer. They are described in detail in Steingrímsson et al. (2020). Here we will give a brief description of the tools through which IGC-Parl will be made accessible.

The concordance tool is powered by the Swedish Language Institute Språkbanken's Korp (Borin et al., 2018) and offers a concordance search using a rich query language[5] (Evert, 2005), enabling users to search by all linguistic features denoted in Section 4.2.

The word frequency database enables users to search by words, canonical forms (lemmas) and fine-grained morphosyntactic PoS-tags. It also supports wildcard searches for each of these search terms, enabling users to see frequency statistics on all words or tags which match a pattern. An example of a wildcard search is shown in Figure 2.

Analysing trends in word occurrence by year can prove useful, for example in research into language change and neologisms. We make the data available in an n-gram viewer, which enables the user to view frequency trends for n-grams up to a length of 3, for both lemmas and word forms as they appear in the text. The user can configure the viewer in a number of ways, for instance to give absolute or relative numbers for each year or display the results as a cu-

mulative or non-cumulative curve. Results can be downloaded, either as SVG graphics or in a comma separated text file. The n-gram viewer is based on the NB n-gram viewer. (Breder Birkenes et al., 2015) All n-grams will be made available for download. Trigrams of length <= 3 are available in their entirety, but with 4- and 5-grams, only those which occur more than 3 times in the corpora are included in the download files.

6. Quantitative Analysis

In total, the corpus contains 218,889,307 tokens in 404,401 speeches, given by 987 different speakers. The Althingi parliamentary records were printed from 1845. They include parliamentary documents and speeches. In recent years, the Althingi has been working on digitising old documents and they intend to go as far back as 1875. Currently, all speeches since 1937 have been made available as well as some of the speeches from 1911 to 1936, which were published on the Althingi website as part of celebrating certain events, e.g. women's suffrage, enacted in 1915. As evident in Figure 6 our corpus reflects this. A reasonable amount of speeches from 1913–1915 are included but there is a gap in the speech collection until 1937, when we finally have a complete set of speeches for each year. As we intend to publish new versions of the corpus annually, which include the most recent data, older speeches will also be included in future versions as they become available.

As the IGC-Parl corpus has been packaged with rich metadata, interesting information about the parliament can easily be congregated. In the following examples we have done so with Python scripts that read through the data. Figure 6 shows the number of words spoken each year in parliament. The columns show the division of word count between male and female parliamentarians. The graph shows us that it isn't until recent years that women have come close to being represented as well as men. By having a gender flag for the parliamentarians, we can study various gender related issues, look into whether men or women are more likely to speak on certain topics, or compare linguistic characteristics or speech length, to name a few. Similar analyses could be done on other parliaments and the comparison could give us valuable insights into gender biases in various countries, at least as they are reflected in parliament.

Enthusiastic followers of the Icelandic parliamentary debates would probably agree that a prominent trait of the Icelandic parliament is that the opposition traditionally speaks more than the ruling coalition, even though there is no tradition for minority coalition governance in Iceland and the

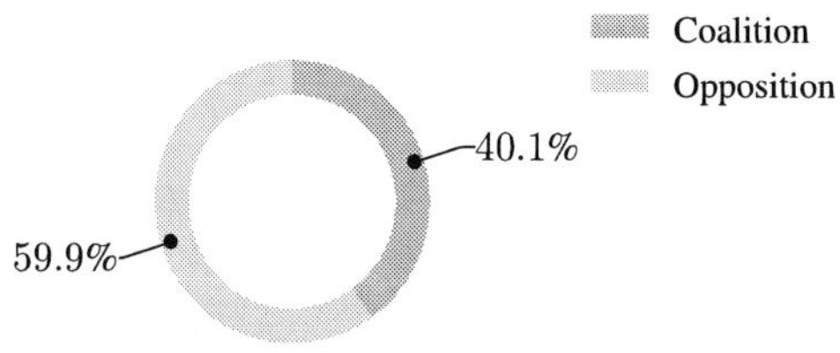

Figure 5: Words spoken by opposition vs. ruling parties

---

[5]The CQP query language: `http://cwb.sourceforge.net/`

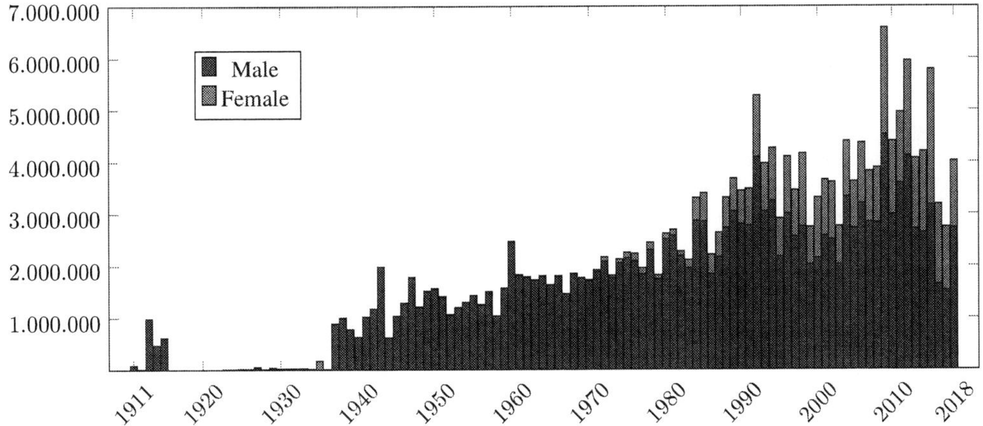

Figure 6: Number of words spoken by year.

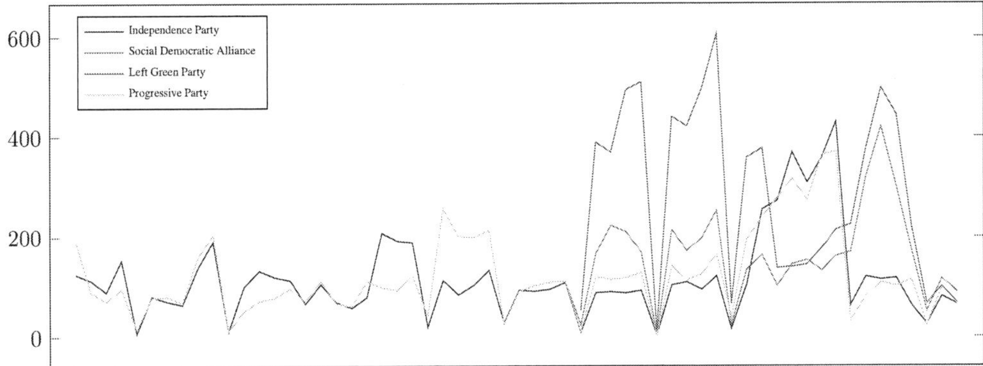

Figure 7: Words spoken on average per day per parliamentarian per parliamentary term from 1970 to 2018

coalition has almost always held the majority. We can test this characteristic of the parliament by using the information the corpus gives us on which parties are in power at which time. We use this information to count speeches and total words spoken by both the opposition and coalition from 1937 when the data is first complete. Figure 5 shows the results and verifies our suspicion.

Figure 7 shows another aspect of this same thing. The graph shows words spoken on average per day, by the average parliamentarian in each of the four largest parties. Each point in the graph stands for a legislative period, lasting from a few weeks and up to five months. The number of meetings in each legislative period varies, with occasional summer legislative periods that have relatively few meetings compared to number of days, explaining the points in the graph where the average for all parties is very low. The graph starts in 1970 and ends in 2018.

The Independence Party and the Progressive Party usually speak less than the Left Greens and the Social Democrats. This may be because they are more often a part of the ruling coalition. An exception to that in 2009–2013 can be seen clearly in the graph as the parliamentarians of these parties had never before spoken as much. When they came back to power they went back to their old ways.

These are only a few examples of how the data can be anal-

ysed. The rich metadata provides abundant research paths for academics and other users to discover.

7. Current and Future Work

While we have published the first version of IGC-Parl[6], an annotated corpus of parliamentary speeches enriched with a variety of relevant metadata, work on Icelandic corpus compilation is ongoing. In subsequent versions of IGC-Parl we want to improve on the metadata even further. Speeches from 1991 onwards have a topic classification, but the topics are only listed in Icelandic. We want to translate the topic listings to English in order to make them more useful for non-Icelandic speakers. A new named entity recogniser is being built for Icelandic. We will use that to add named entity annotation to future versions of the corpus. As we do not know the PoS-tagging and lemmatisation accuracy for this particular corpus we plan to manually create a test set that will allow us to measure the accuracy of the automatic tools. As this corpus is somewhat different from the data the PoS-tagger is trained on, we want to investigate whether there are any systemic errors made in the tagging process. If so, we want to try to alleviate them in later versions of the corpus by adjusting the tagger.

---

[6]`http://hdl.handle.net/20.500.12537/14`

The frequency database tool described in Section 5 will get a more user friendly design and will be optimised for speed. And while the corpus can currently be queried in an n-gram viewer we have plans to allow for more detailed querying, for instance by party affiliation.

Furthermore we intend to add other parliamentary data to the corpus, starting with inquiries and replies to them, resolutions and bills and amendments to them.

As we are trying to adhere to the Parla-CLARIN schema, we will follow the advancement of the scheme and in future versions amend our encoding to be as close to the CLARIN standard for parliamentary corpora as we see fit.

8. Conclusion and Acknowledgements

We have described the compilation of IGC-Parl, the metadata and the composition of the data. The work is funded by the Language Technology Program for Icelandic 2019–2023 (Nikulásdóttir et al., 2020).

9. Bibliographical References

Andrej Pančur, M. and Erjavec, T. (2018). SlovParl 2.0: The Collection of Slovene Parliamentary Debates from the Period of Secession. In Darja Fišer, et al., editors, *Proceedings of the Eleventh International Conference on Language Resources and Evaluation (LREC 2018)*, Paris, France, may. European Language Resources Association (ELRA).

Bjarnadóttir, K., Hlynsdóttir, K. I., and Steingrímsson, S. (2019). DIM: The Database of Icelandic Morphology. In *Proceedings of the 22nd Nordic Conference on Computational Linguistics*, NODALIDA 2019, Turku, Finland.

Borin, L., Forsberg, M., and Roxendal, J. (2018). Korp-the corpus infrastructure of Språkbanken. In *Proceedings of the Eighth International Conference on Language Resources and Evaluation (LREC 2012)*, pages 474–478.

Breder Birkenes, M., Johnsen, L. G., Lindstad, A. M., and Ostad, J. (2015). From digital library to n-grams: NB n-gram. In *Proceedings of the 20th Nordic Conference of Computational Linguistics*, NODALIDA 2015, Vilnius, Lithuania.

Erjavec, T. and Pančur, A. (2019). Introduction to the proposed annotation scheme. ParlaFormat Workshop.

Evert, S. (2005). The CQP query language tutorial. *IMS Stuttgart. CWB version*, 2.

Darja Fišer, et al., editors. (2018). *Proceedings of LREC2018 Workshop ParlaCLARIN: Creating and Using Parliamentary Corpora.*, Paris, France, May. European Language Resources Association (ELRA).

Gartner, R. (2014). A metadata infrastructure for the analysis of parliamentary proceedings. In *Big Humanities Data, The Second IEEE Big Data 2014 Workshop*, Bethesda, Maryland, USA.

Gielissen, T. and Marx, M. (2009). Exemplification of Parliamentary Debates. In *Proceedings of the 9th Dutch-Belgian Information Retrieval Workshop*, DIR 2010, pages 19–25.

Hajlaoui, N., Kolovratnik, D., Väyrynen, J., Steinberger, R., and Varga, D. (2014). DCEP -digital corpus of the European parliament. In *Proceedings of the Ninth International Conference on Language Resources and Evaluation (LREC'14)*, Reykjavik, Iceland, May. European Language Resources Association (ELRA).

Ingólfsdóttir, S. L., Loftsson, H., Daðason, J. F., and Bjarnadóttir, K. (2019). Nefnir: A high accuracy lemmatizer for Icelandic. In *Proceedings of the 22nd Nordic Conference on Computational Linguistics*, NODALIDA 2019, Turku, Finland.

Koehn, P. (2005). Europarl: A Parallel Corpus for Statistical Machine Translation. In *Conference Proceedings: the tenth Machine Translation Summit*, pages 79–86, Phuket, Thailand. AAMT, AAMT.

Loftsson, H., Yngvason, J. H., Helgadóttir, S., and Rögnvaldsson, E. (2010). Developing a PoS-tagged corpus using existing tools. In Francis M. Tyers Sarasola, Kepa et al., editors, *Proceedings of 7th SaLTMiL Workshop on Creation and Use of Basic Lexical Resources for Less-Resourced Languages*, LREC 2010, Valetta, Malta.

Nikulásdóttir, A. B., Guðnason, J., Ingason, A. K., Loftsson, H., Rögnvaldsson, E., Sigurðsson, E. F., and Steingrímsson, S. (2020). Language Technology Programme for Icelandic 2019–2023. In *Proceedings of the Twelfth International Conference on Language Resources and Evaluation (LREC 2020)*. European Language Resources Association (ELRA).

Ogrodniczuk, M. (2018). Polish Parliamentary Corpus. In Darja Fišer, et al., editors, *Proceedings of the Eleventh International Conference on Language Resources and Evaluation (LREC 2018)*, Paris, France, may. European Language Resources Association (ELRA).

Onur Gungor, M. T. and Çağıl Sönmez. (2018). A Corpus of Grand National Assembly of Turkish Parliament's Transcripts. In Darja Fišer, et al., editors, *Proceedings of the Eleventh International Conference on Language Resources and Evaluation (LREC 2018)*, Paris, France, may. European Language Resources Association (ELRA).

Þorsteinsson, V. (2020). Tokenizer for icelandic text. CLARIN-IS, Stofnun Árna Magnússonar.

Pind, J., Magnússon, F., and Briem, S. (1991). *Íslensk orðtíðnibók [The Icelandic Frequency Dictionary]*. The Institute of Lexicography, University of Iceland, Reykjavik, Iceland.

Roukos, Salim, D. G. and Melamed, D. (1995). Hansard French/English LDC95T20.

Stefánsdóttir, L. B. and Ingason, A. K. (2019). Lifespan Change and Style Shift in the Icelandic Gigaword Corpus. In K. Simov et al., editors, *Proceedings of CLARIN Annual Conference 2019*, pages 138–141.

Steingrímsson, S., Helgadóttir, S., Rögnvaldsson, E., Barkarson, S., and Guðnason, J. (2018). Risamálheild: A Very Large Icelandic Text Corpus. In *Proceedings of the Eleventh International Conference on Language Resources and Evaluation (LREC 2018)*, Miyazaki, Japan, May 7-12, 2018. European Language Resources Association (ELRA).

Steingrímsson, S., Kárason, Ö., and Loftsson, H. (2019). Augmenting a BiLSTM tagger with a morphological lexicon and a lexical category identification step. In *Proceedings of Recent Advances in Natural Language Processing*, RANLP 2019, Varna, Bulgaria.

Steingrímsson, S., Barkarson, S., and Örnólfsson, G. T. (2020). Facilitating Corpus Usage: Making Icelandic Corpora More Accessible for Researchers and Language Users. In *Proceedings of the Twelfth International Conference on Language Resources and Evaluation (LREC 2020)*. European Language Resources Association (ELRA).

10. Language Resource References

Marc Alexander and Mark Davies. (2015). *Hansard Corpus 1803-2005*. Available online at http://www.hansard-corpus.org.

Tanja Wissik and Hannes Pirker. (2018). *ParlAT Corpus*. Austrian Centre for Digital Humanities.

Proceedings of ParlaCLARIN II Workshop, pages 18–22
Language Resources and Evaluation Conference (LREC 2020), Marseille, 11–16 May 2020
© European Language Resources Association (ELRA), licensed under CC-BY-NC

Compiling Czech Parliamentary Stenographic Protocols into a Corpus

Barbora Hladká, Matyáš Kopp, Pavel Straňák
Charles University
Faculty of Mathematics and Physics
Prague, Czech Republic
{hladka, kopp, stranak}@ufal.mff.cuni.cz

Abstract

The Parliament of the Czech Republic consists of two chambers: the Chamber of Deputies (Lower House) and the Senate (Upper House). In our work, we focus on agenda and documents that relate to the Chamber of Deputies. Namely, we pay particular attention to stenographic protocols that record the Chamber of Deputies' meetings. Our overall goal is to continually compile the protocols into the TEI encoded corpus ParCzech and make the corpus accessible in a more user friendly way than the Parliament publishes the protocols. In the very first stage of the compilation, the ParCzech corpus consists of the 2013+ protocols that we make accessible and searchable in the TEITOK web-based platform.

Keywords: Parliament of the Czech Republic, Chamber of Deputies, stenographic protocols, TEI encoding, TEITOK

1. Motivation

Parliamentary data is interesting for social and political scientists, data scientists, historians, linguists, journalists and citizens in general. For a wide range of tasks parliamentary data must be easily findable and accessible, encoded according to international standards and, if possible, with rich and correct annotations and metadata. In the fields of Natural Language Processing and Corpus Linguistics, the CLARIN ERIC infrastructure plays a leading role in the task of compilation of parliamentary data into language corpora. They organized the CLARIN-PLUS cross-disciplinary workshop "Working with parliamentary records" held in Sofia, Bulgaria in 2017 that clearly indicated a need for discussion on processing parliamentary data in a wider community.[1] In 2018 the ParlaCLARIN workshop was organized in Miyazaki, Japan and it means a significant step forward in the given discussion (Fišer et al., 2018).

The CLARIN ERIC infrastructure provides the most comprehensive overview of the existing parliamentary corpora and related publications.[2] As of March 2020, there are 34 parliamentary corpora in the overview and its description, size, licence and availability are provided for each of them. In our work we focus on stenographic protocols published by the Chamber of Deputies of the Parliament of the Czech Republic. In the past, two Czech parliamentary corpora have been published: (1) CzechParl is a corpus of stenographic protocols recorded during the meetings of both chambers of the Parliament of the Czech Republic between 1993–2010 (Jakubíček and Kovář, 2010). This corpus contains 82 million tokens and it is available for on-line searching in SketchEngine;[3] (2) The Czech Parliamentary Meetings corpus consists of the recordings from the Chamber of Deputies of the Parliament of the Czech Republic made

between February – August 2011. This corpus contains 88 hours of speech data and their transcriptions. Both the spoken and written data are available for download (Pražák and Šmídl, 2012) and for on-line searching in the KonText concordancer.[4]

Our goal is to make the protocols accessible and searchable in a more user friendly way than the Czech Parliament does. We make them available in the ParCzech corpus that we, in contrast with other corpora in the CLARIN ERIC overview, approach as a live text collection rather than a static collection. This provides interesting aspects of a workflow design, especially into a procedure of regular updates. Regarding data encoding, the works (Erjavec and Pančur, 2019) and (Pančur et al., 2019) inspired us the most. At the same time we looked at the CLARIN ERIC overview from a different angle and created Table 1 including ParCzech.

This paper is organized as follows. In Section 2. we describe the digital repository of the Czech Parliament and the agenda that is available online on the website of the Czech Chamber of Deputies. The details on recording, editing, and publishing the stenographic protocols by the Czech Parliament are explained in Section 3. In Section 4. we describe our procedure to compile the protocols into ParCzech. Section 5. shows how to search ParCzech in the TEITOK web-based platform.

Terminological note The following terms in parliamentary procedures are relevant for our topic. During a *term*, there are *meetings* which are a group of *sittings* and which typically take place in more than one day. For illustration, the 30th meeting in the 8th term of the Czech Chamber of Deputies was a group of 12 sittings.[5] Each meeting has its own agenda and an *agenda item* is discussed in *speeches* that can be made at more than one sitting.

---

[1] https://www.clarin.eu/event/2017/clarin-plus-workshop-working-parliamentary-records
[2] https://www.clarin.eu/resource-families/parliamentary-corpora
[3] https://www.sketchengine.eu/czechparl-corpus-of-czech-parliament

[4] https://lindat.mff.cuni.cz/services/kontext/first_form?corpname=czechparl_2012_03_28_cs_w
[5] On 28, 29, 30, 31 May and 4, 5, 6, 7, 18, 19, 20, 21 June 2019, see https://www.psp.cz/eknih/2017ps/stenprot/030schuz/index.htm

<table>
<thead>
<tr><th rowspan="2">language</th><th rowspan="2">corpus (url if cannot be downloaded)</th><th colspan="6">concordancer</th><th rowspan="2">format</th><th rowspan="2">down load</th></tr>
<tr><th>K</th><th>SE</th><th>Kr</th><th>N</th><th>C</th><th>w</th></tr>
</thead>
<tbody>
<tr><td>Bulgarian</td><td>Corpus of Bulgarian Political and Journalistic Speech (↗)</td><td></td><td></td><td></td><td></td><td></td><td>•</td><td>?</td><td></td></tr>
<tr><td>Croatian</td><td>Croatian parliamentary corpus ParlaMeter-hr 1.0</td><td>•</td><td>•</td><td></td><td></td><td></td><td>•</td><td>TEI</td><td>↓</td></tr>
<tr><td>Czech</td><td>Czech Parliamentary Meeting</td><td>•</td><td></td><td></td><td></td><td></td><td></td><td>XML</td><td>↓</td></tr>
<tr><td></td><td>CzechParl (↗)</td><td></td><td>•</td><td></td><td></td><td></td><td></td><td>?</td><td></td></tr>
<tr><td></td><td>ParCzech</td><td>+T</td><td></td><td></td><td></td><td></td><td></td><td>TEI</td><td>↓</td></tr>
<tr><td>Danish</td><td>The Danish Parliament Corpus 2009–2017, v1</td><td></td><td></td><td></td><td></td><td></td><td></td><td>TEI</td><td>↓</td></tr>
<tr><td>Dutch</td><td>DutchParl</td><td></td><td></td><td></td><td></td><td></td><td>•</td><td>XML</td><td>↓</td></tr>
<tr><td>English</td><td>HanDeSeT: Hansard Debates with Sentiment Tags</td><td></td><td></td><td></td><td></td><td></td><td></td><td>CSV</td><td>↓</td></tr>
<tr><td></td><td>Hansard corpus</td><td></td><td></td><td></td><td></td><td></td><td>•</td><td>?</td><td>↓</td></tr>
<tr><td></td><td>Parliamentary Debates on Europe at the House of Commons 1998–2015 (↗)</td><td></td><td></td><td></td><td></td><td></td><td></td><td>TEI</td><td></td></tr>
<tr><td></td><td>UKParl Dataset</td><td></td><td></td><td></td><td></td><td></td><td></td><td>?</td><td>↓</td></tr>
<tr><td>Estonian</td><td>Transcripts of Riigikogu (Estonian Parliament)</td><td></td><td></td><td></td><td></td><td></td><td>•</td><td>TEI</td><td>↓</td></tr>
<tr><td>Finnish</td><td>Plenary Sessions of the Parliament of Finland</td><td></td><td></td><td>•</td><td></td><td></td><td></td><td>?</td><td></td></tr>
<tr><td>French</td><td>Archives Parlementaires (↗)</td><td></td><td></td><td></td><td></td><td></td><td></td><td>TEI</td><td></td></tr>
<tr><td></td><td>Parliamentary Debates on Europe at the Assemblée nationale 2002–2012</td><td></td><td></td><td></td><td></td><td></td><td></td><td>TEI</td><td>↓</td></tr>
<tr><td>German</td><td>Korpusbasierte Analyse österreichischer Parlamentsreden</td><td></td><td></td><td></td><td></td><td></td><td></td><td>XML</td><td>↓</td></tr>
<tr><td></td><td>ParlAT beta</td><td></td><td></td><td></td><td></td><td></td><td></td><td>CSV</td><td></td></tr>
<tr><td></td><td>Parliamentary Debates on Europe at the Bundestag 1998–2015</td><td></td><td></td><td></td><td></td><td></td><td></td><td>TEI</td><td>↓</td></tr>
<tr><td></td><td>polmineR corpus</td><td></td><td></td><td></td><td></td><td></td><td>•</td><td>TEI</td><td>↓</td></tr>
<tr><td>Greek</td><td>Hellenic Parliament Minutes 1989–1994, 1997–2018</td><td></td><td></td><td></td><td></td><td></td><td></td><td>text</td><td>↓</td></tr>
<tr><td></td><td>Speeches of Politicians in the Greek Parliament</td><td></td><td></td><td></td><td></td><td></td><td></td><td>TXT</td><td>↓</td></tr>
<tr><td>Icelandic</td><td>The Icelandic Parliamentary Corpus</td><td></td><td></td><td>•</td><td></td><td></td><td></td><td></td><td>↓</td></tr>
<tr><td>Latvian</td><td>LinkedSAEIMA (↗)</td><td></td><td>•</td><td></td><td></td><td></td><td></td><td>RDF, CoNLL-U</td><td></td></tr>
<tr><td>Lithuanian</td><td>Lithuanian Parliament Corpus for Authorship Attribution</td><td></td><td></td><td></td><td></td><td></td><td></td><td>CSV</td><td>↓</td></tr>
<tr><td>Norwegian</td><td>Proceedings of Norwegian Parliamentary Debates (↗)</td><td></td><td></td><td></td><td></td><td>•</td><td></td><td>?</td><td></td></tr>
<tr><td></td><td>Talk of Norway</td><td></td><td></td><td></td><td></td><td></td><td></td><td>CSV</td><td>↓</td></tr>
<tr><td>Polish</td><td>Polish Parliamentary Corpus</td><td></td><td></td><td></td><td>•</td><td></td><td></td><td>TEI</td><td>↓</td></tr>
<tr><td>Portuguese</td><td>PTPARL Corpus</td><td></td><td></td><td></td><td></td><td></td><td></td><td>TXT</td><td>↓</td></tr>
<tr><td>Slovenian</td><td>Slovenian parliamentary corpus ParlaMeter-sl 1.0</td><td>•</td><td>•</td><td></td><td></td><td></td><td></td><td>TEI</td><td>↓</td></tr>
<tr><td></td><td>Slovenian parliamentary corpus siParl 1.0</td><td>•</td><td>•</td><td></td><td></td><td></td><td></td><td>TEI</td><td>↓</td></tr>
<tr><td></td><td>Slovenian parliamentary corpus SlovParl 2.0</td><td>•</td><td>•</td><td></td><td></td><td></td><td></td><td>TEI</td><td>↓</td></tr>
<tr><td>Swedish</td><td>Riksdag's Open Data</td><td></td><td></td><td>•</td><td></td><td></td><td></td><td>XML</td><td>↓</td></tr>
<tr><td>7 lang.</td><td>The ParlSpeech V2 data set</td><td></td><td></td><td></td><td></td><td></td><td></td><td></td><td>↓</td></tr>
<tr><td>21 lang.</td><td>Europarl: European Parliament Proceedings Parallel Corpus 1996–2011</td><td></td><td></td><td></td><td></td><td></td><td></td><td>HTML</td><td>↓</td></tr>
</tbody>
</table>

Table 1: A different view on the overview of parliamentary corpora published by the CLARIN ERIC infrastructure on `https://www.clarin.eu/resource-families/parliamentary-corpora` as of 27 March, 2020. For each corpus we provide concordancers through which it is available (**K**-KonText, **SE**-(no)SketchEngine, **Kr**-Korp, **N**-NKJP, **C**-Corpuscle, **w**-dedicated website), its internal format, and an url link if a corpus is available to download. **+T** by ParCzech stands for KonText+TEITOK.

2. Digital repository of the Czech Parliament

Digital repository of the Parliament of the Czech Republic `https://public.psp.cz/en/sqw/hp.sqw?k=82` contains recording of the Assemblies since the earliest time of their existence until the last sitting of parliament. It consists of two parts: Bohemian Diet from its first reported (not directly recorded) acts in 1039 until 1848. Various historical periods have variable recordings, but many do contain transcripts. E.g. for the period 1526–1611 we can see by looking for the first period (1526–1545) (`https://public.psp.cz/eknih/snemy/v010/`) that there is the first correspondence of the Diet and records of the most important acts, mostly elections of Czech kings. After that the content of each Diet follows. The contents are in form of letters, but they are rather detailed and for most assemblies they consists of dozens of documents, arguments and replies, rather well documenting issues of the assembly. There are excuses for not participating due to sickness, there are king's proposals for the diet, diet's replies, e.g. this one concerning help fighting Turks: `https://public.psp.cz/eknih/snemy/v010/1545/t032600.htm`. For this period of 19 years there are 336 documents. Later diets are documented progressively better. For a diet of February 4–19, 1605 there are 46 documents (`https://public.psp.cz/eknih/snemy/v11a/`) Between the years 1611 and 1847 very few documents have been digitised, although the diet was active for the whole time.

From 1848, when the Austrian parliament was reformed and first members of the Bohemian Diet were elected also from citizens, the parliaments and their chambers of first Austrian, later Czechoslovak, and currently Czech Parliaments are available in the repository: `https://public.psp.cz/eknih/index.htm`. For all of these parliaments, protocols of each meeting are available in the repository. For the Austrian period the documents are often in German and are more similar to minutes rather than full transcript.[6] In general, form and quality of the Austrian' era transcripts are very variable, but they might become an interesting resource in future.

Since establishment of the first parliament of the new Czechoslovak Republic in 1918 the available documents are much more extensive. For every sitting, there is a "nest"-style site which has not only full transcripts, but there are also registries of all members of parliament (MOP) and its organs, for each MOP there is a list of their activities in the meetings[7], registry of "parliamentary prints", i.e. documents submitted to the parliament for discussion and vote, etc. lists of committees, and lists of topics in the prints and transcripts. All of these documents are published basically in plain text.[8] This structure remains in general constant all the way until 1989, with only a minor addition of additional documents like invitations to parliamentary sessions.

A substantial improvement of the proceedings has occured with the newly elected House of Deputies for 2006–2010. From the first sitting of this house in addition to transcripts[9], which are necessarily edited at least for fluency of spoken language, also the unedited audio recordings of the sessions are available.[10] Then from the sitting Senate of 2010–2012 also the Senate has improved their data and their transcripts are available in XML (XHTML) with linked votes, audio and even video recordings.[11] A small problem is in the form of published audio and video, which is available for streaming, not for a simple download. However in general we can say that from 2010 all the proceedings of the Parliament of the Czech Republic are available in the rich form of agenda, documents, transcripts of the proceedings, and votes, together with audio recording of the proceedings. All of this can be downloaded from the Digital repository of the Parliament.

3. Stenographic Protocols

The Czech Chamber of Deputies uses stenography to record its meetings like few other countries (Torregrossa, 2016). Stenography allows reporters to take notes during sittings and then they need time to transcribe them listening to the audio recording. The Czech Chamber of Deputies reporters take 10 minute shifts and then they have 80–90 minutes to transcribe their records. The draft versions of stenographic protocols are published online on the same day and it takes several days to do language revisions and get the final versions. Finally the speakers have 2–3 weeks for authorization. Figure 1 presents the protocol that has been already published online but neither correction nor authorization has been done yet.

The language revisions respect differences between spoken and written language. Reporters put focus on incorrect endings and cases, apparently incorrect word order, stuttering, evident slip of the tongue, if not further repaired, excessive use of personal and demonstrative pronouns, word repetition unless it is an intention. On the other hand, editing of factual errors and mistakes is not acceptable. In addition, notes important for capturing the atmosphere of the meeting and the events in the meeting hall are added to the text in brackets only to the extent strictly necessary and as objective as possible. Minor modifications for the purpose of text formatting are permitted. The reporters can neither correct nor replace offensive and indecent words. The speeches

---

[6]Some protocols, e.g. 1866, have not been processed via OCR because they are typeset in fraktur (gothic) font. Interestingly, they are detailed stenographic protocols and have been published in parallel in German and Czech.

[7]C.f. activities of senators (MOP from the upper chamber) with names starting with 'E' in 1925: `https://public.psp.cz/eknih/1925ns/se/rejstrik/jmenny/e.htm`

[8]This level of detail is true for the pre-WWII Czechoslovak parliament and post-war federal parliament. National – Czech and Slovak – assemblies only have transcripts available.

[9]`https://public.psp.cz/eknih/2006ps/stenprot/`

[10]`https://public.psp.cz/eknih/2006ps/audio/2006/`

[11]The first XHTML transcript: `https://www.senat.cz/xqw/webdav/pssenat/original/66197/55769` and linked vote: `https://www.senat.cz/xqw/xervlet/pssenat/hlasy?G=11178&O=8`

must remain undistorted and authentic regardless of their content and political affiliation of their speakers.

Spoken and written language differ in many ways, e.g. speech can use timing, tone, volume, and timbre to add emotional context. In order to provide a complete picture of the event, a corresponding part of the audio recording is available for each stenographic protocol.

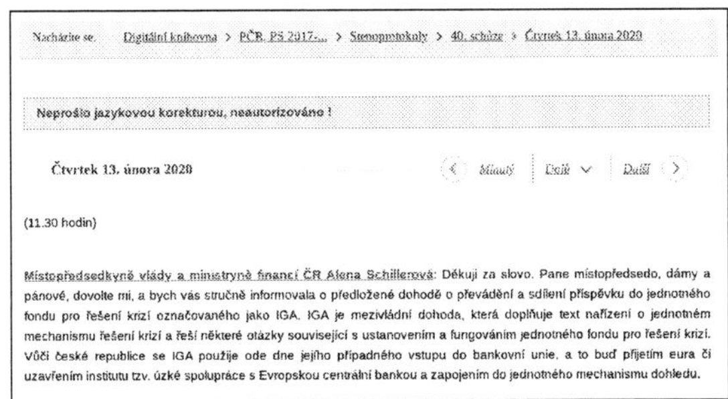

Figure 1: Neither correction nor authorisation of the given stenographic protocol published online has been done yet, see the information *Neprošlo jazykovou korekturou, neautorizováno!* at the top of the screenshot.

4. Compiling the Protocols into a Corpus

We take the following steps in order to compile the stenographic protocols of the Czech Chamber of Deputies into the ParCzech corpus:

Study source data We identified *what works* and *what does not work* in the protocols of each Chamber of Deputies published during the eight parliamentary terms.[12] Namely we focused on the features of author identification, links to the authors, links to the agenda items, spoken interpellation, availability of audio recordings, browsing the data. Since most of the features work for the protocols between 2013–present we have decided to compile this subset of the protocols first.

Get and encode source data We downloaded the 2013+ protocols and converted them into the ParlaCLARIN TEI based format.[13] Since that moment we call this collection the ParCzech corpus.

One TEI document corresponds to one agenda item. We label the documents in a way that describes a hierarchy of terms, meetings, sittings, and agenda items. All meetings are numbered from 001 onwards for each term, sittings from 01 onwards for each meeting, agenda items from 001 onwards for each meeting. For illustration, the document 2013-001-01-005 is a protocol of speeches on the fifth agenda item (005) made in the first sitting (01) of the first meeting (001) of the term that started in 2013 (2013). The document 2013-001-01-003b.u is a protocol of speeches on the third agenda item made in multiple parts and b stands for the second part; the suffix u stands for an unauthorized version.

---

[12] 1993–1996, 1996–1998, 1998–2002, 2002–2006, 2006–2010, 2010–2013, 2013–2017, 2017–present

[13] https://clarin-eric.github.io/parla-clarin/#sec-intro

It may happen that one agenda item is being discussed more than once during a current sitting. In other words, an agenda item discussion can be interrupted with a discussion on a different agenda item. But it does not affect our strategy to store one agenda item in a single TEI document. Sitting openings are stored in single TEI documents. The data scrapper is implemented as a Perl script downloading both the newly published protocols (i.e. not authorized yet) and the authorized protocols.

The version of 2013–present ParCzech consists of in 4,689 TEI documents containing 136,888 speeches, 1,312,897 sentences and 23,360,798 tokens.

The Czech Chamber of Deputies publishes audio recordings as mp3 files on its website. We have not aligned these audio files with the TEI documents yet.

Process ParCzech We enrich ParCzech automatically by morphological and named-entity annotations using the procedures MorphoDita[14] and NameTag[15], resp. (Straková et al., 2014). We run MorphoDita with the model MorfFlex CZ (Straka and Straková, 2016) and NameTag with the CNEC model (Straka and Straková, 2014). NameTag classifies entities into a set of 42 classes (called "types") with a very detailed characterization and these fine-grained classes are merged into 7 super-classes (called "supertypes"). In comparison with the ParlaCLARIN TEI elements, the repertoire of the NameTag classes is richer and therefore we introduce new TEI elements not included in the ParlaCLARIN TEI format recommendations.

5. ParCzech in TEITOK

TEITOK is a web-based platform for viewing, creating, and editing corpora with both rich textual mark-up and linguistic annotation.[16] It communicates with the KonText search engine allowing evaluation of simple and complex queries, displaying their results as concordance lines, computing frequency distribution and further work with language data.[17] The ParCzech corpus is downloadable and accessible in TEITOK at

```
http://hdl.handle.net/11234/1-3174
```

Figure 2 illustrates four different options over which users can browse ParCzech (sitting date, meeting, term, authorized). For example, when browsing over the sitting date users can see that four items of the fifth meeting in the term 2013–2017 were on the agenda on 21 January 2014.

TEITOK uses the Corpus Query Processor (CQP) to query corpora in the CQP query language (CQL).[18] Figure 3 illustrates a query builder that provides an easy way to define queries in CQL. At present, users can formulate queries on words, lemma, part-of-speech tags, named entities, and speakers.

---

[14] http://ufal.mff.cuni.cz/morphodita

[15] http://ufal.mff.cuni.cz/nametag

[16] http://teitok.corpuswiki.org

[17] https://lindat.mff.cuni.cz/services/kontext/corpora/corplist

[18] http://cwb.sourceforge.net/index.php

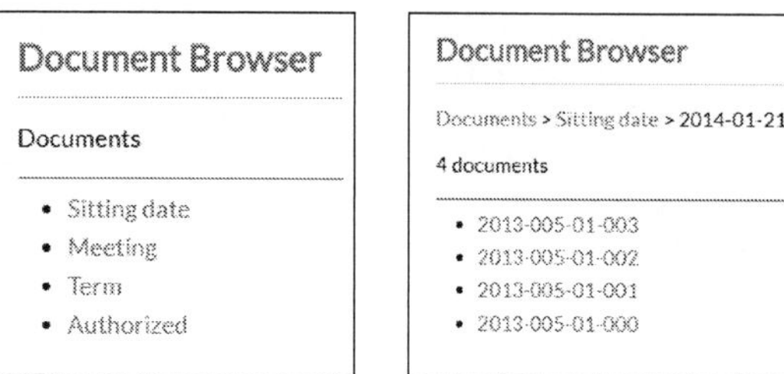

Figure 2: Browsing the ParCzech corpus in TEITOK

Figure 3: TEITOK interface to query ParCzech

6. Conclusion

Publishing the proceedings in the form of coherent and annotated dataset is also important from the perspective of data accessibility. While the Library of the Parliament of the Czech Republic has done a very good job in publishing all of the material, it is still available in a complicated and easily broken form. Making it all available as not only an online searchable service, but also a downloadable and citable collection available with a PID via a certified data repository will significantly improve the accessibility of the data and its availability for further research.

We have designed and implemented a procedure to compile the Czech stenographic protocols into a corpus which we call the ParCzech corpus. The corpus is accessible and searchable in the TEITOK tool and it is directly downloadable. However, our compilation pipeline is not fully tuned. Mainly we have to concentrate on studying the protocol flow in the Digital repository of the Parliament of the Czech Republic since it affects the procedure of ParCzech regular updates. Once we fix it, we will focus on interlinking ParCzech with other data sources.

Acknowledgements

We wish to thank Maarten Janssen, the author of TEITOK, for his advice on the stenographic protocol representation and on uploading the protocols into TEITOK. This work has been using language resources and tools developed and/or stored and/or distributed by the LINDAT/CLARIAH-CZ project of the Ministry of Education, Youth and Sports of the Czech Republic (project LM2018101).

7. Bibliographical References

Erjavec, T. and Pančur, A. (2019). Parla-CLARIN: TEI guidelines for corpora of parliamentary proceedings, September. https://doi.org/10.5281/zenodo.3446164.

Darja Fišer, et al., editors. (2018). *Proceedings of LREC2018 Workshop ParlaCLARIN: Creating and Using Parliamentary Corpora*. European Language Resources Association (ELRA), Paris, France.

Jakubíček, M. and Kovář, V. (2010). CzechParl: Corpus of Stenographic Protocols from Czech Parliament. In *Proceedings of Recent Advances in Slavonic Natural Language Processing, RASLAN 2010*, pages 41–46.

Straková, J., Straka, M., and Hajič, J. (2014). Open-Source Tools for Morphology, Lemmatization, POS Tagging and Named Entity Recognition. In *Proceedings of 52nd Annual Meeting of the Association for Computational Linguistics: System Demonstrations*, pages 13–18, Baltimore, Maryland, June. Association for Computational Linguistics. http://www.aclweb.org/anthology/P/P14/P14-5003.pdf.

Torregrossa, G. (2016). The production of parliamentary reports – a research about the methods used in different countries. IPRS. https://issuu.com/iprs/docs/torregrossa2016.

8. Language Resource References

Pančur, A., Erjavec, T., Ojsteršek, M., Šorn, M., and Blaj Hribar, N. (2019). Slovenian parliamentary corpus siParl 1.0 (1990–2018). Slovenian language resource repository CLARIN.SI. http://hdl.handle.net/11356/1236.

Pražák, A. and Šmídl, L. (2012). Czech Parliament Meetings. LINDAT/CLARIAH-CZ digital library at the Institute of Formal and Applied Linguistics (ÚFAL), Faculty of Mathematics and Physics, Charles University. http://hdl.handle.net/11858/00-097C-0000-0005-CF9C-4.

Straka, M. and Straková, J. (2014). Czech models (CNEC) for NameTag. LINDAT/CLARIAH-CZ digital library at the Institute of Formal and Applied Linguistics (ÚFAL), Faculty of Mathematics and Physics, Charles University. http://hdl.handle.net/11858/00-097C-0000-0023-7D42-8.

Straka, M. and Straková, J. (2016). Czech models (MorfFlex CZ 161115 + PDT 3.0) for MorphoDiTa 161115. LINDAT/CLARIAH-CZ digital library at the Institute of Formal and Applied Linguistics (ÚFAL), Faculty of Mathematics and Physics, Charles University. http://hdl.handle.net/11234/1-1836.

Proceedings of ParlaCLARIN II Workshop, pages 23–27
Language Resources and Evaluation Conference (LREC 2020), Marseille, 11–16 May 2020
© European Language Resources Association (ELRA), licensed under CC-BY-NC

Unfinished Business: Construction and Maintenance of a Semantically Tagged Historical Parliamentary Corpus, UK Hansard from 1803 to the present day

Matthew Coole, Paul Rayson, John Mariani
Lancaster University
Lancaster, UK
{m.coole, p.rayson, j.mariani}@lancaster.ac.uk

Abstract

Creating, curating and maintaining modern political corpora is becoming an ever more involved task. As interest from various social bodies and the general public in political discourse grows so too does the need to enrich such datasets with metadata and linguistic annotations. Beyond this, such corpora must be easy to browse and search for linguists, social scientists, digital humanists and the general public. We present our efforts to compile a linguistically annotated and semantically tagged version of the Hansard corpus from 1803 right up to the present day. This involves combining multiple sources of documents and transcripts. We describe our toolchain for tagging; using several existing tools that provide tokenisation, part-of-speech tagging and semantic annotations. We also provide an overview of our bespoke web-based search interface built on LexiDB. In conclusion, we examine the completed corpus by looking at four case studies making use of semantic categories made available by our toolchain.

Keywords: Corpus, Construction, Hansard, Semantic Annotation

1. Introduction

Parliamentary discourse is of concern not only to political and linguistic scholars but also social charities and community groups. The transcriptions of speeches and discussions in the UK Houses of Lords and the Commons are better known as Hansard. Recent reports from these proceedings are freely available online. Historical transcriptions are available in the form of the Historical Hansard corpus which includes the transcriptions from 1803-2005. Previously the SAMUELS[1] (Semantic Annotation and Mark-Up For Enhancing Lexical Searches) project has researched tokenising and tagging this corpus (Wattam et al., 2014). As political engagement grows daily alongside the Hansard corpus transcripts, bridging this gap from 2005 to the present and maintaining an up to date, fully tokenised and tagged version of this dataset becomes increasingly relevant and important to improve search functionality and timeliness.

This paper presents the process, tools and output of our efforts to build a complete corpus of Hansard that contains linguistic and semantic annotations and runs right up to the present day. We also describe how this corpus is made available through a bespoke search interface built on top of the corpus database LexiDB. Through the use of our framework, the latest data from Hansard is continually downloaded, tagged and indexed in the database daily, meaning we have a live version of the parliamentary proceedings that is always up to date.

There are other forms of the Hansard corpus available online. Mark Davies provides access to the historical portion of Hansard up to 2005 through an online interface [2]. The primary advantage over this is our corpus has data from the latest parliamentary debates right up to the present day. The Hansard at Huddersfield[3] project has been updated to include all contributions up to 2019. However, whilst this data is presented in an attractive interface it is not linguistically tagged with semantic tags or POS (part-of-speech) tags making it more difficult to search for linguistic features based on such tags.

2. Background

In recent years, more and more nations have had their parliamentary discourse curated into a corpus format. This has inevitably involved various methods of cleaning the source data and transcriptions. Sometimes this is a simple task when the original data is consistently formatted using XML or another easy to interpret form. This may be simply mapping from one format to another such as the case of SLov-Parl 2.0 (Pančur et al., 2017) converting between HTML and XML. Sometimes the process may be more involved, such as parsing PDF source documents that may even be scans of the original handwritten paper transcripts.

Transcriptions for UK Hansard are made available online daily[4] and are available in XML format. Although easy to parse, the data within this XML format is not clean and is very sparsely documented with no consistent schema to process many aspects of the documents, particularly regarding the metadata. Previous work on the Parliamentary Discourse[5] and SAMUELS[6] projects had provided a cleaned-up version of the data prior to 2005. This put the data into a single text file per member contribution (speech or similar). The metadata for each contribution was then recorded in a separate TSV (tab-separated values) file containing information such as the member name, date of the contribution, current parliament sitting, house session etc. This made for

---

[1] `https://www.gla.ac.uk/schools/critical/`
`research/fundedresearchprojects/samuels/`
[2] `https://www.english-corpora.org/hansard/`
[3] `https://hansard.hud.ac.uk/site/index.php`
[4] `https://hansard.parliament.uk/`
[5] `https://www.gla.ac.uk/schools/critical/`
`research/fundedresearchprojects/`
`parliamentarydiscourse/`
[6] `https://www.gla.ac.uk/schools/critical/`
`research/fundedresearchprojects/samuels/`

easier consumption of the source texts for linguistic tagging and annotation whilst still retaining the metadata in a form that could be easily searched and cross-referenced.

Other efforts have been made to add semantic topics to British Parliamentary speeches. Research (Nanni et al., 2019) grouping all speeches from the houses into semantic topics based on the content of the contribution provides a means of searching within Hansard for speeches not only based on MP information but also based on the topic discussed. This work utilised the publication of the Hansard corpus from another initiative, TheyWorkForYou [7] (run by MySociety[8]) provides a version of the Hansard transcripts back to 1918 which is cleaned with disambiguated MPs names and affiliations allowing for easier searching of this metadata when compared to that provided in the Historic Hansard corpus from the SAMUELS project.

3. Data collection

The Historical Hansard corpus covers transcriptions from 1803 - 2005 in both the House of Lords and the House of Commons. This data is freely available online [4][0] to anyone who wishes to use it. Previously the historic portion of the Hansard corpus has been processed through Lancaster University's linguistic toolchain (described below). This historic section of the corpus consists of just under 1.7 billion words (when tokenised through CLAWS) in around 7.5 million files.

For post-2005 data, several sources are available. The parliamentary website provides Atom feeds to allow for daily transcripts to be downloaded, but their API is not particularly useful in retrieving individual speeches from specific dates. TheyWorkForYou provides a means of accessing raw scraped XML from speeches back to 1919 as well as an open-source parser for cleaning the source XML data. Using this as well as a script provided by the Hansard at Huddersfield project all missing data after 2005 was retrieved and added to the original historic data to create a complete corpus of Hansard from 1803 onwards. The additional data consisted of approximately 315 million additional tokens in 4,302 files bringing the total corpus to approximately two billion words (the modern data contains several member contributions per file as opposed to the historic data which was divided into a single member's contribution per file).

The post-2005 data was brought as close as possible to being in line with the format produced from the SAMUELS project for Historic Hansard. Each source XML file contains multiple contributions from a single sitting of one of the houses. Each contribution was split into a separate file (consistent with Historic Hansard). This created around 1.2 million additional files which brought the total number of files in the corpus up to around 8.8 million. Each contribution file is stored in the original plain text as a TXT file and a tagged version in TSV format. TSV files were used as opposed to other XML based formats such as TEI based ParlaClarin format[9] to remain consistent with the output of

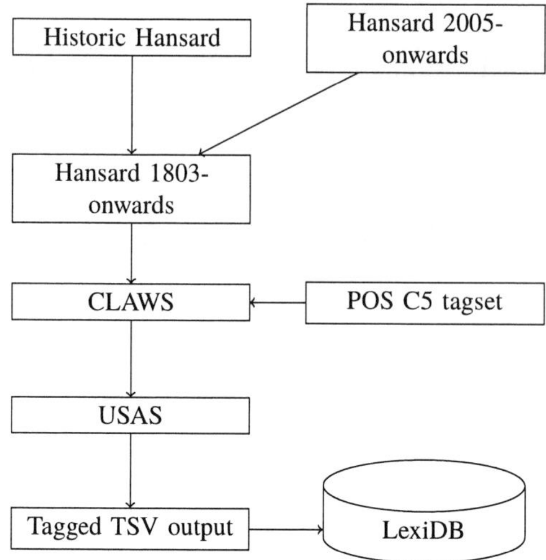

Figure 1: Annotation Processing pipeline

the SAMUELS project. From the source XML file metadata was extracted to produce a similar supplementary TSV as is available with Historic Hansard. From the source XML, the date, member name, current parliament and sitting were extracted. In addition to this, we also extracted the PimsId (Parliamentary Information Management System ID) as these allow us to link to the open parliament site [10] and can provide means of linking to resources on the semantic web.

4. Tool Chain

4.1. Processing pipeline

4.1.1. CLAWS

CLAWS (Constituent Likelihood Automatic Word-tagging System) (Garside, 1987) is a part-of-speech (POS) tagger that also functions as a tokeniser. POS tagging is the most common form of linguistic annotation and CLAWS performs this operation on English text and has been used to tokenise and POS tag many different corpora in the past including the British National Corpus (BNC)[11](Leech et al., 1994). CLAWS outputs a vertical format where each line corresponds to a single token (the smallest meaningful unit of text) and includes a POS tag based on the C5 tagset[12]. This tagset consists of 62 tag codes e.g. NN1 (singular noun), PNX (reflexive noun) etc. CLAWS has an error-rate of only 1.5%, is the defacto standard for British corpora such as the BNC (Garside and Smith, 1997), Mark Davies' BYU English corpora and was the tagger used in the SAMUELS project.

4.1.2. USAS

USAS (UCREL Semantic Analysis System) (Rayson et al., 2004) semantically tags text using a semantic tagset[13] based on 21 main discourse fields. The major fields include categories such as; emotion, money & commerce, science & technology, food & farming etc. The tagset is tiered with

---

[7] http://parser.theyworkforyou.com/hansard.html

[8] https://www.mysociety.org/

[9] https://github.com/clarin-eric/parla-clarin

[10] https://api.parliament.uk/

[11] http://www.natcorp.ox.ac.uk/

[12] http://ucrel.lancs.ac.uk/claws5tags.html

[13] http://ucrel.lancs.ac.uk/usas/semtags.txt

each of these main 21 domains containing a number of subgroups[14]. In total there are 232 semantic tags. USAS can make use of CLAWS' vertical POS tagged output and produce output in various formats such as TSV. The English tagger is around 91% accurate, and it has been extended to multiple languages beyond English (Piao et al., 2016), and experiments are ongoing to incorporate neural and deep learning methods (Ezeani et al., 2019).

4.2. Corpus Interface

4.2.1. Overview

The data produced by the above pipeline is then indexed and stored in a LexiDB (Coole et al., 2016) instance. LexiDB is used as previous work (Coole et al., 2015) has shown other database technologies struggle to handle language corpora of the scale constructed here. LexiDB was specifically designed to handle corpus data in a way that allows it to both scale-out and be queried in a manner akin to other corpus data systems. The advantage of LexiDB is as further parliamentary data becomes available the database can easily be added to regularly, even as often as daily. This makes it feasible to run the processing pipeline whenever new data becomes available online[15] making for a truly "live", semantically tagged version of parliamentary debates available at all times.

4.2.2. Web Interface

A web interface[16] to the LexiDB instance hosting the compiled data was built to allow access to the full annotated corpus. This interface allows for several corpus queries to be run;

- Concordance search
- NGrams
- Word Lists
- Collocations
  - Log-likelihood
  - Mutual Information

Each of these query types has various options for filtering and sorting. Beyond this, a multitude of visualizations are available ranging from histograms for term occurrence over time to sunburst diagrams for exploring n-grams. Figure 4 shows the web interface.

The search bar allows for all of the annotation layers added to the data in the processing pipeline to be queried for. The query syntax takes the form of a regular expression over token stream and uses JSON query by example objects to represent tokens. A full in-depth guide to this syntax is available online[17]. The syntax will seem intuitive to corpus linguists and those already familiar with CQL (Corpus Query Language) used by CWB, CQPweb and SketchEngine, although the syntax differs from CQL in many ways, it is a result of combining JSON and regular expression syntax.

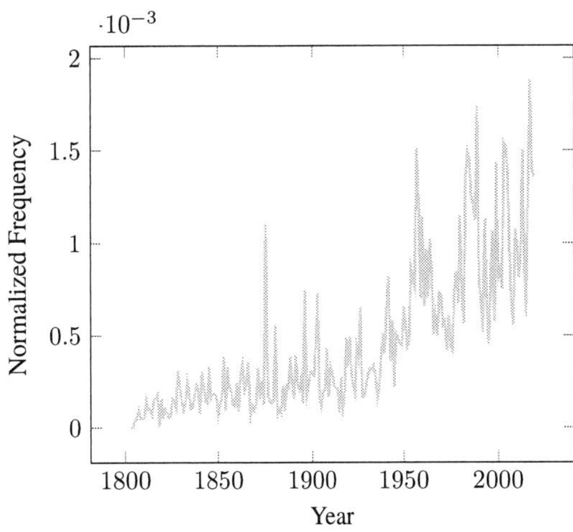

Figure 2: Semantic Category Y (Science & Technology) over time

5. Semantic Exploration

With the corpus complete and semantic tags available from 1803 onwards, we can examine various changes in the discourse based on the semantic categories available to us. In this vein, we look at four case studies examining the change in these semantic domains within both houses over time.

5.1. Science & Technology

The first semantic category examined is Science & Technology (Y*). This category includes two tags; Science & technology in general (Y1) and Information technology and computing (Y2). Figure 2 illustrates the change in this category over time. The plot is based on sub-sampling around 500 contributions per year and then the frequency is normalized as a proportion of all semantic tags that year. We can see a general trend that the discourse across both houses is becoming more and more frequently part of this semantic category. Digging beyond this we can observe how variations or spikes in the normalised frequency become bigger the later in the corpus we go. This could suggest Science & Technology can become hot topics of debate coinciding with major world incidence or advances in technology. Each of these spikes could be analysed in turn to examine what may have caused the discourse to shift towards this category at that time.

5.2. Numbers & Measurement

Numbers & Measurements (USAS tagged N*.*) contains various tags relating to maths and measurements; Mathematics (N2), Measurement: Distance (N3.3), Measurement: Area (N3.6) etc. Interestingly when comparing the semantic category of Science & Technology to that of Numbers & Measurement (Figure 3) we find that the trend of the normalised frequency of both generally increasing over time is true up until the late 20th century. Alarmingly at this point, the usage of numbers and measurements in both houses drops (proportionally to other semantic categories). One might expect as society moves towards greater scientific and technological understanding that there would be a continued increase in usage of specific measurements and statistics in

---

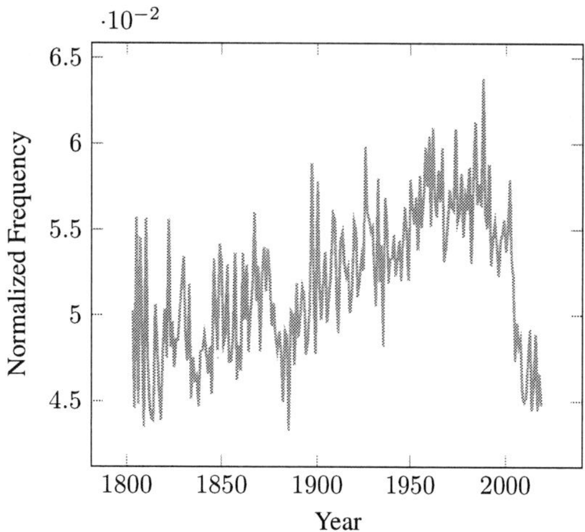

Figure 3: Semantic Category N (Numbers and Measurement) over time

discourse. This sudden decline entering the 21st century could indicate that politicians are becoming less precise when discussing issues and policies and not using precise figures, measurements or estimates and using vaguer language.

5.3. War & Warfare

The semantic category G3 (Warfare, defence and the army; weapons) is shown in the interface's histogram visualization[18]. This category represents a wider semantic field compared to the word "war" and the trends between this term and the semantic category can be compared over time. As can be seen in Figure 4 both the semantic category and the term "war" have peaks around both world wars as would be expected. Interestingly though through the latter part of the 20th century the G3 semantic category noticeably rises to a greater extent than the term "war", this could be investigated further through a concordance analysis as to why politicians are speaking more about topics relating to war than specifically mentioning "war", or are using terms metaphorically. This is a good example of the kind of exploration of this corpus that is possible with our web interface.

5.4. COVID-19

Another visualization possible through our web interface is the ability to produce word clouds based on collocation metrics. Figure 5 shows a word cloud based on a general search for coronavirus; `(covid|COVID)-19|[Cc]oronavirus` and using the log-likelihood metric for collocations around this search term, the higher the metric the larger word appears. This includes the top 150 collocations of the search and is a good starting point for linguists to explore what is being said in this area before performing a more fine-grained analysis.

6. Conclusion

We have presented here our research to update the UK Hansard corpus. Our main contributions are: 1) a fully

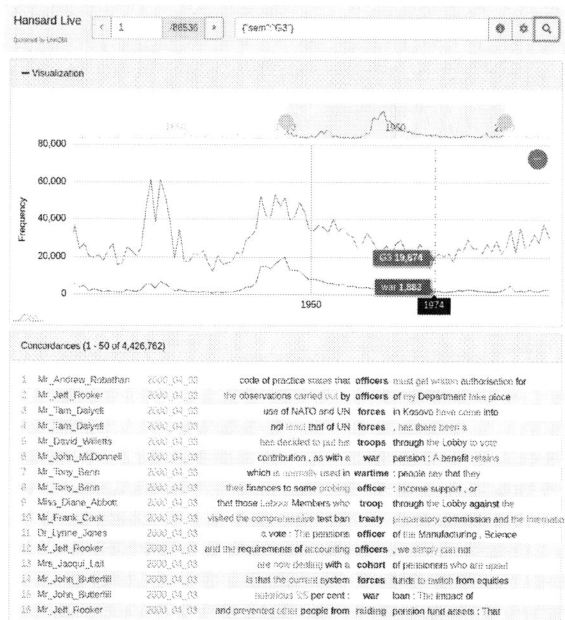

Figure 4: Web Interface showing War & G3 Semantic Tag searches

Figure 5: COVID-19 Wordcloud

tagged version of the Hansard corpus from 1803 up to the present data that is tokenised, POS tagged and semantically annotated 2) an NLP framework for annotation that can be fully automated and will be used going forward to keep our linguistically annotated version of the Hansard corpus up to date with new data as transcriptions from parliament become available daily 3) a search interface that allows for linguistic queries to be performed against the corpus as well as providing visualizations to better understand changes in political discourse over time. We will also make the entire semantically tagged corpus available for download through a link on our web interface page[19], observing the same licences as for the untagged data.

7. Acknowledgements

This research conducted by the lead author is funded at Lancaster University by an EPSRC Doctoral Training Grant. The SAMUELS project was funded by the Arts and Humanities Research Council in conjunction with the Economic and Social Research Council (grant reference AH/L010062/1) from January 2014 to April 2015.

---

[18]https://www.amcharts.com/

[19]http://ucrel.hansard-l.lancs.ac.uk

8. Bibliographical References

Coole, M., Rayson, P., and Mariani, J. (2015). Scaling out for extreme scale corpus data. In 2015 IEEE International Conference on Big Data, pages 1643–1649. IEEE.

Coole, M., Rayson, P., and Mariani, J. (2016). lexiDB: A scalable corpus database management system. In 2016 IEEE International Conference on Big Data (Big Data), pages 3880–3884. IEEE.

Ezeani, I., Piao, S., Neale, S., Rayson, P., and Knight, D. (2019). Leveraging pre-trained embeddings for welsh taggers. In Proceedings of the 4th Workshop on Representation Learning for NLP (RepL4NLP-2019), pages 270–280, Florence, Italy, August. Association for Computational Linguistics.

Garside, R. and Smith, N. (1997). A hybrid grammatical tagger: CLAWS4. *Corpus Annotation: Linguistic Information from Computer Text Corpora*, pages 102–121.

Garside, R. (1987). The CLAWS word-tagging system. *The Computational analysis of English: A corpus-based approach. London: Longman*, pages 30–41.

Leech, G., Garside, R., and Bryant, M. (1994). CLAWS4: the tagging of the British National Corpus. In COLING 1994 Volume 1: The 15th International Conference on Computational Linguistics.

Nanni, F., Menini, S., Tonelli, S., and Ponzetto, S. P. (2019). Semantifying the UK Hansard (1918-2018). In 2019 ACM/IEEE Joint Conference on Digital Libraries (JCDL), pages 412–413. IEEE.

Pančur, A., Šorn, M., and Erjavec, T. (2017). Slovenian parliamentary corpus SlovParl 2.0.

Piao, S., Rayson, P., Archer, D., Bianchi, F., Dayrell, C., El-Haj, M., Jiménez, R.-M., Knight, D., Křen, M., Löfberg, L., Nawab, R. M. A., Shafi, J., Teh, P. L., and Mudraya, O. (2016). Lexical coverage evaluation of large-scale multilingual semantic lexicons for twelve languages. In Proceedings of the Tenth International Conference on Language Resources and Evaluation (LREC'16), pages 2614–2619, Portorož, Slovenia, May. European Language Resources Association (ELRA).

Rayson, P., Archer, D., Piao, S., and McEnery, T. (2004). The UCREL semantic analysis system. In Proceedings of the workshop on Beyond Named Entity Recognition Semantic labelling for NLP tasks in association with 4th International Conference on Language Resources and Evaluation (LREC 2004), pages 7–12.

Wattam, S., Rayson, P., Alexander, M., and Anderson, J. (2014). Experiences with parallelisation of an existing NLP pipeline: Tagging hansard. In Proceedings of the Ninth International Conference on Language Resources and Evaluation (LREC'14), pages 4093–4096, Reykjavik, Iceland, May. European Language Resources Association (ELRA).

The siParl corpus of Slovenian parliamentary proceedings

Andrej Pančur, Tomaž Erjavec

Institute of Contemporary History, Department of Knowledge Technologies, Jožef Stefan Institute

Privoz 11, SI-1000 Ljubljana, Slovenia, Jamova cesta 39, SI-1000 Ljubljana, Slovenia

andrej.pancur@inz.si, tomaz.erjavec@ijs.si

Abstract

The paper describes the process of acquisition, up-translation, encoding, annotation, and distribution of siParl, a collection of the parliamentary debates from the Assembly of the Republic of Slovenia 1990–2018, covering the period from just before Slovenia became an independent country in 1991, and almost up to the present. The entire corpus, comprising over 8 thousand sessions, 1 million speeches and 200 million words was uniformly encoded in accordance with the TEI-based Parla-CLARIN schema for encoding corpora of parliamentary debates, and contains extensive meta-data about the speakers, a typology of sessions etc. and structural and editorial annotations. The corpus was also linguistically annotated using state-of-the-art tools. siParl is open source and maintained on GitHub with its major versions archived in the CLARIN.SI repository. It is also available for linguistic and content analysis through the on-line CLARIN.SI concordancers, thus offering an invaluable resource for scholars studying Slovenian political history.

Keywords: Slovenian parliamentary corpus, Text Encoding Initiative, StanfordNLP

1. Introduction

The unique content, structure and language of records of parliamentary debates are all factors make them an important object of study in a wide range disciplines in digital humanities and social sciences, such as political science (Van Dijk, 2010), sociology (Cheng, 2015), history (Pančur and Šorn, 2016), discourse analysis (Hirst et al., 2014), sociolinguistics (Rheault et al., 2016), and multilinguality (Bayley, 2004). Despite the fact that parliamentary discourse has become an increasingly important research topic in various fields of digital humanities and social sciences in the past 50 years (Chester and Bowring, 1962; Franklin and Norton, 1993), it has only recently started to acquire a truly interdisciplinary scope (Bayley, 2004). Recent developments enable cross-fertilization of linguistic studies with other disciplines and in-depth exploration of institutional uses of language, interpersonal behavior patterns, interplay between language-shaped facts, and reality-prompted language ritualisation and change (Ihalainen et al., 2016).

The most distinguishing characteristic of records of parliamentary debates is that they are essentially transcriptions of spoken language produced in controlled and regulated circumstances. For this reason, they are rich in invaluable (sociodemographic) meta-data. They are also easily available under various Freedom of Information Acts set in place to enable informed participation by the public and to improve effective functioning of democratic systems, making the datasets even more valuable for researchers with heterogeneous backgrounds.

This has motivated a number of national as well as international initiatives (for an overview, see Fišer and Lenardič (2018)) to compile, process and analyze parliamentary corpora. They are available for most European countries, with the UK's Hansard Corpus being the largest (1.6 billion tokens) and spanning the longest time period (1803–2005) while corpora from other countries are significantly smaller (most comprise between 10 and 100 million tokens) and cover significantly shorter periods (mostly from the 1970s onward).

There have also been two parliamentary corpora compiled in Slovenia, in particular the SlovParl corpus (Pančur et al., 2018) with about 10 million words, which contains minutes of the Assembly of the Republic of Slovenia for the legislative period 1990–1992 when Slovenia became an independent country, and the Parlameter corpus (Fišer et al., 2019) with about 40 million words, which covers the seventh mandate (2014–2018) of the Slovenian parliament. Both corpora are available under CC BY licences via the CLARIN.SI repository of language resources (Pančur et al., 2017; Dobranić et al., 2019).

In this paper we present the siParl corpus, which was made using the same basic workflow as for the SlovParl corpus, but encompasses, in addition to SlovParl, i.e. the period 1990–1992, also all the years up to 2018, leading to an (almost) comprehensive Slovenian parliamentary corpus, with close to 200 million words, making it one of the larger available parliamentary corpora.

Version 1.0 of this corpus was compiled and made available in the CLARIN.SI repository in 2019 (Pančur et al., 2019), while in this paper we present siParl version 2.0, which is also available in the repository (Pančur et al., 2020) and includes the same text but, in contrast to version 1.0, has much improved manually checked metadata, has been re-encoded to comply with the Parla-CLARIN recommendation for encoding of parliamentary corpora (Erjavec and Pančur, 2019), and has been newly linguistically annotated using state-of-the-art tools.

The rest of the paper is structured as follows: Section 2. overviews the compilation of the corpus and gives information on the corpus structure and size, Section 3. introduces the Parla-CLARIN encoding of the corpus, Section 4. explains its linguistic annotation, Section 5. describes how the corpus is distributed, and Section 6. gives some conclusions and directions for further research.

2. Corpus compilation and structure

In the design of siParl corpus, we attempted to satisfy the following desiderata:

Proceedings of ParlaCLARIN II Workshop, pages 28–34
Language Resources and Evaluation Conference (LREC 2020), Marseille, 11–16 May 2020
© European Language Resources Association (ELRA), licensed under CC-BY-NC

1. **Multidisciplinary:** The corpus must be useful for as many disciplines as possible. To attain this goal, the siParl corpus (as well as this paper) was created in close cooperation between the Slovenian DARIAH and CLARIN infrastructures.

2. **All-inclusive:** In addition to parliamentary debates, other types of parliamentary papers are also planned to be included.

3. **Long-term:** Since such large-scale plans can't be realized during the period of a short-term research project, these activities should be financed as part of the work of long-term research infrastructures.

4. **Open science:** All previous principles can be optimally realized in accordance with the principles of open science, i.e. the corpus should be made available under FAIR principles[1].

The transcriptions of parliamentary debates of the National Assembly of the Republic of Slovenia are available as HTML files on the web pages of National Assembly[2]. With the help of BeautifulSoup[3] and Python we scraped the wanted data from their website.

The uniform structure of documents with parliamentary debates is, in principle, well suited for automatic annotation. However, for the case of our source documents, it turned out that the HTML files for the period 1990–1996 do not contain born-digital text, thus being differently structured from the rest and had to be processed separately. The later documents also have problematic HTML markup, as layout and other typographical aspects of source text (bold, italic, underline, indent, uppercase, punctuation, spacing) are not always consistently applied. Therefore, when converting from HTML to XML, a rather complex and very time-consuming (the effort estimated at about 1.2 FTE) semi-automatic annotation needed to be performed in several steps, where each step contained:

1. developing XSLT stylesheets for automatic annotation;

2. developing XPath and regular expressions to search for annotation errors;

3. manual correction of identified errors.

It should also be noted that significant effort was invested in obtaining speaker metadata, such as their place and date of birth, the chronology of their party membership, link to their Wikipedia article etc., and that this information is also included in the corpus.

Parliamentary debates for a particular nation typically have a quite uniform structure, which fluctuates very little in time (Marx, 2009) and this also applies to Slovenian parliamentary debates. By analysing representative samples we arrived at the following general structure of parliamentary proceedings, given below with the minimal and maximal occurrences of structural elements:

---

[1] https://www.go-fair.org/fair-principles/
[2] https://www.dz-rs.si
[3] https://www.crummy.com/software/
BeautifulSoup/

Level	Count
Legislative periods	8
Sessions	8,571
Days	11,351
MPs	660
Speakers	8,418
Speeches	1,083,233
Words	200,406,464
Sentences	11,019,550
Words	195,296,618
Tokens	228,152,632

Table 1: Basic statistics of the corpus

- Document (1, n)
  - Table of contents (0, 1)
  - List of speakers (0, 1)
  - Index (0, 1)
  - Annex (0, n)
  - Meeting (1, n)
    - Non-verbal content (0, n)
    - Topic (1, n)
      - Non-verbal content (0, n)
      - Speech (1, n)
      - Non-verbal content (0,n)
      - Paragraph (1, n)
      - Non-verbal content (0,n)

However, inside this general structure, that of individual documents is very flexible. They might contain all meetings of all parliamentary chambers in one year, one meeting that lasts for several days, or only one day of an interrupted meeting. A document may contain the table of contents, the list of speakers, the topic index and annexes (session papers, legislation), or these might be present in separate documents. Non-verbal content of parliamentary debates (i.e. metadata about the transcription, such as information about the meeting and chairperson, outcome of a vote, actions like applause, etc.) can be present anywhere in the structure of the meeting. Transition from one topic to another can occur during the chairman's speech.

On the basis of the encoded corpus we computed some basic statistics over siParl, which are given in Table 1. The first part of the table contains a summary of the main aspects of the corpus, with the number of words encompassing the complete corpus. The second part concerns the summary of the automatic linguistic annotation (further detailed in Section 4.), where it should be noted that this annotation was preformed only on the transcription proper, i.e. the non-verbal content was omitted from this annotation.

Table 2 gives similar information but separately for each of the eight legislative periods, where we also make the split between the sittings of the National Assembly and that of other working bodies, such as various commissions; for these we give the number of such bodies for each period. It should be noted that the "Words" column here contains all the text, including that of non-verbal items.

Legislative period	Organisation	No. of organisations	Sessions	Days	Speakers	MPs	Items of agenda	Speeches	Non-verbal items	Words
1990—1992	National Assembly	3	234	608	521	242	5,154	59,062	120,824	11,131,908
1992—1996	National Assembly	1	94	462	315	101	2,864	66,555	152,698	11,698,884
1996—2000	National Assembly	1	76	430	359	105	3,256	55,852	133,164	10,763,395
	Working Bodies	27	1,274	1,711	1,268	108	6,327	155,514	216,135	17,953,666
2000—2004	National Assembly	1	89	303	296	105	2,636	56,157	91,089	10,358,962
	Working Bodies	27	1,129	1,405	1,291	102	4,855	126,014	187,105	16,408,922
2004—2008	National Assembly	1	82	283	237	102	2,770	63,443	79,326	13,312,828
	Working Bodies	25	1,211	1,300	1,886	101	4,779	115,260	175,972	18,323,287
2008—2011	National Assembly	1	84	233	191	103	2,340	51,381	62,262	11,712,103
	Working Bodies	25	1,204	1,308	2,144	102	4,508	82,380	123,984	17,031,791
2011—2014	National Assembly	1	96	196	202	114	1,912	37,073	43,925	8,205,794
	Working Bodies	28	1,136	1,125	1,994	111	3,831	68,777	99,783	14,784,252
2014—2018	National Assembly	1	104	288	207	101	2,809	52,268	61,837	14,516,417
	Working Bodies	22	1,758	1,699	2,697	100	5,606	93,497	139,834	24,204,255

Table 2: Basic statistics regarding different legislative periods

3. Corpus encoding

As mentioned, many researchers have already compiled corpora of parliamentary proceedings. However, these corpora are encoded in a variety of different annotation schemes, limiting their interchange and re-use. In order to overcome this problem, the CLARIN research infrastructure organised a workshop in 2019[4] at which the idea and draft of a common annotation scheme for encoding corpora of parliamentary proceedings was introduced, the participants presented their own experiences with encoding parliamentary corpora and gave their comments to the draft proposal. On this basis, guidelines and an XML schema, called Parla-CLARIN, was developed (Erjavec and Pančur, 2019), which is meant for encoding of parliamentary corpora for the purposes of scholarly investigations, and that could serve as a common storage and interchange format for such corpora. These recommendations attempt to take into account the following aspects of parliamentary corpora:

- Structure: legislative periods, sessions, topics, speeches, transcription variants

- Metadata: mandates, titles, parliamentary bodies, locations, dates and times

- Speakers: sex, date of birth, education, party membership, links to external resources

- Political parties: name(s), history, relations

- Speeches: speaker, text, comments, verbal and non-verbal interruptions

- Linguistic annotation: PoS tagging, word normalisation, named entity tagging, syntactic parsing etc.

- Multimedia: audio and video, facsimile of original transcript

The Parla-CLARIN recommendations are implemented as a parameterisation of the TEI Guidelines (TEI Consortium, 2011), which are XML-based recommendations for encoding texts for scholarly purposes. As opposed to most other such recommendations, the TEI Guidelines have the ambition to be applicable to texts in any language, of any date, and without restriction on form or content. There are a number of advantages of taking the TEI as the foundation of Parla-CLARIN. The recommendation does not need to specify and document a large number of elements, but only narrow down the choices offered by TEI and exemplify their use on concrete examples. As the CLARIN workshop showed, a number of existing parliamentary corpora are already encoded in some variant of TEI, making the conversion into a common TEI based-format much easier. The TEI parameterisation proposed for Parla-CLARIN allows a wide range of parliamentary proceedings to be encoded, while making explicit recommendations on the manner of encoding various phenomena.

Parla-CLARIN is written as a TEI ODD document, i.e. as a TEI document that contains both explanatory prose and the definition of the schema in the TEI ODD language. This document can be automatically converted either to a HTML view of the prose and schema parts, and to an XML schema. The recommendations are maintained on GitHub[5] from where they can be cloned, or read on the equivalent github.io pages.

---

[4] https://www.clarin.eu/blog/clarin-parlaformat-workshop

[5] https://github.com/clarin-eric/parla-clarin/

The presented siParl corpus is the first complete corpus that has been encoded according to the Parla-CLARIN recommendation, also in the hope that it will serve as a best-practice exemplar. Of course, siParl does not contain all the encoding supported by the Parla-CLARIN recommendation (e.g. multimedia, verbal interruptions), however, it does have rich metadata and linguistic annotation, so it can serve as a good example for the encoding recommendation. We next give some examples from the Parla-CLARIN encoded corpus[6]. First, complex metadata is encoded in various elements available in the teiHeader element, such as taxonomies and various types of lists offered by TEI. Figure 1 gives the example of the start of the event list element that contains the Slovene and English names of the eight legislative periods, treated as events, and their start and end dates; crucially, each period is also given its ID, which can then be referred to by other elements.

```
<listEvent>
 <head>Legislative periods</head>
 <event xml:id="DZ.1"
  from="1992-12-23" to="1996-11-27">
  <label xml:lang="sl">1. mandat</label>
  <label xml:lang="en">Term 1</label>
 </event>
 <event xml:id="DZ.2"
   from="1996-11-28" to="2000-10-26">
  <label xml:lang="sl">2. mandat</label>
  <label xml:lang="en">Term 2</label>
 </event>
   ...
```

Figure 1: Encoding of legislative periods.

Figure 2 illustrates the encoding of speakers, where, again, each person is given their ID that can then be referred to in the speeches, and then contains the person's basic metadata and their chronologically marked role(s) in the parliament with — where relevant — party affiliation(s), followed by link(s) to external resources, in particular, Wikipedia articles in Slovene, and, where available, also in English.

```
<person xml:id="ŠpiletičBogomir">
 <persName>
  <surname>Špiletič</surname>
  <forename>Bogomir</forename>
 </persName>
 <sex value="M"/>
 <birth when="1961-11-01"/>
 <death when="2013-06-17"/>
 <affiliation role="MP" ana="#DZ.2" ref="#DZ"
  from="1996-11-28" to="2000-10-26"/>
 <affiliation role="member" ana="#DZ.2"
  ref="#party.SDS.1"
  from="1996-11-28" to="2000-10-26"/>
 <idno type="wikimedia"
   xml:lang="sl">https:...</idno>
</person>
```

Figure 2: Encoding of person metadata.

---

[6]Note that for illustrative purposes some details of the encoding have been omitted, and the lines split, sometimes in places that would lead to ill-formed data.

Next, Figure 3 gives the encoding of one political party with its ID, name in Slovene and English, its acronym, the period of its existence, and link(s) to Wikipedia articles.

```
<org xml:id="party.SDS.1"
 role="political_party">
 <orgName full="yes"
  xml:lang="sl">Socialdemokratska
  stranka Slovenije</orgName>
 <orgName full="yes" xml:lang="en">Social
  Democratic Union of Slovenia</orgName>
 <orgName full="init">SDS</orgName>
 <event from="1989-02-16" to="2003-09-19">
  <label xml:lang="en">existence</label>
 </event>
 <idno type="wikimedia"
   xml:lang="sl">https:...</idno>
 <idno type="wikimedia"
   xml:lang="en">https:...</idno>
</org>
```

Figure 3: Encoding of party metadata.

Finally, Figure 4 gives the start of the body of one parliament session. The non-verbal events, i.e. transcription metadata is encoded in the note element, which are of various types, e.g. the first one giving the time when the session came to order and the second introducing the speaker. Each speech is marked by the utterance element, which gives the reference to the ID of the speaker and, in the analysis attribute, the reference to the role of the speaker inside the session.

Each speech is divided into segments, i.e. paragraphs as distinguished in the source transcriptions. These, in siParl, then have pure textual content with the exception of the gap element, which indicates that a part of the speech is missing, also giving the reason.

```
<body>
 <div>
  <note type="time">Seja se je pričela ob
  9.30 uri.</note>
  <note type="speaker">PREDSEDNIK RAFAEL
  KUŽNIK:</note>
  <u who="#KužnikRafael" ana="#chair">
  <seg>
   <gap reason="inaudible"/> in potem
   še točko razno.
    ...
```

Figure 4: Encoding of the transcription.

4. Linguistic annotation

The siParl corpus is available in two variants. The first, as introduced in the previous section, and manitaned on GitHub, contains meta-data, structural annotations, non-verbal items and speeches, and the plain-text of their segments. The second version is identical to the first, except that the segments have been linguistically annotated: each is tokenised, sentence segmented, part-of-speech tagged, lemmatised, parsed, and tagged with named entities. Such annotations significantly expand the possibilities of corpus analysis, in particular they allow to mount the corpus into web-based concordancers, such as those of the CLARIN.SI infrastructure, which then support complex queries over sequences of token annotations and displaying their concordancers, frequency lists, keyword lists of selected parts of the corpus based on the metadata etc.

The main linguistic annotation of the corpus was performed by CLASSLA-StanfordNLP[7] (Ljubešić and Dobrovoljc, 2019), a fork of the well-known StanfordNLP library[8] (Qi et al., 2018), which, inter alia, supports part-of-speech tagging, lemmatisation and dependency parsing. As opposed to StanfordNLP, the CLASSLA-StanfordNLP fork introduces some extensions, such as using an external dictionary while performing lemmatisation, and training the tagger and lemmatiser on more data than available in Universal Dependencies treebanks.

The CLASSLA-StanfordNLP pipeline obtains significantly better performance than previous tools for Slovenian, e.g. the accuracy of predicting the fine-grained PoS tags was improved from the previous 94.21% (using a CRF tagger trained on the same resources) to 97.06%.

We have annotated the corpus for fine-grained part-of-speech, i.e. morphosyntactic descriptions (MSD) using the MULTEXT-East[9] (Erjavec, 2012) schema for Slovenian, as well as with the part-of-speech and morphological features in the Universal Dependencies formalism for Slovenian (Dobrovoljc et al., 2017). The corpus was also lemmatised, important for Slovenian, as it is a highly inflecting language. Finally, the tool also parsed the corpus using the Universal Dependencies formalism. The CLASSLA-StanfordNLP models used for morphosyntactic annotation, lemmatisation and parsing are available from the CLARIN.SI repository (Ljubešić, 2020c; Ljubešić, 2020b; Ljubešić, 2020a).

The corpus was also annotated for named entities, using the Janes-NER tool [10], which is CRF-based and uses a rather standard feature set relevant for identifying named entities, as well as distributional information in form of Brown clusters (Brown et al., 1992). The evaluation of the tool (Fišer et al., 2018) showed that it has an average F1 score of 0.69, with the "other" class having the lowest F1 = 0.30, followed by organisations with F1 = 0.56, locations with F1 = 0.80, and the person class having the highest F1 = 0.92.https://rdcu.be/7RX4

Figure 5 illustrates the encoding of segments with added linguistic analyses. Each segment is composed of sentences, and these of words and punctuation symbols; the fact that adjacent tokens are not separated by a space is indicated by the join attribute. Each token is then annotated by its MULTEXT-East MSD as the value of the ana attribute and using the extended pointer syntax offered by TEI; in short, an MSD with the "mte" prefix in effect points to the definition of the MSD which gives its decomposition into a feature structure containing its attributes and their

---

values. The Universal Dependencies annotation is given as the value of the msd attribute. The syntactic dependencies are stored in the link group element, which contains links that connect the head and argument of the dependency relation, itself given in the ana attribute; again, the extended pointer syntax is used, to point to the full name of of each relation.

```
<seg xml:id="...seg8">
 <s xml:id="...seg8.s1">
  <gap reason="inaudible"/>
  <w xml:id="...seg8.s1.t1" ana="mte:Pr-nsa"
   msd="UposTag=PRON|Case=Acc|..."
   lemma="kar">Kar</w>
  <w xml:id="...seg8.s1.t2" ana="mte:Vmbm2p"
   join="right" msd="UposTag=VERB|.."
   lemma="izvoliti">izvolite</w>
  <pc xml:id="...seg8.s1.t3" ana="mte:Z"
   msd="UposTag=PUNCT">,</pc>
  <w xml:id="...seg8.s1.t4" ana="mte:Cs"
   join="right" msd="UposTag=SCONJ"
   lemma="da">da</w>
  <pc xml:id="...seg8.s1.t5" ana="mte:Z"
   msd="UposTag=PUNCT">.</pc>
  <linkGrp corresp="#...seg8.s1"
   targFunc="head argument" type="UD-SYN">
    <link ana="ud-syn:obj"
     target="#...seg8.s1.t2 #...seg8.s1.t1"/>
    <link ana="ud-syn:root"
     target="#...seg8.s1 #...seg8.s1.t2"/>
    <link ana="ud-syn:punct"
     target="#...seg8.s1.t4 #...seg8.s1.t3"/>
    <link ana="ud-syn:discourse"
     target="#...seg8.s1.t2 #...seg8.s1.t4"/>
    <link ana="ud-syn:punct"
     target="#...seg8.s1.t2 #...seg8.s1.t5"/>
  </linkGrp>
 </s>
</seg>
```

Figure 5: Linguistic annotation of the siParl corpus segment "*Kar izvolite, da.*"

5. Availability and maintenance

In accordance with our fourth basic principle (open science), we have made sure that the corpus is openly available, can be further developed in a collaborative fashion, has been converted into several immediately usable formats and, for the purposes of digital humanities and social sciences, also available through web applications.

As mentioned, the plain text version of the Parla-CLARIN encoded corpus is accessible and maintained on the DARIAH-SI GitHub repository[11]. This is also the place for users to post issues about the corpus or even send pull requests. It should be noted that while this project does not, due to its size, contain the linguistically annotated corpus, it does contain a folder with example documents and the scripts for annotation and conversion.

As mentioned, the major 2.0 version of the corpus is also available via the CLARIN.SI repository[12] (Pančur et al.,

---

[7] https://github.com/clarinsi/classla-stanfordnlp

[8] https://stanfordnlp.github.io/stanfordnlp/

[9] http://nl.ijs.si/ME/

[10] https://www.github.com/clarinsi/janes-ner

[11] https://github.com/DARIAH-SI/siParl

[12] http://hdl.handle.net/11356/1300

2020) under the Creative Commons CC BY licence. This repository item comprises six datasets:

1. the Parla-CLARIN encoded plain-text corpus (essentially a copy of the corpus from GitHub);

2. the Parla-CLARIN encoded linguistically analysed corpus;

3. the linguistically analysed corpus in the so called vertical format, used by various concordancers (this is a much simpler format to use than the source TEI, but does not contain all the information from the source);

4. the text of the linguistically analysed corpus in the CONLL-U format, used by the Universal Dependencies project;

5. the plain text of the linguistically analysed corpus;

6. TSV files giving the metadata of all sessions / speeches in the corpus.

The linguistically annotated version of siParl has also been mounted under the two concordancers available at CLARIN.SI, namely KonText and noSketch Engine, enabling on-line exploration of this and other corpora. The two concordancers are open source and both use the same Manatee back-end (Rychlý, 2007) and set of indexed corpora, but provide different front-ends. Apart from visual differences, KonText supports log-in via the authentication and authorization infrastructure (AAI), and, in fact, allows only basic functionality without logging in. However, log-in enables the user to personalise the visual appearance of the concordancer, save sub-corpora and the query history. On the other hand, noSketch Engine does not support log-in, so all its functionality is available to anonymous users, however, this also has the disadvantage of not allowing personalisation of the interface etc. As both concordancers use the same back-end, they also support querying via the powerful CQL query language, enabling searching via logical combinations of annotations, using regular expression, etc.

6. Conclusions

The paper presented siParl, a corpus of Slovenian parliamentary debates spanning the complete history of Slovenia as an independent country up to 2018. The corpus is fairly large with about 200 million words, and is, given the large amount of manual editing, fairly error-free. siParl 2.0 has been encoded according to the TEI-based Parla-CLARIN annotation scheme, is linguistically annotated with state-of-the-art tools for Slovenian, and is openly available via the CLARIN.SI repository and concordancers.

The corpus development is a good example of the possibilities of cooperation between the two distinct, but related research infrastructures, namely the Slovenian DARIAH and CLARIN, which is esp. obvious in the various distribution modes and formats of the corpus; here it should be noted that we also plan to mount the corpus in a form amiable for reading and browsing in the DARIAH-SI digital library and interconnect the corpus there with the one available via the concordancers.

In further work we plan to extend the corpus in three directions: include in it, in addition to the parliamentary debates, also other types of parliamentary papers, such as voting results, legislation, and summary records of meetings; extend it to include the materials from 2019 and 2020; and to include materials from before 1991, i.e. from the time when Slovenia was a part of the Socialist Republic of Yugoslavia. We also plan to further refine the encoding in combination with updating the Parla-CLARIN recommendation, which might become necessary when we consider other corpora of parliamentary debates to be included as exemplars for the proposed encoding.

Finally, we plan to make some effort in popularising the corpus among potential users from the fields of history, political science and linguistics, using the DARIAH-SI and CLARIN.SI dissemination networks and various local events.

Acknowledgements

We would like to thank the anonymous reviewers for their helpful suggestions on how to improve the paper. The work presented here was funded by the Slovenian research infrastructures DARAH-SI and CLARIN.SI and by the Slovenian Research Agency within the research program P2-0103 "Knowledge Technologies", and research infrastructure program I0-0013 "Slovenian historiography research infrastructure".

7. Bibliographical References

Bayley, P. (2004). *Cross-cultural perspectives on parliamentary discourse*, volume 10. John Benjamins Publishing.

Brown, P. F., Desouza, P. V., Mercer, R. L., Pietra, V. J. D., and Lai, J. C. (1992). Class-based n-gram models of natural language. *Computational linguistics*, 18(4):467–479.

Cheng, J. E. (2015). Islamophobia, muslimophobia or racism? parliamentary discourses on Islam and Muslims in debates on the minaret ban in Switzerland. *Discourse & Society*, 26(5):562–586.

Chester, D. N. and Bowring, N. (1962). *Questions in parliament*. Clarendon Press.

Dobrovoljc, K., Erjavec, T., and Krek, S. (2017). The universal dependencies treebank for Slovenian. In *Proceedings of the 6th Workshop on Balto-Slavic Natural Language Processing*, pages 33–38, Valencia, Spain, April. Association for Computational Linguistics.

Erjavec, T. and Pančur, A. (2019). Parla-CLARIN: TEI guidelines for corpora of parliamentary proceedings. In *TEI members meeting: What is text, really? TEI and beyond. Book of Abstracts*. University of Graz, September. https://gams.uni-graz.at/o:tei2019.157.

Erjavec, T. (2012). MULTEXT-East: morphosyntactic resources for Central and Eastern European languages. *Language Resources and Evaluation*, 46(1):35–57. https://doi.org/10.1007/s10579-011-9174-8.

Fišer, D., Ljubešić, N., and Erjavec, T. (2018). The Janes project: language resources and tools for Slovene user generated content. *Language Resources and Evaluation.* `https://rdcu.be/7RX4`.

Fišer, D. and Lenardič, J. (2018). Parliamentary corpora in the CLARIN infrastructure. In *Selected papers from the CLARIN Annual Conference 2017, Budapest, 18–20 September 2017*, pages 75–85. Linköping University Electronic Press.

Fišer, D., Ljubešić, N., and Erjavec, T. (2019). Parlameter – a corpus of contemporary Slovene parliamentary proceedings. *Prispevki za novejšo zgodovino*, 59(1):70–98. `http://ojs.inz.si/pnz/article/view/327/615`.

Franklin, M. N. and Norton, P. (1993). *Parliamentary Questions: For the Study of Parliament Group.* Oxford University Press, USA.

Hirst, G., Feng, V. W., Cochrane, C., and Naderi, N. (2014). Argumentation, ideology, and issue framing in parliamentary discourse. In *ArgNLP*.

Ihalainen, P., Ilie, C., and Palonen, K. (2016). *Parliament and Parliamentarism: A Comparative History of a European Concept.* Berghahn Books.

Ljubešić, N. and Dobrovoljc, K. (2019). What does Neural Bring? Analysing Improvements in Morphosyntactic Annotation and Lemmatisation of Slovenian, Croatian and Serbian. In *Proceedings of the 7th Workshop on Balto-Slavic Natural Language Processing*, pages 29–34, Florence, Italy, August. Association for Computational Linguistics.

Marx, M. (2009). Long, often quite boring, notes of meetings. In *ESAIR '09: Proceedings of the WSDM '09 Workshop on Exploiting Semantic Annotations in Information Retrieval*, pages 46–53, Barcelona, Spain, February.

Pančur, A. and Šorn, M. (2016). Smart Big Data: Use of Slovenian Parliamentary Papers in Digital History. *Prispevki za novejšo zgodovino/Contributions to Contemporary History*, 56(3):130–146.

Pančur, A., Šorn, M., and Erjavec, T. (2018). SlovParl 2.0 : The collection of Slovene parliamentary debates from the period of secession. In Darja Fišer, et al., editors, *Proceedings of LREC2018 Workshop ParlaCLARIN: Creating and Using Parliamentary Corpora*, pages 8–14, Paris, France, May. European Language Resources Association (ELRA). `http://lrec-conf.org/workshops/lrec2018/W2/summaries/4_W2.html`.

Qi, P., Dozat, T., Zhang, Y., and Manning, C. D. (2018). Universal dependency parsing from scratch. In *Proceedings of the CoNLL 2018 Shared Task: Multilingual Parsing from Raw Text to Universal Dependencies*, pages 160–170, Brussels, Belgium, October. Association for Computational Linguistics.

Rheault, L., Beelen, K., Cochrane, C., and Hirst, G. (2016). Measuring emotion in parliamentary debates with automated textual analysis. *PloS one*, 11(12):e0168843.

Rychlý, P. (2007). Manatee/Bonito - A Modular Corpus Manager. In *1st Workshop on Recent Advances in Slavonic Natural Language Processing*, pages 65–70, Brno. Masarykova univerzita.

TEI Consortium, e. (2011). *TEI P5: Guidelines for Electronic Text Encoding and Interchange.* TEI Consortium. `http://www.tei-c.org/P5/`.

Van Dijk, T. A. (2010). Political identities in parliamentary debates. *European Parliaments under Scrutiny. Discourse strategies and interaction practices*, pages 29–56.

8. Language Resource References

Dobranić, Filip and Ljubešić, Nikola and Erjavec, Tomaž. (2019). *Slovenian parliamentary corpus ParlaMeter-sl 1.0.* Jožef Stefan Institute, distributed via the Slovenian language resource repository CLARIN.SI, `http://hdl.handle.net/11356/1208`.

Ljubešić, Nikola. (2020a). *The CLASSLA-StanfordNLP model for for UD dependency parsing of standard Slovenian.* Jožef Stefan Institute, distributed via the Slovenian language resource repository CLARIN.SI, `http://hdl.handle.net/11356/1258`.

Ljubešić, Nikola. (2020b). *The CLASSLA-StanfordNLP model for lemmatisation of standard Slovenian 1.1.* Jožef Stefan Institute, distributed via the Slovenian language resource repository CLARIN.SI, `http://hdl.handle.net/11356/1286`.

Ljubešić, Nikola. (2020c). *The CLASSLA-StanfordNLP model for morphosyntactic annotation of standard Slovenian.* Jožef Stefan Institute, distributed via the Slovenian language resource repository CLARIN.SI, `http://hdl.handle.net/11356/1251`.

Pančur, Andrej and Šorn, Mojca and Erjavec, Tomaž. (2017). *Slovenian parliamentary corpus SlovParl 2.0.* Institute of Contemporary History, distributed via the Slovenian language resource repository CLARIN.SI, `http://hdl.handle.net/11356/1167`.

Pančur, Andrej and Erjavec, Tomaž and Ojsteršek, Mihael and Šorn, Mojca and Blaj Hribar, Neja. (2019). *Slovenian parliamentary corpus siParl 1.0 (1990-2018).* Institute of Contemporary History, distributed via the Slovenian language resource repository CLARIN.SI, `http://hdl.handle.net/11356/1236`.

Pančur, Andrej and Erjavec, Tomaž and Ojsteršek, Mihael and Šorn, Mojca and Blaj Hribar, Neja. (2020). *Slovenian parliamentary corpus siParl 2.0 (1990-2018).* Institute of Contemporary History, distributed via the Slovenian language resource repository CLARIN.SI, `http://hdl.handle.net/11356/1300`.

Proceedings of ParlaCLARIN II Workshop, pages 35–39
Language Resources and Evaluation Conference (LREC 2020), Marseille, 11–16 May 2020
© European Language Resources Association (ELRA), licensed under CC-BY-NC

Who Mentions Whom? Recognizing Political Actors in Proceedings

Lennart Kerkvliet, Jaap Kamps, Maarten Marx
Universiteit van Amsterdam
lennart.kerkvliet@student.uva.nl, {kamps, maartenmarx}@uva.nl

Abstract

We show that it is straightforward to train a state of the art named entity tagger (spaCy) to recognize political actors in Dutch parliamentary proceedings with high accuracy. The tagger was trained on 3.4K manually labeled examples, which were created in a modest 2.5 days work. This resource is made available on github. Besides proper nouns of persons and political parties, the tagger can recognize quite complex definite descriptions referring to cabinet ministers, ministries, and parliamentary committees. We also provide a demo search engine which employs the tagged entities in its SERP and result summaries.

Introduction

Parliamentary proceedings containing edited verbatim transcripts of debates can be seen as semistructured documents which convey *who said what (to whom) and in which capacity*[1]. Much of the work around ParlaClarin has been devoted to 1) *extracting* this structure from un- or partially structured textual formats like PDF, HTML or Word, and 2) defining an XML schema in which this structure can be encoded in an efficient manner preferably fitting every possible proceedings format. Several projects have shown that this extraction process is feasible for large diachronic corpora (Beelen et al., 2017; Palmirani and Vitali, 2011; Marx et al., 2010; Fišer et al., 2018; Blätte and Blessing, 2018). The main reason that this can be done is that parliamentary proceedings are predominantly based on the Hansard model, and tend to change very little during the years.

So the problem of *who says what* has been solved and we can ask complex information retrieval queries like *when did members from party X start speaking about immigration?* But we cannot yet ask the similar structured query which asks for speeches about immigration and *mentioning* a member of party X. This query is difficult because of two reasons: 1) member of party X refers to a set of persons which changes over time, and 2) these persons can be named in a number of different ways. The first problem can be solved using a parliamentary database indicating who was a member of which party in which period. The second is harder, especially in politics in which speakers can be rather creative in naming fellow MPs.[2]

The problem of "who mentions whom" can be solved using *named entity recognition* techniques (Cardie and Wilkerson, 2008; Lample et al., 2016) and then these recognized entities can be used in search systems following techniques from *entity oriented information retrieval* (Balog, 2018). In this paper we show that this process is feasible with off-the-shelf NLP and IR technology with a modest investment in creating training material. Concretely, the research described here is done to answer the following two questions:

1. How effective and accurate are off-the-shelf named entity recognition techniques when applied to parliamentary proceedings?
2. How easily can named entity annotations in parliamentary proceedings be integrated in a parliamentary search engine (both indexing and SERP), and how useful is this extra layer of meta data?

Main findings

An out of the box NER engine like spaCy[3] trained on a newspaper corpus performs very poorly on Dutch proceedings. However, creating a training corpus which generalizes well and leads to quite acceptable recognition scores is feasible in a few days work and can be done by non experts.

The recognized entities are not just *named entities* but also the more interesting (especially in proceedings) *definite descriptions* referring to political actors like ministers of X or committees on Y, which are annotated as persons and organizations, respectively.

Next to political actors we also showed that recognizing other entities like monetary amounts and laws is feasible.

Incorporating named entity information in an existing Elastic Search search engine is straightforward both for indexing and improving the search engine result page (SERP). Easily implemented features include faceted search using entities, highlighting of entities in search snippets, entity histograms ("entity clouds"), and diachronic histograms of entities (like Google ngram viewer).

A panel of 3 academic parliamentary historians rated the extra search engine functionality based on the extracted political actors on average with a 7.5 on a scale between 1 and 10.

Resources The manually annotated set of sentences used to train the NER tagger is available at https://github.com/maartenmarx/DutchParlNer. A search engine for Dutch parliamentary proceedings which employs the tagged entities is located at http://ner.politicalmashup.nl.

---

[1]We put the *to whom* in between brackets because this is not in all cases obvious. In the Dutch proceedings of plenary debates it is however clear who is *interrupting* whom and complete interuptions (and answers from the MP or cabinet member who was interupted) are transcribed.

[2]For instance, in the UK, "the Honourable Member for..." followed by the name of their constituency or as either "the Honourable gentleman" or "the Honourable lady". If the MP being addressed is a member of the same party they are referred to as "my Honourable friend". See http://news.bbc.co.uk/democracylive/hi/guides/newsid_82000/82149.stm.

---

[3]https://spacy.io/

Related work

Named entity recognition (NER) is a key task for many information processing algorithms like question answering and relation extraction, and has been studied in several evaluation platforms like CoNNL and MUC. We refer to (Nadeau and Sekine, 2007) for an older survey covering the traditional techniques (rule based, learned classifiers, conditional random fields) and to (Lample et al., 2016) for a survey covering the newer neural approaches based on transfer learning and word embeddings.

A common problem with NER taggers is that they perform often very well on the type of data on which they are trained, but perform (very) poorly on data from another domain. This has been observed for the special domain of parliamentary proceedings and led to several papers describing special approaches, which we will reference here. (Grover et al., 2008) describes a rule based system developed for OCRed historical documents which is tested on UK Hansard proceedings from the period 1814-1817. (Bick, 2004) contains a rule based system developed for modern Danish proceedings, and (Bojārs et al., 2019) for modern Latvian proceedings. The latter use NER tagging and linking to Wikipedia to turn the proceedings into a linked data graph. NER tagging with the Stanford parser[4] has been applied to German (Faruqui et al., 2010) and Slovenian (Pančur and Šorn, 2016) proceedings. A semantic web information retrieval system for proceedings of the european parliament built on top of MongoDB is presented in (Onyimadu et al., 2012). A combination of entity recognition and linking (to Wikipedia) on Dutch proceedings is presented in (Olieman et al., 2015) which builds a system on top of DBpedia SpotLight and the Dutch NER tagger FROG.

Method

Data set

We created a hand labeled dataset consisting of 5.536 sentences taken from Dutch plenary and committee proceedings from 2018-2019. These sentences consisted of 86.206 tokens and contained 3.579 named entities, often consisting of multiple tokens. These sentences are available in the spaCy train format[5] in the github repository belonging to this paper. Table 1 lists the number of manually labeled entities per class.

Creating the data set

The data set was created using active learning. This greatly sped up the annotation process which took in total 20 hours for one person. To bootstrap the process we used a list of current MPs and cabinet members and a list of ministries and parliamentary committees, turned this into a regular expression and matched that on the sentences in the corpus. We then trained spaCy with these automatically annotated

examples and then manually checked and corrected the output. After correcting a few hundred sentences, the model was trained again with the corrected (now hand-labeled) examples, and this process was repeated a number of times until all sentences were hand-labeled. This way of working saves time because acknowledging that an example is correct or not can be done with one click, in contrast to marking entities in a text manually. In addition, the annotator perceived that the NER tagger improved after each round, and that this made his work more enjoyable and rewarding. All location names (e.g. cities, countries, mountains etc.) were considered Geo-political entities (GPE class) irrespective of the context they appeared in. The annotations were done by one annotator.

Named entity recognition with spaCy

spaCy features an extremely fast statistical entity recognition system, that assigns labels to contiguous spans of tokens. The default model identifies a variety of named and numeric entities, including persons, companies, locations, organizations and products[6].

For Dutch, a single statistical model (`nl_core_news_sm`) is available, trained on the Lassy corpus (van Noord et al., 2013). We used this as our baseline model. We then retrained this model with the additional training data described in section .

Political Actor Centric SERP

We created a search engine for 10 years of Dutch plenary and committee proceedings using Elasticsearch with a standard *Search Engine Result Page (SERP)* based on recommendations in (Hearst, 2009). Using the recent *mapper annotated text* plugin[7] in Elasticsearch it is easy to index and use tagged ngrams. Elasticsearch indexes the additional list of "tags" as occurring at exactly the same position as the original string in the text and so these tags can be used in several tasks like highlighting, faceted search, and complex "phrase" queries combining tags and keywords (e.g. entity oriented search like "Europe Cabinet_Member").

We added three extra features based on the tagged political actors (Balog, 2018):

1. Highlighting of political actors in result snippets. See Figure 1.

2. Diachronic histograms of number of mentions per year per political actor in the returned hits given a query. See Figure 2.

3. "Word" clouds containing the top 30 most mentioned political actors in the returned hits given a query.

In the interface we used consistent color coding to indicate the class of the entity, e.g., always blue for persons, red for organizations and yellow for locations.

---

[4]https://nlp.stanford.edu/software/lex-parser.shtml

[5] For example, `["Geert Wilders is partijleider van de PVV", [[0, 13, "PERSON"], [37, 40, "ORG"]]`

[6]https://spacy.io/usage/linguistic-features#named-entities

[7] https://www.elastic.co/blog/search-for-things-not-strings-with-the-annotated-text-plugin

Table 1: Number of manually annotated entities per entity type in our data set.

Type	Description	Number
PERSON	People, including fictional	1163
NORP	Nationalities or religious or political groups	149
FAC	Buildings, airports, highways, bridges, etc	11
ORG	Companies, agencies, institutions, etc	954
GPE	Countries, cities, states	395
EVENT	Named hurricanes, battles, wars, sports events, etc	31
LAW	Named documents made into laws	76
DATE	Absolute or relative dates or periods	261
PERCENT	Percentage, including "%"	59
MONEY	Monetary values, including unit	75
ORDINAL	"first", "second", etc	142
CARDINAL	Numerals that do not fall under another type	262
Total		3579

Figure 1: Result snippet with highlighting of political actors.

Results

Quantitative evaluation

We compare the precision (P), recall (R) and the F1 score obtained by the trained NER tagger to the out of the box spaCy baseline (trained using the *nl_core_web_sm* model, currently the only model available for Dutch). We use the following evaluation setup: we created a random 80% train, 20% test split; trained the model on the train set and computed P, R and F1 scores on the test set. We repeated this 8 times and compute for each NER class the average score over these 8 trials. The score for the baseline was computed in the same manner. The evaluation uses the *strict* method: an annotation of an NE is correct if it exactly coincides with the gold standard annotation. In other words, if both annotations have the same staring B token, and the same sequence of following I tokens.

Table 2 contains the scores for each NER class for the baseline and the trained model[8]. The micro averaged F1 score increases from 49.2 to 90.1. All increases, except for the classes DATE and PERCENT are significant. Concentrating on the political actor classes PERSON and ORG, we see that the untrained baseline model is cautious with a low recall and a bit higher precision, while recall and precision are on par for the trained model. The often quite complex organization names are harder to recognize than the person.

Qualitative evaluation

A panel of 3 academic parliamentary historians were asked to rate the three extra political actor centered features, which were shown in section : highlighting of entities in result snippets, entity word clouds, and entity time lines. They did this during a real task on a search engine filled with 10 years of Dutch plenary and committee proceedings.

They rated the extra search engine functionality based on the extracted political actors on average with a 7.5 on a scale between 1 and 10. The raw scores were (8,8,7) for the entity highlighting, (7,8,8) for the entity clouds, and (9,7,8) for the entity time lines.

Conclusions

We have shown that an off-the-shelf named entity recognizer trained with an easy to obtain set of examples performs rather well on parliamentary proceedings. Of interest is that it is able to learn to detect complex definite descriptions of committees, ministries and other parliamentary bodies, usually consisting of several tokens.

Employing these tagged named entities in an existing search

---

[8] We did not train the classes FAC, EVENT and CARDINAL.

Figure 2: Google ngram-viewer style display of the number of mentions per year for a number of political actors.

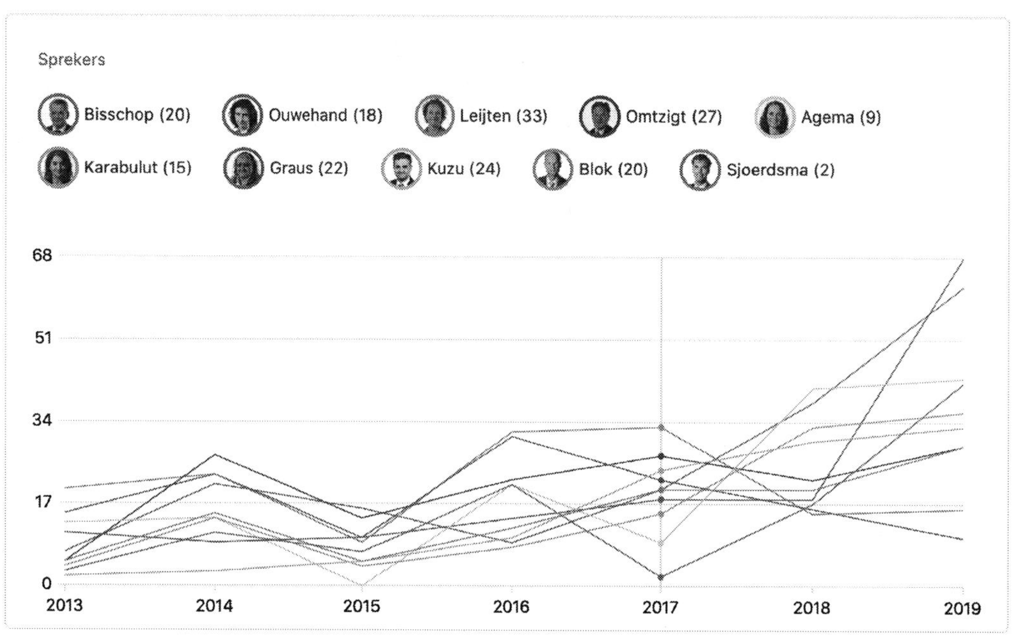

Table 2: Precision (P), Recall (R) and F1 scores for each NER class for the baseline and trained models.

(a) Baseline Model

Type	P	R	F_1
PERSON	16.1	6.2	9.0
ORG	58.8	37.1	45.5
MONEY	17.9	4.8	7.5
LAW	50.0	4.3	7.8
GPE	60.4	87.5	71.4
NORP	50.2	89.7	64.1
DATE	80.3	86.5	83.2
PERCENT	97.3	96.4	96.8
ORDINAL	91.52	95.90	93.60

(b) Trained Model

Type	P	R	F_1
PERSON	93.8	91.9	92.8
ORG	82.9	85.3	84.1
MONEY	95.1	93.0	93.9
LAW	81.7	76.5	78.6
GPE	92.5	90.5	91.4
NORP	85.0	85.7	85.2
DATE	89.3	90.9	90.1
PERCENT	97.6	96.4	97.0
ORDINAL	96.9	95.4	96.1

new types of entities. It would be of interest to see whether it is possible to distinguish *political actors* within the classes of persons and organizations.

Previous work has shown that using transfer learning techniques with unsupervised learned embeddings like BERT or ELMO can significantly outperform state of the art NER approaches (Peng et al., 2019; Devlin et al., 2018). We expect that similar gains can be reached with proceedings data.

We have not touched upon the obvious next step which is the *reconciliation of entities*, that is, linking the named entity in a text to the correct unique object that it refers to. Even though proceedings seem to be often cleaned compared to the verbatim transcript (with the official names of actors like ministries replacing more colloquial mentions), there is still quite some variance in ways of referring to the same object. Also political entities like ministries or committees frequently change their name[9]. Keeping the links from entities to unique objects up to date, correct and complete is one of the hardest things in a dynamic political information system, simply because it asks for continuous manual labor by experts.

engine is easy and was evaluated positively by professional users.

Future work

A nice feature of spaCy is the ease with which one can train

---

[9]In the Netherlands, the ministry of Justice changed its name from *Veiligheid en Justitie* to *Justitie en Veiligheid*, which costed 2M Euro (Volkskrant, 2020).

Bibliographical References

Balog, K. (2018). *Entity-oriented search*. Springer.

Beelen, K., Thijm, T. A., Cochrane, C., Halvemaan, K., Hirst, G., Kimmins, M., Lijbrink, S., Marx, M., Naderi, N., Rheault, L., et al. (2017). Digitization of the Canadian parliamentary debates. *Canadian Journal of Political Science/Revue canadienne de science politique*, 50(3):849–864.

Bick, E. (2004). A named entity recognizer for danish. In *LREC*. Citeseer.

Blätte, A. and Blessing, A. (2018). The GermaParl corpus of parliamentary protocols. In *Proceedings of the Eleventh International Conference on Language Resources and Evaluation (LREC 2018)*.

Bojārs, U., Darǧis, R., Lavrinovičs, U., and Paikens, P. (2019). Linkedsaeima: A linked open dataset of latvia's parliamentary debates. In *International Conference on Semantic Systems*, pages 50–56. Springer.

Cardie, C. and Wilkerson, J. (2008). Text annotation for political science research. *Journal of Information Technology & Politics*, 5(1):1–6.

Devlin, J., Chang, M.-W., Lee, K., and Toutanova, K. (2018). Bert: Pre-training of deep bidirectional transformers for language understanding. *arXiv preprint arXiv:1810.04805*.

Faruqui, M., Padó, S., and Sprachverarbeitung, M. (2010). Training and evaluating a german named entity recognizer with semantic generalization. In *KONVENS*, pages 129–133.

Darja Fišer, et al., editors. (2018). *Proceedings of LREC2018 Workshop ParlaCLARIN: Creating and Using Parliamentary Corpora.*, Paris, France, May. European Language Resources Association (ELRA).

Grover, C., Givon, S., Tobin, R., and Ball, J. (2008). Named entity recognition for digitised historical texts. In *LREC*.

Hearst, M. A. (2009). *Search User Interfaces*. Cambridge University Press, USA, 1st edition.

Lample, G., Ballesteros, M., Subramanian, S., Kawakami, K., and Dyer, C. (2016). Neural architectures for named entity recognition. *arXiv preprint arXiv:1603.01360*.

Marx, M., Aders, N., and Schuth, A. (2010). Digital sustainable publication of legacy parliamentary proceedings. In *Proceedings of the 11th Annual International Digital Government Research Conference on Public Administration Online: Challenges and Opportunities*, pages 99–104.

Nadeau, D. and Sekine, S. (2007). A survey of named entity recognition and classification. *Lingvisticae Investigationes*, 30(1):3–26.

Olieman, A., Kamps, J., Marx, M., and Nusselder, A. (2015). A hybrid approach to domain-specific entity linking. *CoRR*, abs/1509.01865.

Onyimadu, O., Nakata, K., Wang, Y., Wilson, T., and Liu, K. (2012). Entity-based semantic search on conversational transcripts semantic. In *Joint International Semantic Technology Conference*, pages 344–349. Springer.

Palmirani, M. and Vitali, F. (2011). Akoma-Ntoso for legal documents. In *Legislative XML for the semantic Web*, pages 75–100. Springer.

Pančur, A. and Šorn, M. (2016). Smart big data: use of slovenian parliamentary papers in digital history. *Contributions to Contemporary History*, 56(3):130–146.

Peng, Y., Yan, S., and Lu, Z. (2019). Transfer learning in biomedical natural language processing: An evaluation of BERT and ELMo on ten benchmarking datasets. In *Proceedings of the 18th BioNLP Workshop and Shared Task*, pages 58–65.

van Noord, G., Bouma, G., Van Eynde, F., de Kok, D., van der Linde, J., Schuurman, I., Sang, E. T. K., and Vandeghinste, V., (2013). *Large Scale Syntactic Annotation of Written Dutch: Lassy*, pages 147–164. Springer, Berlin, Heidelberg.

Volkskrant. (2020). Van Veiligheid en Justitie naar Justitie en Veiligheid: naamswijziging ministeries kost kabinet miljoenen. https://www.volkskrant.nl/nieuws-achtergrond/van-veiligheid-en-justitie-naar-justitie-en-veiligheid-naamswijziging-ministeries-kost-kabinet-miljoenen b88129af. Accessed: 2020-02-01.

Proceedings of ParlaCLARIN II Workshop, pages 40–43
Language Resources and Evaluation Conference (LREC 2020), Marseille, 11–16 May 2020
© European Language Resources Association (ELRA), licensed under CC-BY-NC

Challenges of Applying Automatic Speech Recognition for Transcribing EU Parliament Committee Meetings: A Pilot Study

Hugo de Vos and Suzan Verberne

Institute of Public Administration and Leiden Institute of Advanced Computer Science, Leiden University
h.p.de.vos@fgga.leidenuniv.nl, s.verberne@liacs.leidenuniv.nl

Abstract

We tested the feasibility of automatically transcribing committee meetings of the European Union parliament with the use of Automatic Speech Recognition techniques. These committee meetings contain more valuable information for political science scholars than the plenary meetings since these meetings showcase actual debates opposed to the more formal plenary meetings. However, since there are no transcriptions of those meetings, they are a lot less accessible for research than the plenary meetings, of which multiple corpora exist. We explored a freely available ASR application and analysed the output in order to identify the weaknesses of an out-of-the box system. We followed up on those weaknesses by proposing directions for optimizing the ASR for our goals. We found that, despite showcasing acceptable results in terms of Word Error Rate, the model did not yet suffice for the purpose of generating a data set for use in Political Science. The application was unable to successfully recognize domain specific terms and names. To overcome this issue, future research will be directed at using domain specific language models in combination with off-the-shelf acoustic models.

Keywords: Automatic Speech Recognition, European Union Parliament, Political Science

1. Introduction

The plenary meetings of the European Parliament have been a thankful study object (Glavaš et al., 2019; Hollink et al., 2018) both in Natural Language Processing (NLP) and in Political Sciences (Greene and Cross, 2017). The recordings and transcripts of these meetings contain rich information about the decision processes of the EU. This research is facilitated by the availability of the data: A large quantity of speeches is available in a standardized format that is relatively easy to come by. For example via the LinkedEP project (Aggelen van et al., 2017) or the Europarl corpus (Koehn, 2005).

However, for political scientists, the relevance of these data is limited, because of the way the plenary meetings are structured. Plenary meetings consist of short (often one-minute) speeches that are mostly read from paper. Such speeches are well prepared and thought out, and speaking times are very limited. There is no room for any interruptions or other means to directly react to what is happening on the floor. In other words: there is no actual debate. The plenary sessions of the EU can be considered a case of formal language use, as opposed to spontaneous speech. Because of their limited length and the formal language use, the speeches only contain superficial information about the topics discussed and very limited information about the position of the meeting participants towards these topics.

Much more interesting sources of information about processes in the EU parliament are the EU parliament *committees*, in which matters are discussed on a more technical level. These domain specific meetings are where the actual debate takes place: specific issues are debated with more detail than in the plenary meetings. EU committees consist of Members of the European Parliament (MEPs) and are centered around core topics within the EU, such as Civil Liberties, Justice and Home Affairs (LIBE committee) or Internal Market and Consumer Protection (IMCO).[1]

The problem of the meetings of the committees is that, contrary to the plenary meetings, there are no transcriptions of those meetings. Only a coarse agenda and minutes are available. This severely limits how well this data can be used for political research, because it is only possible to find the meetings based on metadata. Moreover, listening to the audio files is time-consuming and therefore unfit for any larger scale research.

It is for this reason that we set up this project of transcribing the committee meetings using Automatic Speech Recognition (ASR) with the aim of creating a corpus that is relevant to political researchers. This will make large scale analyses of this rich data collection possible, and allows for political research that goes beyond the available but shallow plenary meetings.

In this paper we discuss results obtained in a pilot on the automatic transcription of the EU parliamentary committee meetings. We studied whether it is feasible to automatically transcribe committee meetings with sufficient quality to be used in political research.

2. Data

The input data consist of audio recordings of the meetings of EU parliamentary committees that were retrieved from the official database of recorded meetings.[2]

The recordings are (almost) entirely in English. If a speaker talks English, their audio recording is directly recorded in the audio file. If a speaker does speak an other language than English, then the first few words of the speaker can be

---

[1] For a full list of EU parliamentary committees consult https://www.europarl.europa.eu/committees/en/parliamentary-committees.html

[2] https://www.europarl.europa.eu/ep-live/en/committees/search

heard after which the sound is overlayed with the recording of an interpreter speaking in English.

2.1. Data sampling

We selected the audio recordings of 5 random meetings of the LIBE committee of the EU parliament. In total these 5 recordings had a length of 9 hours and 51 minutes. Of those 5 meetings we manually transcribed the first 15-20 minutes as reference material, leading to 1 hour and 20 minutes of manually transcribed audio which constituted a total of 7902 words. An average of 100 words per minute might seem low, but this is due to a lot of silences, for example when a new speaker needs to walk to the microphone.

2.2. Manual transcription

Manual transcription for the purpose of ASR evaluation was not done from scratch but by editing the output of the ASR-application (See Section 3.1. for description of the application). We realize that this way of transcribing might insert biases in the transcription. Yet for the purpose of this pilot we think it does suffice. During the transcription a few special elements were used:

- If a section of the audio was inaudible or the exact thing said could not be understood this was transcribed as ****.

- The parts where the first few words of a non English speaking speaker were heard before the sound of the entire sequence before interpreter started was described as a single instance of **FOREIGN**, since we were no to recognize the different words in a foreign language.

3. Methods

3.1. ASR application

For transcribing the sound files we used the English Automatic Speech Recognition Webservice (based on the Kaldi framework), developed at the University of Twente, version 0.1[3]. This webservice is based on the KALDI framework for speech recognition (Povey et al., 2011). It was trained on the TED-LIUM data set[4], which is a data set of transcribed TED-talks. This is especially beneficial for our case since the model is able to dealing with non native speakers of English.

3.2. Evaluation

To evaluate the quality of the ASR for our data we used the Word Error Rate (WER) on our manually transcribed sample. This is a common metric for measuring and comparing the quality of ASR-systems (Chiu et al., 2018; Toshniwal et al., 2018). The WER is based on the Levenshtein distance, which defines the minimal edit distance between two strings. For this minimal edit distance, the number of insertions, deletions and substitutions divided by the total number of words:

$$\text{WER} = \frac{\text{Substitutions} + \text{Deletions} + \text{Insertions}}{\text{Total nr of words}} \quad (1)$$

4. Results

The results are summarized in Table 1. The table indicates that the ASR quality is reasonably good with WERs between 5 and 14. We think that these results provide us with a decent baseline, especially given the specificity of the domain (see Section 5.) and the fact that all of the speakers in our sample were non-native speakers of English and that the model was not tuned for this. As a comparison, the WER reported for end-to-end ASR (Hadian et al., 2018) on the 300-hour Switchboard corpus is 9.3; the best WER reported for the LibriSpeech test-other set is 5.0 and for the LibriSpeech test-clean set it is 2.2.[5]

Table 1 also shows that the WER differs quite largely between the five topics, with the Justice scoreboard being the most difficult to transcribe. An inspection of the output indicates that this is mainly due to variation in speaker pronunciation (some speakers are easier to understand than others), and the amount of technical language, which is particularly low in the topic 'Appointment of vice-chairs'.

Topic	# transcribed words	WER
Appointment of vice-chairs	2294	5.15
Justice scoreboard	1092	13.19
Visa code	1815	6.61
Eurojust evaluation	1442	9.43
Legal Assitance for MEPs	1259	8.11

Table 1: WER values for the five manually transcribed texts

5. Error Analysis

Although the WERs presented above are a promising start, there are some issues that could seriously limit the usefulness of the transcriptions for political research and need attention by future ASR developments for this domain.

5.1. Person Names

In order for the data to be relevant for political research, the correct recognition of person names is essential. A lot of political science research is centered around questions involving people, roles, parties, and their contributions (Simaki et al., 2018). However, the recognition of names is a challenge for our generic ASR system.

In total 48 times a name was mentioned in our sample, yet only one time the name was recognized correctly, which was in the following context:

Dear colleagues dear friends. Dear <u>Alexander.</u>

---

[3]The webservice is available from https://webservices-lst.science.ru.nl

[4]https://www.openslr.org/19/

[5]Results on these tasks are listed on https://paperswithcode.com/task/speech-recognition

Examples of incorrectly recognized names were more abundant. For example in:

> *This is one of the greatest successes of this committee of its secretariat and Emilio De Capitani sitting next to me the head of it.*

which was recognized as:

> *This is one of the greatest successes of this committee of its secretariat in dick up a county sitting next to me the head of it.*

What becomes clear from this example is that apart from the name every word was recognized correctly. However, without a correctly recognized name, this sentence becomes close to incomprehensible, let alone useful for political research.

Another example where a name was miss-recognized is:

> *We have for the rapporteur Axel Voss among us.*

which was recognized as:

> *We have what the rapporteur access among us.*

In this example also words besides the name Axel Voss are misrecognized, yet only changing the word *access* for *Axel Voss* will make the sentence more or less understandable, showing again the detrimentality of correctly recognizing names.

5.2. Institution names

Apart from person names, also institution names appear to be hard to recognize. One of the transcribed fragments is about the Eurojust[6] institution. Eurojust was mentioned a total of 12 times in 1442 transcribed words yet it was never recognized correctly. For example

> *(...) and present the Eurojust annual report two thousand and thirteen (...)*

was recognized as

> *(...) and presenter you just annual report two thousand and thirteen (...)*

5.3. Domain-specific terms

Another type of words that is often not recognized are specific jargon terms from the EU. One of the transcribed fragments was about new legislation regarding EU visas: the visa code. Although the word *visa* was correctly recognized 14 out of 35 times, the phrase *visa code* was only correctly identified 1 out of 12 times.
This again forms a problem for political science research. If one of the most important terms of a documents is not recognized properly this will affect any further analysis on the content of the meetings.

---

[6]European Union Agency for Criminal Justice Cooperation.

6. Next steps

We presented the results from a pilot studying the feasibility of automatically transcribing EU committee meetings for the sake of political research. We are following-up on this work on two directions: adapting ASR, and downstream analysis of the resulting transcripts.

6.1. Improving the ASR

Modern ASR-systems consist of three or four parts: an acoustic model, a language model a decoder and often a vocabulary. The latter is sometimes implicit to the language model. The acoustic model is typically a deep neural network that is trained to map an acoustic signal to symbols (either graphemes or phonemes) representing the sounds. The output of this model is a string of symbols that is transcribed into a sequence of words by the decoder. This decoder compares the string of characters with a language model. A language model contains information about what the probability of occurrence is of words and word sequences (Chan et al., 2016). Based on the information of the acoustic model and the language model, the decoder determines what word is the most likely (Synnaeve et al., 2019).

Adapting an ASR-pipeline towards a specific domain can be done in all the components: the acoustic model, the language model, the vocabulary and the decoder.

For our application we will achieve the domain adaptation by adding a domain-specific language model and vocabulary. The reason for this is that most errors can be ascribed to out-of-vocabulary terms. If a term is not in the language model or underrepresented in the language model, an ASR-system will be unable to recognize it.[7] In the case of names of persons and institutions, most of them will not have been present in the corpus that a generic language model is trained on. The result is that the decoder will not consider those words when analyzing the output of the acoustic model. A word such as *visa* might be in the training corpus of a generic ASR language model, but it will be less common than in the EU-domain and also occur in different contexts within the EU than outside the EU. Therefore it will also be more often disregarded as the most likely term.

We can leverage the availability of written documents from the European Union to train a domain-specific language model. For example, all the transcripts from plenary meetings of the EU parliament can be used for this purpose, since they are readily available: for example via the LinkedEP project (Aggelen van et al., 2017).

6.2. Analysis of the transcripts

Once we have a collection of reliable transcripts of the meetings of the EU parliament committees, we plan to ex-

---

[7]The alternative, training a domain-specific, acoustic model would require large amounts of time and resources: hundreds of hours of transcribed acoustic data would be needed, together with substantial computational power (Synnaeve et al., 2019).

plore a number of interesting research directions. In this section we will paint some of the possibilities.

Opinion mining and stance analysis We plan to use the data set to mine the opinions and standpoints of different MEPs over time. This falls within a tradition in Political Science of measuring positions of actors based on texts. This can either be a position towards a specific subject (Lopez et al., 2017) or in the larger political spectrum, for example on a right-left scale (Lowe et al., 2011). Such analyses can be made extra interesting in the case of this particular data. Members of these committees are not only affiliated to their committees, but also to national political parties, European political fractions and in some extent also to their home country. Linking the textual database to other databases holding these affiliations will add interesting dimensions that can provide for exciting new research.

Topic modelling Other research possibilities with this data set would include (dynamic) topic modeling (Blei and Lafferty, 2006). It would be a novel research direction to explore what the main topics are prevalent within and between committees over time.

7. Conclusion

In this paper we explored the possibility of generating a corpus of transcriptions of EU parliament committee meetings using a generic ASR system. We conclude that the system we used shows promising results, yet does not suffice. However, we deem it possible to make adaptations towards a working system. The main problems are recognizing names and domain-specific terms that are outside the vocabulary of a generic system. For this reason, our next steps are to train a domain-specific language model and vocabulary, leveraging the large amount of written EU documents available. Our long-term aim is to enable researchers in the field of political science and public administration to better analyze the EU policy processes with the help of automated text analyses.

8. Bibliographical References

Blei, D. M. and Lafferty, J. D. (2006). Dynamic topic models. In *Proceedings of the 23rd international conference on Machine learning*, pages 113–120.

Chan, W., Jaitly, N., Le, Q., and Vinyals, O. (2016). Listen, attend and spell: A neural network for large vocabulary conversational speech recognition. In *2016 IEEE International Conference on Acoustics, Speech and Signal Processing (ICASSP)*, pages 4960–4964. IEEE.

Chiu, C.-C., Sainath, T. N., Wu, Y., Prabhavalkar, R., Nguyen, P., Chen, Z., Kannan, A., Weiss, R. J., Rao, K., Gonina, E., et al. (2018). State-of-the-art speech recognition with sequence-to-sequence models. In *2018 IEEE International Conference on Acoustics, Speech and Signal Processing (ICASSP)*, pages 4774–4778. IEEE.

Glavaš, G., Nanni, F., and Ponzetto, S. P. (2019). Computational analysis of political texts: Bridging research efforts across communities. In *Proceedings of the 57th annual meeting of the association for computational linguistics: Tutorial abstracts*, pages 18–23.

Greene, D. and Cross, J. P. (2017). Exploring the political agenda of the european parliament using a dynamic topic modeling approach. *Political Analysis*, 25(1):77–94.

Hadian, H., Sameti, H., Povey, D., and Khudanpur, S. (2018). End-to-end speech recognition using lattice-free mmi. In *Interspeech*, pages 12–16.

Hollink, L., van Aggelen, A., and van Ossenbruggen, J. (2018). Using the web of data to study gender differences in online knowledge sources: the case of the european parliament. In *Proceedings of the 10th ACM Conference on Web Science*, pages 381–385.

Lopez, J. C. A. D., Collignon-Delmar, S., Benoit, K., and Matsuo, A. (2017). Predicting the brexit vote by tracking and classifying public opinion using twitter data. *Statistics, Politics and Policy*, 8(1):85–104.

Lowe, W., Benoit, K., Mikhaylov, S., and Laver, M. (2011). Scaling policy preferences from coded political texts. *Legislative studies quarterly*, 36(1):123–155.

Povey, D., Ghoshal, A., Boulianne, G., Burget, L., Glembek, O., Goel, N., Hannemann, M., Motlicek, P., Qian, Y., Schwarz, P., Silovsky, J., Stemmer, G., and Vesely, K. (2011). The kaldi speech recognition toolkit. In *IEEE 2011 Workshop on Automatic Speech Recognition and Understanding*. IEEE Signal Processing Society, December. IEEE Catalog No.: CFP11SRW-USB.

Simaki, V., Paradis, C., and Kerren, A. (2018). Evaluating stance-annotated sentences from political blogs regarding the brexit: a quantitative analysis. *ICAME Journal*, 42(1).

Synnaeve, G., Xu, Q., Kahn, J., Grave, E., Likhomanenko, T., Pratap, V., Sriram, A., Liptchinsky, V., and Collobert, R. (2019). End-to-end asr: from supervised to semi-supervised learning with modern architectures. *arXiv preprint arXiv:1911.08460*.

Toshniwal, S., Kannan, A., Chiu, C.-C., Wu, Y., Sainath, T. N., and Livescu, K. (2018). A comparison of techniques for language model integration in encoder-decoder speech recognition. In *2018 IEEE Spoken Language Technology Workshop (SLT)*, pages 369–375. IEEE.

9. Language Resource References

Aggelen van, Astrid and Hollink, Laura and Kemman, Max and Kleppe, Martijn and Beunders, Henri. (2017). *The debates of the european parliament as linked open data*. IOS Press.

Koehn, P. (2005). Europarl: A parallel corpus for statistical machine translation. In *MT summit*, volume 5, pages 79–86. Citeseer.

Proceedings of ParlaCLARIN II Workshop, pages 44–50
Language Resources and Evaluation Conference (LREC 2020), Marseille, 11–16 May 2020
© European Language Resources Association (ELRA), licensed under CC-BY-NC

Parsing Icelandic Alþingi Transcripts:
Parliamentary Speeches as a Genre

Kristján Rúnarsson, Einar Freyr Sigurðsson
The Árni Magnússon Institute for Icelandic Studies
Árnagarði við Suðurgötu, IS-102
krunars@hi.is, einar.freyr.sigurdsson@arnastofnun.is

Abstract

We introduce a corpus of transcripts from Alþingi, the Icelandic parliament. The corpus is syntactically parsed for phrase structure according to the annotation scheme of the Icelandic Parsed Historical Corpus (IcePaHC). This addition to IcePaHC makes it more diverse with respect to text types and we argue that having a syntactically parsed corpus facilitates research on different types of texts. We furthermore argue that the speech corpus can be treated somewhat like spoken language even though the transcripts differ in various ways from daily spoken language. We also compare this text type to other types and argue that this genre can shed light on their properties. Finally, we show how this addition to IcePaHC has helped us identify and solve issues with our parsing scheme.

Keywords: parliamentary corpus, parliamentary transcripts, text types

1. Introduction

In this paper we discuss a corpus of Icelandic Alþingi parliamentary speeches, syntactically parsed for phrase structure.[1] The corpus, which contains approx. 60,000 words, is parsed in accordance with the Icelandic Parsed Historical Corpus (IcePaHC) (Wallenberg et al., 2011).[2] This new addition to IcePaHC makes it more diverse with respect to genres of texts. We chose unprepared speeches to make the parliamentary speech corpus more coherent and closer to reflecting actual spoken language.

In this paper, we first of all argue that having a syntactically parsed corpus facilitates research on different text types. It is therefore crucial for us to have the parliamentary speeches parsed in the same way as the other 1 million words found in IcePaHC.

Secondly, we focus on the properties of the unprepared speeches we chose for the corpus. We argue that they can be treated like spoken language in important ways, though they differ in various ways from "regular" spoken language. Thirdly, we argue that the text type under discussion can shed light on other text types. For example, long clauses containing many words seem to be one of the characteristics not only of the parliamentary speeches but also of religious texts, whereas clauses in narratives tend to be much shorter. Finding common traits in the speeches and the religious texts may help us discover the defining characteristics of these two genres.

Furthermore, we will show examples of how this new addition to IcePaHC has helped us identify and solve issues with our parsing scheme.

The paper is structured as follows: In Section 2 we give a brief description of IcePaHC. Section 3 discusses the parliamentary transcripts and looks at parliamentary speeches as a text type as opposed to other genres. Section 4 discusses how the addition of parliamentary transcripts has impacted the annotation scheme of IcePaHC. Section 5 concludes the paper.

2. IcePaHC

The Icelandic Parsed Historical Corpus (IcePaHC) (Wallenberg et al., 2011; Rögnvaldsson et al., 2012) is a collection of parsed texts containing 1 million running words from the 12th through the 21st centuries. It is annotated according to a scheme based on that of the Penn Parsed Corpora of Historical English (https://www.ling.upenn.edu/hist-corpora/) (Kroch and Taylor, 2000; Kroch et al., 2004) using the annotation tool Annotald (Ecay et al., 2018), after preprocessing, including lemmatization and preliminary parsing, using IceNLP (http://icenlp.sourceforge.net/) — see Loftsson (2008), Loftsson and Rögnvaldsson (2007) and Ingason et al. (2008) — as well as various scripts developed specifically for IcePaHC.

IcePaHC has been designed to capture the Icelandic language in various contexts with regard to time period and subject matter. The texts have been selected so as to be presumably written each mainly by a single author and the length of the excerpts has been decided so that they are short enough that many diverse texts could be included, while still providing adequate coverage of the authors' internal grammar.

IcePaHC aims to include texts in each of several genres (narratives, religion, biographies, science, law) from every century from the 12th century to the present, but currently includes mainly narratives and religious texts. There is also a need for still more types of texts from different authors and times dealing with diverse subjects. The new additions to IcePaHC are genres not previously included, namely parliamentary transcripts and news articles. This paper focuses on the parliamentary transcripts and discusses their importance as a text type.

---

[1] The creation of the parsed corpus of parliamentary speeches is part of a bigger project named "Universal Treebanking" (Einar Freyr Sigurðsson PI), funded by the Strategic Research and Development Programme for Language Technology 2019–2020 in which IcePaHC is also being converted to a Universal Dependencies scheme.

[2] The parsed Icelandic Alþingi parliamentary speech corpus is available along with the rest of IcePaHC at https://github.com/antonkarl/icecorpus.

3. The Parliamentary Transcripts

3.1. The Nature of the Texts and Their Selection

The parliamentary transcripts are from a small set of only four speakers that have been chosen so as to represent both male and female speakers of different generations: Steingrímur J. Sigfússon (b. 1955), Þorgerður Katrín Gunnarsdóttir (b. 1965), Helgi Hrafn Gunnarsson (b. 1980) and Björt Ólafsdóttir (b. 1983).[3] An important secondary consideration was the existence of enough material from each speaker from a similar time, in this case between 2011 and 2015.

The transcripts, which were extracted from the Icelandic Gigaword Corpus (Steingrímsson et al., 2018), were chosen from among responses rather than prepared speeches, so as to better represent spontaneous speech. The transcripts have, however, been edited by parliamentary secretaries for publication, so the text we have to work with is not pure speech. This is a drawback, especially if the intention is to examine in detail the structure of spoken language as opposed to written language, e.g., getting accurate statistics about the relative prevalence of specific features. Nevertheless, it has been evident in the annotation process that certain features mainly associated with spoken language appear frequently in the transcripts despite the apparent tendency of the editing process to make them more concise and regularly structured and adhere more closely to the norms of formal written language.

It may also be noted that published novels such as are included in IcePaHC's narratives category also go through an editing process with similar aims and tendencies to that of parliamentary speeches before being published, so they too do not perfectly represent the speaker's idiolect.

There are also other circumstances in favor of the parliamentary speeches including ease of access to both text and original audio, lack of copyright restrictions and individual authorship (indisputable in the case of responses, apart from editor changes), which aligns very well with the design goals of IcePaHC.

3.2. Comparison with Other Text Types

It was our belief that there would be important differences between the parliamentary transcripts and the existing IcePaHC corpus, and that constructions might be found there that are not found, or are significantly less common, in other more formal text types.

As expected, the parliamentary transcripts differ from previously added IcePaHC texts in several ways. Disfluencies, fragment answers (i.e., shortened answers to questions), resumptive elements, clefts and arguments shared by conjoined clauses (instances of which might be analysed as right node raising) are some of the phenomena which occur frequently in the parliamentary transcripts.

Adding new text types may also help us understand the nature of other text types, because there are many linguistic factors that could conceivably be affected by the genre. Several factors may be unique for a text type, while others might be shared with other text types.

For example, as discussed in Section 3.4, we see that there is a notable similarity between the parliamentary speeches and religious texts, in contrast to narrative texts. Such findings may reveal something of the nature of these texts, and comparisons of this kind can spark new research, e.g., in sociolinguistics.

In Sections 3.3–3.7 we discuss various linguistic features of the parliamentary transcripts.

3.3. Disfluencies

We can expect to find disfluencies of various sorts – such as breaks, false starts and repetitions – to a much higher degree in spoken language than in written texts that are carefully planned and thought through. These include breaks where a sentence or a phrase breaks off or is not finished. An example from our Alþingi corpus is shown below.

(1)   Ég veit ekki alveg hvernig ætti að vinna þetta tiltekna frumvarp frekar vegna þess að **það er svo**, – nú vantar mig aftur íslenska orðið fyrir „brutal" –

'I don't know exactly how this particular bill should be further worked on because **it is so [BREAK]** – now I need again the Icelandic word for "brutal"'

The speaker in this example breaks off when describing the bill as he cannot remember the Icelandic word for English *brutal*. Such breaks are marked specially in the parsing scheme and can therefore be easily found.

The unprepared speeches in our corpus, being spontaneous and not written beforehand, do in fact contain a higher total number of breaks than all the rest of IcePaHC. Even though the parliamentary speech corpus only contains around 60,000 running words, as opposed to the 1 million words of IcePaHC, it has 14 breaks whereas IcePaHC has only 5. It is possible that there is some inconsistency in parsing between the speeches and the rest of IcePaHC but this nonetheless suggests that breaks are more frequently found in the speeches due to their nature as spoken language.

3.4. Clause Length

Matthíasson (1959) argues that parliamentary speeches tend to contain exceptionally many subordinate clauses as a result of their nature, with, e.g., the speeches often being spontaneous.[4] Matthíasson (1959, 206) furthermore claims that increased frequency of subordinate clauses results in longer matrix clauses. It is quite straightforward to investigate the length of clauses with our parsed corpus and we can compare the speeches with other genres, namely narrative and religious texts. When we look at the relative frequency of the three text types (see Figure 1), it turns out that the proportion of short clauses, with four to eight words, is much higher in the narratives. Religious texts and the parliamentary speeches exhibit a similar proportion of longer clauses, on the other hand, as opposed to narrative texts whose longer clauses are proportionally less frequent, as can be clearly seen in Figure 1.

---

[3] Helgi Hrafn Gunnarsson and Steingrímur J. Sigfússon's speeches were selected as their language had been investigated before; see Stefánsdóttir (2016) and Stefánsdóttir and Ingason (2018).

[4] Verifying Matthíasson's claim should now be possible as different types of subordinate clauses (complement clauses, relative clauses, adverbial clauses, etc.) are all parsed in the corpus.

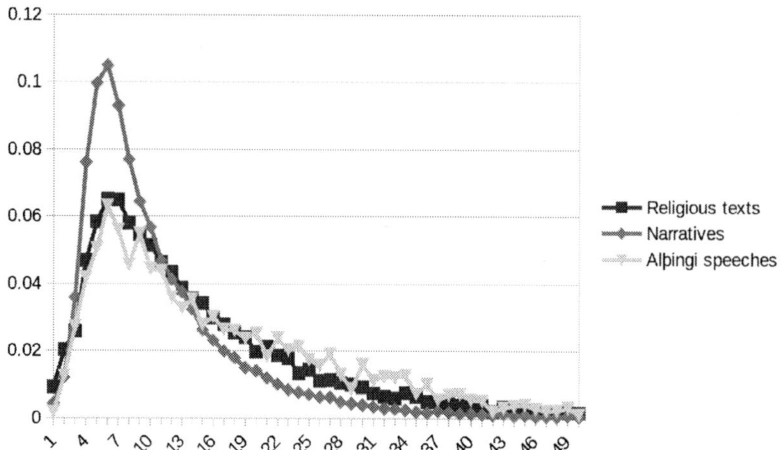

Figure 1: Relative frequency distribution of lengths (in words) of root clauses in different text types (religious texts, narrative texts, parliamentary speeches).

3.5. Resumptive Elements

The resumptive element *þá* 'then' is frequently found in the parliamentary transcripts immediately following left-dislocated subordinate clauses headed by *ef* 'if', *þegar* 'when', *þótt* 'even', *þó (að)* 'even', *þrátt (fyrir að)* 'despite', etc.

(2) en ef fólk   vill   fara á hausinn **þá**   er það
     but if people wants.to go bankrupt **then** is that
     væntanlega möguleiki   líka.
     presumably a.possibility too

Some such use of the resumptive *þá* has been linked to spoken language (Thráinsson, 2005, 578) and we have in fact noticed that it is sometimes deleted in the transcripts, presumably because it is frowned upon to an extent. This use is, nonetheless, quite frequently found in our parliamentary speech corpus as well as in other texts in IcePaHC from all periods.

However, we find a certain use of resumptive elements in the transcripts that we do not in other texts in IcePaHC. In some cases, resumptive *þá* is immediately preceded by *að*.[5] *Að* can be many things in Icelandic syntax, such as a preposition, an infinitival marker or a complementizer. Without going into details, it is presumably a complementizer in the *að þá* construction.

(3) Vandinn er auðvitað sá að þegar menn tala um
     hin ósnortnu víðerni, sem því miður gerast nú ansi
     fágæt og Ísland býr yfir sumum þeirra, sennilega
     stærstu ósnortnu víðernum í Evrópu, a.m.k. í Vestur-
     Evrópu, **að þá** er skilgreiningin sú að þar [...]
     'The problem is of course that when people talk
     about the untouched wilderness, which unfortu-
     nately are now becoming quite rare and Iceland has
     got some of them, probably the biggest untouched
     wilderness in Europe, at least in Western Europe,
     that then the definition is that there...'

Thráinsson (2005, 578) mentions the use of resumptive *að þá*, taking it to be even more connected to spoken language use than *þá*. The use of resumptive *þá* and *að þá* merits further research but for now it suffices to point out that the use of resumptive *að þá* found in the parliamentary speeches is indicative of the spoken language trait of this particular text type.

3.6. Topic Expressions

Topic-introducing expressions seem to be relatively frequent in the parliamentary speeches as opposed to other text types in IcePaHC. These are expressions starting with words like *varðandi* 'regarding', *að því er varðar* 'regarding', *hvað varðar* 'as regards', *hvað viðkemur* 'as regards'. To give an example, there are 42 instances of matrix clauses starting with the topic introducer *varðandi* in our parliamentary corpus, as in (4), but none in other IcePaHC texts.[6]

(4)   **Varðandi aukna kostnaðarþátttöku sjúklinga** líst
       mér að sjálfsögðu illa á hana.
       '**Regarding an increased cost participation of pa-
       tients**, I do not, of course, like it.'

This is something that needs further investigation. That is, are such topic introducers more frequent in spoken language than written texts? This shows a clear need for more parsed transcripts of spoken language. We therefore leave this for future research.

3.7. Words Indicative of Informal Register

When we try to figure out the properties of a certain text type, it is worth looking at the individual words used as well as the syntax. For that purpose, we do not need to rely on a syntactically parsed corpus as we can search for particular words in other corpora such as the Icelandic Gigaword Corpus (IGC; https://malheildir.arnastofnun.is/) (Steingrímsson et al., 2018). Svavarsdóttir (2007, 38–39) looks at word use

---

[5] For a syntactic analysis, see Jónsson (2019).

[6] It should be noted that we would not expect to find this particular expression in older texts in IcePaHC.

in three corpora of different types; she discusses words that are found in spoken language dialogues and to some degree in what she calls informal texts (diaries, etc.) but not, or to a much lesser degree, in rather formal, written texts (newspaper texts). Looking through her list of words, we note that she mentions, for example, *ókei* 'okay', which is neither found in her formal nor informal text corpus. There are, however, 16 instances of *ókei* in the spoken language corpus she reports on. Searching IGC, we find several instances of the word *ókei* in parliamentary transcripts, which without a doubt does not belong to a formal register.

Note that while we are arguing that the Icelandic parliamentary speeches share various properties with other types of spoken language, we are not arguing that parliamentary speeches are like any other type of (informal) spoken language. Members of parliament sometimes use loanwords from other languages, like English, which they often ask the audience to excuse (by adding a phrase like *svo ég sletti* 'so I use a foreign word/expression'); this may be indicative of a somewhat formal setting. We will not look further into this for now.

4. Development of the Annotation Scheme

The prevalence of certain features has prompted a deeper look into the way syntactic structure is analysed and annotated in IcePaHC, both shedding light on old issues that had never been definitively settled during earlier work on IcePaHC and bringing new issues to our attention.

The situation of IcePaHC is peculiar in that its annotation scheme (http://linguist.is/icelandic_treebank/) is derived from one developed for historical English texts (https://www.ling.upenn.edu/hist-corpora/) (Kroch and Taylor, 2000; Kroch et al., 2004). While the fact that it has been developed for Early Modern and Middle English rather than just contemporary English has made the annotation scheme more suitable for Icelandic, there are still important features of Icelandic that affect the practicability of specific analytical choices that have been retained from the Penn Parsed Corpora of Historical English (PPCHE) scheme.[7]

In particular, Icelandic is a highly inflected language, much more so than English, especially with regard to case. While the English of PPCHE, especially Middle English, does have some limited case inflection, it is a language in transition and it is not always clear to what degree inflection exists and case has generally not been annotated. By contrast, Icelandic shows a clear distinction between the cases and cases have been annotated in IcePaHC.

This affects the analysis of presumed instances of right node raising and that of comparative phrases which have been presumed to contain a prepositional phrase.

4.1. Right Node Raising

One issue where Icelandic does not seem to conform to the scheme is that of right node raising. An English example from Postal (1974, 126) is shown in (5).

(5)   Jack may be—and Tony certainly is—a werewolf.

Here, the NP *a werewolf* applies to the two matrix clauses, i.e., *Jack may be a werewolf* and *Tony certainly is a werewolf*.[8]

The parsing scheme employed in IcePaHC has presumed that the second clause in right node raising is parenthetical and that its rightmost element is raised so as to appear in the appropriate place in the encompassing prior clause. This analysis has been inherited from PPCHE. While it might be practical for English, it causes problems when applied to Icelandic, because the evidence clearly shows that it is the second clause which governs the case of the shared constituent and not the former. If the shared phrase has been moved (with argument movement), it would be expected to acquire its case from the governor of the place it was moved to, and if it has not been moved it should likewise retain the appropriate case for its position. An analysis involving right node raising is shown below where the dashed line rectangle marks the parenthetical clause (IP-MAT-PRN).

```
( (IP-MAT (NP-SBJ (PRO-N Við)) 'we'
  (BEDI vorum) 'were'
  (PP (P í) 'in'
    (NP (ADJ-D miklu) 'much'
      (N-D sambandi) 'contact'
      (PP (P við) 'with'
        (IP-MAT-PRN (CONJ og) 'and'
          (NP-SBJ *con*)
          (VBDI fengum) 'got'
          (NP-OB1 (NP (ADJ-A góða) 'good'
            (N-A leiðsögn)) 'guidance'
            (CONJP (CONJ eða) 'or'
              (NP (ADJ-A góða) 'good'
                (N-A áminningu))) 'reminder'
          (CP-REL *ICH*-1))
          (PP (P frá-frá))) 'from'
        (NP (NPR-D Sambandi) 'association'
          (NP-POS (ADJ-G íslenskra)
                      'Icelandic-GEN'
            (NS-G sveitarfélaga))
                'municipalities-GEN'
  ))))
  (CP-REL-1 (WNP-2 0)
    (C sem) 'which'
      (IP-SUB (NP-SBJ *T*-2)
        (NEG ekki) 'not'
        (BEDI var) 'was'
        (VAN svarað))) 'answered'
(, ,-,)))
```

In this example, one and the same NP, *Sambandi íslenskra sveitarfélaga*, applies to two clauses; it is simultaneously, in a way, the object of two prepositions, *við* and *frá*, and the question is how best to account for that within the scheme. The NP headed by *Sambandi* is in the dative case as the preposition *frá* assigns dative to its complement, but according to the analysis above it ends up in a PP with the

---

[8] Without going into details of the original account in Postal (1974), right node raising "places a double of the sequence [i.e. the phrase which is identical in both clauses] on the right, by Chomsky adjunction, and deletes all original occurrences" (p. 126).

preposition *við* 'with', which should govern the accusative case. Furthermore, there is an extraposed relative clause (CP-REL) belonging to the parenthetical clause (IP-MAT-PRN), but it ends up having to be raised to the outer main clause because it appears after the raised NP.

We therefore came up with a different scheme which appears to fit the Icelandic pattern better:

```
( (IP-MAT (IP-MAT (NP-SBJ (PRO-N Við))
      (BEDI vorum)
      (PP (P í)
        (NP (ADJ-D miklu)
        (N-D sambandi)
        (PP (P við)))))
    (CONJP (CONJ og)
      (IP-MAT (NP-SBJ *con*)
        (VBDI fengum)
        (NP-OB1 (NP (ADJ-A góða)
          (N-A leiðsögn))
          (CONJP (CONJ eða)
            (NP (ADJ-A góða)
              (N-A áminningu)))
          (CP-REL *ICH*-1))
        (PP (P frá)
          (NP (NPR-D Sambandi)
            (NP-POS (ADJ-G íslenskra)
              (NS-G sveitarfélaga))))
        (CP-REL-1 (WNP-2 0)
          (C sem)
          (IP-SUB (NP-SBJ *T*-2)
            (NEG ekki)
            (BEDI var)
            (VAN svarað)))))
    (, ,-,)))
```

Here, the shared NP appears in a PP with a preposition governing the correct case, and instead of a parenthetical clause, the two matrix clauses are conjoined in the most usual way, using a conjunction phrase.

4.2. Resumptive NPs in Comparative Clauses

Another issue that has been identified as a problem in IcePaHC is the treatment of comparative constructions of the form *<COMP ADJ/ADV> than ..., so/as <ADJ/ADV> as ...*, etc., also inherited from PPCHE. These constructions are parsed as adjectival or adverbial phrases containing a prepositional phrase, where the preposition is the word *than* or *as* (in Icelandic *en*, *og*) that immediately follows the head adjective/adverb. In case a subordinate clause with a gap corresponding in function to the head follows, the complement of the preposition is a complementizer phrase containing the subordinate clause IP, as in the following example:

```
(ADJP (ADJR-N helgari) 'holier'
  (PP (P en) 'than'
    (CP-CMP (WADJP-2 0)
      (C 0)
      (IP-SUB (ADJP *T*-2)
        (NP-SBJ (OTHERS-N aðrir) 'other'
        (ADJ-N helgir) 'holy'
        (NS-N menn)))))) 'men'
```

While this two-layer PP/CP combination might seem odd it is in line with the treatment of various other subordinate clause types in IcePaHC and the Penn Parsed Corpora of Historical English. However, when, instead of gap, an overt phrase corresponding to the antecedent is used, the structure is simplified, as shown in the following example, where the pronoun *sig* corresponds to the prior NP *engan betri vin*:

```
(IP-SUB (NP-SBJ (NPR-N Gróa)) 'Gróa'
  (VBDS ætti) 'had'
  (NP-OB1 (Q-A engan) 'no'
    (ADJR-A betri) 'better'
    (N-A vin) 'friend'
    (PP *ICH*-4))
  (ADVP-LOC (ADV hér) 'here'
    (PP (P á) 'on'
      (NP (N-D jörðu)))) 'earth'
  (PP-4 (P en) 'than'
    (NP (PRO-A sig)))) 'him/her'
```

From an English-speaking, or caseless, point of view, this seems to work rather well and even to confirm the appropriateness of calling the traditionally termed subordinating conjunctions prepositions, which may otherwise seem idiosyncratic. For Icelandic, however, the grammatical case of the supposed prepositional complement shows that it cannot be a direct complement to the preposition, since a preposition governs a specific case, but the phrases in question do not take their case from any preposition, but rather agree in case with their antecedents.

This prompted us to include the CP-CMP in such constructions as well, allowing for an IP therein where the phrase could fill the same role as its antecedent. That raised another issue: how does the WH-phrase in the CP connect to the subordinate clause? The following shows an attempt at this, using a dummy adverbial phrase (ADVP) that has no clear semantic role or connection to the antecedent:

```
( (IP-IMP (VBPI Nýtum) 'let's utilize'
  (ADVP (ADV þá)) 'then'
  (NP-OB1 (N-A tíma$) 'time'
    (D-A $nn)) 'the'
  (PP (RP fram) 'forward'
    (P að) 'to'
    (NP (ADJS-D næstu) 'next'
    (NS-D þingkosningum)
        'parliamentary elections'
    (, ,-,)
    (CP-REL (WNP-1 0)
      (C sem) 'which'
      (IP-SUB (NP-SBJ *T*-1)
        (RDPI verða) 'will be'
        (ADVP (ADV vonandi)) 'hopefully'
        (ADVP (ADVR fyrr) 'sooner'
        (PP (P en) 'than'
          (CP-CMP (WADVP-2 0)
            (C 0)
            (IP-SUB (ADVP *T*-2)
              (ADVP (ADVR síðar)))) 'later'
        )))))))
  (. .-.)))
```

A possible solution to the problem was found in another CP construction – the relative clause. The following example shows a resumptive NP, *spítalann* 'the hospital', being used in lieu of a gap in a relative clause.

```
( (IP-MAT (ADVP (ADVS Helst)) `chiefly'
  (BEPI er) `is'
  (NP-SBJ (PRO-N það)) `it'
  (NP-PRD
    (NPR-N Landspítali$) `National Hospital'
    (D-N $nn)) `the'
  (CP-CLF (WNP-1 0)
    (C sem) `which'
    (IP-SUB (NP-SBJ (PRO-N við)) `we'
      (VBPI sjáum) `see'
      (CP-THT (C að) `that'
        (IP-SUB (NP-SBJ *exp*)
          (NP-ADV (NP-ADV (N-A ár) `year'
            (PP (P frá) `from'
              (NP (N-D ári))))) `year'
          (, ,-,)
          (BEPI er) `is'
          (NEG ekki) `not'
          (DAN gert) `done'
          (ADVP
            (ADV nægjanlega) `adequately'
            (ADV vel)) `well'
          (PP (P við) `to'
            (NP-RSP-1
              (N-A spítala$) `hospital'
              (D-A $nn))))))) `the'
  (. .-.)))
```

This analysis is based on that of the PPCHE; it is also used particularly in the Penn audio-aligned corpora (Tortora et al., 2017; Tortora et al., 2020) and has been used in IcePaHC before. The WH-phrase is generally considered to have been moved from the IP and in a relative clause corresponds to the antecedent that the relative clause speaks about. In comparative clauses there is also a comparative phrase that is an antecedent to the CP. Using the same method of connecting the phrase that corresponds to the antecedent to the WH-phrase neatly ties together the treatment of different types of CP in gapped and ungapped variants.

```
( (IP-IMP (VBPI Nýtum) `let's utilize'
  (ADVP (ADV þá)) `then'
  (NP-OB1 (N-A tíma$) `time'
    (D-A $nn)) `the'
  (PP (RP fram) `forward'
    (P að) `to'
    (NP (ADJS-D næstu) `next'
    (NS-D þingkosningum)
        `parliament elections'
  (, ,-,)
  (CP-REL (WNP-1 0)
    (C sem) `which'
    (IP-SUB (NP-SBJ *T*-1)
      (RDPI verða) `will be'
      (ADVP (ADV vonandi)) `hopefully'
      (ADVP (ADVR fyrr) `sooner'
      (PP (P en) `than'
        (CP-CMP (WADVP-2 0)
          (C 0)
          (IP-SUB (ADVP-RSP-2
                  (ADVR síðar))) `later'
      )))))))
  (. .-.)))
```

5. Conclusion

We have established that the Icelandic Parsed Historical Corpus benefits from the addition of parliamentary transcripts by demonstrating their unique qualities while also showing their potential relationships to other types of text. Furthermore, we have found that adding new types of texts inspires us to improve our analysis in unanticipated ways. We are currently working on a further addition to the treebank, and it is our hope that even more text types will be added in the future so that it represents as good a cross-section of the language as possible.

6. Acknowledgements

This project is funded by the Strategic Research and Development Programme for Language Technology, grant no. 180020-5301.

We would also like to thank the three anonymous reviewers for their comments on the paper.

7. Bibliographical References

Ingason, A. K., Helgadóttir, S., Loftsson, H., and Rögnvaldsson, E. (2008). A Mixed Method Lemmatization Algorithm Using a Hierarchy of Linguistic Identities (HOLI). In Bengt Nordström et al., editors, Advances in Natural Language Processing. 6th International Conference, GoTAL 2008 Gothenburg, Sweden, August 25–27, 2008 Proceedings, pages 205–216, Berlin. Springer.

Jónsson, J. G. (2019). The XP-*þá*-construction and V2. In Ken Ramshøj Christensen, et al., editors, The Sign of the V: Papers in Honour of Sten Vikner, pages 341–360, Aarhus University. Department of English School of Communication and Culture.

Loftsson, H. and Rögnvaldsson, E. (2007). IceParser: An incremental finite-state parser for Icelandic. In Proceedings of the 16th Nordic Conference of Computational Linguistics (NODALIDA 2007), pages 128–135, Tartu, Estonia, May. University of Tartu, Estonia.

Loftsson, H. (2008). Tagging Icelandic text: A linguistic rule-based approach. *Nordic Journal of Linguistics*, 31:47–72.

Matthíasson, H. (1959). Setningaform og stíll. Bókaútgáfa Menningarsjóðs, Reykjavík.

Postal, P. M. (1974). On Raising. One Rule of English Grammar and its Theoretical Implications. MIT Press, Cambridge, MA.

Stefánsdóttir, L. B. and Ingason, A. K. (2018). A high definition study of syntactic lifespan change. *University of Pennsylvania Working Papers in Linguistics*, 24.1:169–178. https://repository.upenn.edu/pwpl/vol24/iss1/20/.

Stefánsdóttir, L. B. (2016). Breytingar á framburði. Með hliðsjón af félagslegum þáttum. B.A. thesis, University of Iceland, Reykjavík. http://hdl.handle.net/1946/24333.

Svavarsdóttir, Á. (2007). Talmál og málheildir — talmál og orðabækur. *Orð og tunga*, 9:25–50.

Thráinsson, H. (2005). Setningar. Handbók um setningafræði. Íslensk tunga III. Almenna bókafélagið, Reykjavík.

8.   Language Resource References

Ecay, A., Beck, J., and Ingason, A. K. (2018). Annotald. Version 1.3.10. http://annotald.github.io.

Kroch, A. S. and Taylor, A. (2000). Penn-Helsinki Parsed Corpus of Middle English. CD-ROM. Second Edition. Size: 1.3 million words.

Kroch, A. S., Santorini, B., and Delfs, L. (2004). Penn-Helsinki Parsed Corpus of Early Modern English. CD-ROM. First Edition. Size: 1.8 million words.

Rögnvaldsson, E., Ingason, A. K., Sigurðsson, E. F., and Wallenberg, J. (2012). The Icelandic Parsed Historical Corpus (IcePaHC). In Proceedings of the Eighth International Conference on Language Resources and Evaluation, LREC 2012, Istanbul, Turkey.

Steingrímsson, S., Helgadóttir, S., Rögnvaldsson, E., Barkarson, S., and Guðnason, J. (2018). Risamálheild: A Very Large Icelandic Text Corpus. In Proceedings of the Eleventh International Conference on Language Resources and Evaluation, LREC 2018, Miyazaki, Japan.

Tortora, C., Santorini, B., Blanchette, F., and Diertani, C. (2017). The Audio-Aligned and Parsed Corpus of Appalachian English (AAPCAppE), version 0.1. www.aapcappe.org. Size: 1.8 million words.

Tortora, C., Cutler, C., Haddican, B., Newman, M., Santorini, B., and Diertani, C. (2020). Corpus of New York City English (CUNY-CoNYCE). https://conyce.commons.gc.cuny.edu/.

Wallenberg, J. C., Ingason, A. K., Sigurðsson, E. F., and Rögnvaldsson, E. (2011). Icelandic Parsed Historical Corpus (IcePaHC). Version 0.9. http://www.linguist.is/icelandic_treebank.

Proceedings of ParlaCLARIN II Workshop, pages 51–57
Language Resources and Evaluation Conference (LREC 2020), Marseille, 11–16 May 2020
© European Language Resources Association (ELRA), licensed under CC-BY-NC

Identifying Parties in Manifestos and Parliament Speeches

Costanza Navarretta, Dorte Haltrup Hansen
Centre for Language Technology, Department of Nordic Studies and Linguistics
University of Copenhagen Emil Holms Kanal 2
2300 Copenhagen S, DK
{costanza,dorteh}@hum.ku.dk

Abstract

This paper addresses differences in the word use of two left-winged and two right-winged Danish parties, and how these differences, which reflect some of the basic stances of the parties, can be used to automatically identify the party of politicians from their speeches. In the first study, the most frequent and characteristic lemmas in the manifestos of the political parties as well as their language complexity are analysed. The analysis shows inter alia that the most frequently occurring lemmas in the manifestos reflect either the ideology or the position of the parties towards specific subjects, confirming for Danish preceding studies of English and German manifestos. Successively, we scaled our analysis applying NLP methods to the transcribed speeches by members of the same parties in the Parliament (Hansards) and trained machine learning algorithms in order to determine to what extent it is possible to predict the party of the politicians from the speeches. The speeches are a subset of the Danish Parliament corpus 2009–2017. The best results of the classification experiments gave a weighted F1-score of 0.57. These results are significantly better than the results obtained by the majority classifier (weighted F1-score = 0.11) and by chance results. They show that the party of the politicians can be distinguished from their speeches in nearly 60% of the cases, even if they debate about the same subjects and thus often use the same terminology. In the future, we will include the subject of the speeches in the prediction experiments.

Keywords: Parliament Speeches, Machine learning, Corpus analysis

1. Introduction

This paper concerns the relation between political parties' stances and the words the parties use as well as applying natural language processing methods and classification algorithms in order to identify the party of Parliament members from their speeches. The language of politicians has been analysed by researchers from various disciplines such as linguistics, rhetoric and political sciences. Moreover, the digital availability of parliament debates, party manifestos and other political data has extended this research to other fields such as computational linguistics and computer science, while political science researchers are using NLP methods and tools in order to test their theories about political opinions and investigate new aspects of political discourse taking advantage of big data technologies.

Being able to distinguish the party of politicians when they talk about important issues such as economy, culture and immigration investigating whether politicians follow their party's positions in practice is one of the long term-aims of the present research. On the short term, it is interesting to find out to which extent politicians use party specific terminology when they speak in the parliament reflecting eventual differences in their parties manifestos. Therefore, we extracted and analysed frequent lemmas in the political manifestos of four political parties in Denmark applying NLP techniques on the manifestos as a way to present differences and similarities in the positions of the four parties. Successively, we scale the study up applying NLP methods to the transcriptions of the parliament speeches of members of the same parties and training classifiers on the resultig data in order to determine the party of politicians from their speeches. We also investigate which features and algorithms perform best on this task. To our best knowledge, this is the first work, at least for Danish, in which NLP techniques are applied to Parliament speeches in order to automatically predict the party of the speakers.

The paper is organised as follows. Firstly, we discuss related research in section 2., secondly we describe the manifestos that we used in our qualitative analysis and the Hansards which were the data in our machine learning experiments (section 3.). Thirdly, we present the qualitative analysis of the manifestos (section 4.) and in section 5. we account for the prediction experiments and their evaluation. Finally, in section 6. we conclude and present future work.

2. Related Studies

The past decades researchers from different disciplines have addressed political discourse taking advantage of the digital availability of political texts and speeches and of NLP tools for processing them. On the one hand, large collection of political data have been collected and/or annotated, e.g. the collection of Hansards from different countries [1] , among many (Alexander and Davies, 2015; Hansen et al., 2018) and outside Europe, e.g. the Canadian bilingual Hansards (Germann, 2001) and the New Zealand's Hansards[2]. Moreover, party manifestos have been collected and annotated in the Comparative Manifesto Project (Merz et al., 2016), and projects associated with the Comparative Agendas Project[3] have manually classified political speeches into domain specific classes. On the other hand, researchers have used raw or annotated data in or der to determine the policy preferences of a number of political parties e.g. (Zirn, 2014; Zirn et al., 2016) and applied

---

[1] A list of these corpora is under `https://www.clarin.eu/resource-families/parliamentary-corpora`.

[2] `https://www.parliament.nz/en/pb/hansard-debates/`.

[3] `https://www.comparativeagendas.net/in`.

sentiment analysis techniques to Hansards in different languages in order to extract the politicians' stances towards particular subjects, e.g. (Onyimadu et al., 2014; Abercrombie and Batista-Navarro, 2018). Similarly, (Schumacher et al., 2019) have applied sentiment analysis to a collection of speeches by Danish and Dutch politicians at party congresses in order to determine over time the number of positive and negative words used by the different parties.

Some researchers propose to count the number of metaphors used by politicians in their speeches for identifying their political ideology (Landtsheer, 2009). The metaphors used in speeches are also studied in order to distinguish the language of male and female politicians in Italy(Ahrens, 2009). Other researchers have used more simple linguistic data such as word scores obtained from political texts in order to determine the political positions of parties over specific dimensions such as economy and culture in other political texts. For example, Laver et al. (2003) determine word scores from British and German parties' manifestos in order to classify political positions in different manifestos produced by the same political parties. They also found that the words used in manifestos cannot be used to classify political speeches in e.g. parliament since the language in manifestos and in parliament speeches is quite different. Slapin and Proksch (2008) use word occurrences in order to estimate political positions in German manifestos. Diermeier et al. (2012) apply support vector machines to the speeches of conservative and liberal politicians in the US Senate in order to find the words that characterize each group mostly. They conclude that cultural terms are more distinctive than economic ones when differentiating the two groups. We follow this line of research of using word- and sentence-based scores for distinguish political discourse by different parties in our analysis of the manifestos.

More recently, the use of word embedding for analysing political speeches has been addressed (Denny and Spirling, 2018) as a better way to determine the semantics of political speeches than word scores since word embeddings account for the context in which words appear. Rheault and Cochrane (2020) apply therefore word embeddings in order to determine the ideology positions of the left and right wing over time in large British, Canadian and U.S.A. parliament corpora. They assess their results against various indicators from e.g. party manifestos, surveys and roll-call votes.

Differing from the preceding studies, in our classification experiments we use NLP techniques applied to Parliament speeches in order to predict the party of the speakers. We do not consider aspects such as sentence length and punctuation marks, since the speeches were converted to written texts by the Parliament language department and punctuation marks and sentence decision are not part of the original speeches. We apply machine learning on our data, but not deep learning since we do not have large-scale parliament data from many decades as it is the case for e.g. in the study by Rheault and Cochrane (2020). Moreover, the political situation in Denmark is different from that of countries such as U.S.A. and Great Britain were there is a clear ideological difference between left and right wing parties. In Denmark, the distinction between left and right parties are often not very strong and parties from the left and the right have common positions on some subjects. For example, the two largest left- and right-wing parties are often accused of being too similar in the Parliament. For these reasons, it is interesting to investigate whether different parties can be in fact distinguished from the speeches of their members.

3. The data

The party manifestos (*principprogrammer*) and the Hansards we address concern the following four Danish parties:

- Dansk Folkeparti (DF, The Danish People's Party) a nationalist party which supports right-wing governments,

- Venstre (V, The Liberal Party) which is the largest right-wing liberal party

- Socialdemokratiet (S, The Social Democratic Party), the largest centre-left party supported by most left-wing parties

- Enhedslisten (Ø, The Red-Green Alliance), the most left-oriented party in the Danish Parliament.

The last twenty years, the Danish prime ministers have belonged to The Liberal Party or The Social Democratic Party. On the contrary, The Danish People's Party and The Red-Green Alliance have never been part of a Government, but they have been very active in the media and in the Parliament debates.

3.1. The manifestos

The party manifestos are interesting since they describe in general terms the ideology of a party and therefore they have been investigated in many projects, e.g. (Merz et al., 2016; Zirn et al., 2016; Laver et al., 2003). In this work, we downloaded the currently valid manifestos from the four parties' homepages. They were published between 2002 – 2017 since parties change their manifestos with varying frequency. In table 1 the length and the publishing date of the four manifestos are given . The oldest and shortest mani-

Party manifesto	Tokens	Year
The Danish People's Party	1132	2002
The Red-Green Alliance	8015	2014
The Social Democratic Party	8835	2017
The Liberal Party	9241	2006

Table 1: Length and year of the manifestos

festo is from The Danish People's Party. The second oldest manifesto, The Liberal Party's one, is also the longest manifesto, while the length of the two most recent manifestos, The Social Democratic Party's and The Red-Green Alliance's ones, are slightly shorter than that of The Liberal Party.

3.2. The Hansards

The dataset of our second study is part of the Danish Parliament Corpus 2009–2017. It consists of the Hansards of the sittings in the Chamber of the Danish Parliament. The corpus is available as a collection through the Danish CLARIN research infrastructure [4] which is part of the European Research Infrastructure for Language Resources and Technology, CLARIN [5]. The corpus consists of xml-files, each covering the Hansards of a parliamentary year which runs from October to June. The xml-files contain metadata providing information about the meetings, the speeches, the name of the speakers, their role (member, minister, chairman), their party and the timing of the speeches as well as the speeches' text. The Hansards contain the exact transcripts of the speeches with the exception of some editing, transforming the spoken speeches into syntactically coherent written texts. In the Hansards factual errors and slips of the tongue are for example corrected and spoken language characteristics such as filled pauses and retractions are not recorded. A more comprehensive description of the corpus is in (Hansen et al., 2018).

The Danish Parliament Corpus consists of approx. 41 million running words and 182,192 speeches. For this work we used a subset of the corpus also used in a preceding study act to the automatic classification of speeches in general domains (Hansen et al., 2019). In this study we only include the speeches by ordinary Parliament members excluding speeches by ministers since these only belonged to the two parties, The Liberal Party and The Social Democratic Party.

4. An analysis of the manifestos

The manifestos were tokenized, PoS-tagged and lemmatized (Jongejan and Damianis, 2009) with the Centre for Language' tools for processing Danish available at the Danish CLARIN infrastructure[6]. In table 2, we report for each manifesto: the number of running words, the number of lemmas, the number of lemmas which only occur in the specific manifesto (unique lemmas), their percentage with respect to the number of lemmas in the manifesto, and finally the manifestos' LIX-score. The LIX-score was originally proposed by (Björnsson, 1968) as a readability score and is often used in the Nordic countries. However, it is also one of the features that has been found useful to characterize the authors of texts, e.g. (Pennebaker et al., 2007). The LIX-score is calculated as $LIX = \frac{W}{S} + \frac{LW \cdot 100}{W}$, where W is the number of words, S is the number of sentences, and LW is the number of long words, that is words that consists of more than 6 letters. The LIX-score formular is similar to e.g. the Flesch-Kincaid Grade Reading Level and other readability scores (see e.g. (Zhou et al., 2017) for a comparison of various readability scores), which do not include text external evidence such as the frequency of words, or syntax, e.g. information on subordinate clauses. We only use it as an extra factor in the comparison of the four manifestos. Since the manifestos are written by professionals, the LIX-score to some extent reflects the chosen complexity of the manifesto texts with respect to the target audience. Unfortunately, this score cannot be used as a feature for analyzing the speeches from the parliament, since sentence length, delimited by punctuation marks, is not a natural property of spoken language. The Social Democratic Party's manifesto has the lowest LIX score, followed by The Danish People's Party's manifesto. The highest LIX score is that of The Red-Green Alliance's manifesto. Not surprisingly, the manifesto of The Danish People's Party contains the lowest number of unique lemmas since it is the shortest one, while the difference between the number of unique lemmas in the manifestos of The Social Democratic Party and The Liberal Party and their length are not related. In fact, the former manifesto contains approx. 400 tokens less than the second, but has relatively fewer unique lemmas.

The five most frequent adjectival, verbal and nominal lemmas and their relative frequency with respect to the lemma's class in each manifesto were extracted and they are shown in table 3 while table 4 shows the three most frequent unique lemmas in each manifesto. Auxiliary verbs were not included in table 3 .

It is not surprising that some of the frequent lemmas in the table are common to more manifestos. However, many of the frequently occurring lemmas and most of the unique frequent lemmas reflect clearly the political stance of the party. This is especially the case for the manifesto of the most right- and left-winged parties. More specifically, The Danish People's Party's manifesto contains many times the adjective *Danish*[7] and *free*, the substantive *democracy* and *country* and the verb *secure*, while the most frequent unique lemmas for this party are *christianity*, *cultural heritage* and *health care* reflecting the main stance of the party: the defense of the Danish culture, religion, and democracy against the influence of non christian immigrants as well as the need for keeping the Danish welfare system. The Red-Green Alliance's manifesto on the other hand contains many occurrences of the lemmas *socialist*, *capitalist*, *capitalism*, *create*, *work*, and *movement* which point towards the party's ideology aiming towards a socialist state and against capitalism. Similarly, the most frequently occurring lemmas in The Liberal Party's manifestos are partly common to those of the other right-winged party and partly characteristic of their liberal ideology, e.g. *free*, *freedom*, *possibility*, *secure*. Moreover, their most frequent unique lemmas are *liberal* and *liberalism* and *police* which reflect their liberal ideology and their intention to secure a strong policy as middle against criminality, one of the themes in the party's manifesto. Finally, the manifesto of the social democrats contains many lemmas common to the manifestos of the other parties, while the most frequent unique lemmas show their general plan of ensuring a social model and integrating the legal immigrants in the Danish society. This reflects the position of the party in the parliament (center-left) and the fact that the social democrats' attitude towards e.g. immigrants the past years has become more similar to that of the right-winged parties.

---

[4] https://clarin.dk.
[5] https://clarin.eu.
[6] https://clarindk/toolchains-wizard.jsp.

[7] The occurrences of the adjective in the party's name were removed from the frequency numbers.

Party	Token	Lemma	UniqLemma	% Uniq	LIX
Danish People's Party	1132	389	83	21.3	47.02
Red-Green Alliance	8015	1294	514	39.7	50.05
Social Democratic Party	8835	1286	469	36.5	39.22
Liberal Party	9241	1668	825	49.5	49.45

Table 2: Number of tokens, lemmas, unique lemmas and LIX of manifestos

Danish People's Party					
%	ADJ	%	VERB	%	NOUN
20.56	dansk (Danish)	3.55	ønske(wish)	6.91	land (country)
4.67	stor (big)	2.37	sikre (secure)	3.62	folk (people)
3.74	høj (high)	2.37	følge (follow)	2.30	folkestyre (democracy)
3.74	fri (free)	21.78	udvikle (develop)	1.97	borger (citizen)
2.80	offentlig (public)	1.18	værdsætte (value)	1.64	udvikling (development)
Red-Green Alliance					
%	ADJ	%	VERB	%	NOUN
4.34	socialistisk (socialist)	3.04	skabe (create)	4.46	menneske (human)
4.34	al (all)	3.04	arbejde (work)	3.22	samfund (society)
3.72	demokratisk (democratic)	1.13	leve (live)	3.10	Kapitalisme (capitalism)
3.22	stor (big)	1.13	se (see)	1.49	land (country)
2.48	økonomisk (economic)	1.13	stå (stand)	1.49	arbejde (work)
Social Democratic Party					
%	ADJ	%	VERB	%	NOUN
8.19	god (good)	2.78	skabe (create)	3.37	verden (world)
5.42	al (all)	2.71	gøre (do)	2.93	land (country)
4.50	mange (many)	2.08	sikre (secure)	2.60	menneske (human)
3.34	stor (big)	1.39	tro (believe)	2.48	fælleskab (community)
2.77	social (social)	1.18	gå (go)	1.66	mulighed (possibility)
Liberal Party					
%	ADJ	%	VERB	%	NOUN
5.48	fri (free)	4.43	sikre (secure)	2.06	menneske (human)
5.02	offentlig (public)	1.33	give (give)	1.83	borger (citizen)
4.46	god (good)	1.14	ønske (wish)	1.78	mulighed (possibility)
4.00	al (all)	1.01	udvikle (develop)	1.78	frihed (freedom)
3.81	enkelt (few)	1.01	skabe (create)	1.69	samfund (society)

Table 3: Most frequent lemmas and % of same in the word class

Partys manifesto	1.unique	2.unique	3.unique
Danish People's Party	kristendom (christianity)	kulturarv (cultural heritage)	sundhedspleje (health care)
Red-Green Alliance	socialistisk (socialist)	kapitalistik (capitalist)	bevægelse (movement)
Social Democratic Party	sammenhængskraft (cohesion)	samfundsmodel (society's mode)l	integration (integration)
Liberal Party	liberal (liberal)	frisind (tolerance/liberalism)	politi (police)

Table 4: Most frequent unique lemmas in the parties' manifestos

A manual analysis of all the unique lemmas in the manifestos shows also that while the manifesto of the Danish People's Party addresses the general themes which are connected with the party's ideology, the manifestos of the other three parties, and especially of the social democrats and liberals, also address general political domains such as the environment, the economy and the education policy. Concluding, the analysis of the most frequently occurring lemmas in the four Danish parties' manifestos show that manifestos' lemma frequencies are a useful feature for extracting the political stance of the political parties confirming the importance of word-related scores investigated in party manifestos in other countries, e.g. (Laver et al., 2003; Slapin and Proksch, 2008).

5. The Prediction experiments

As noticed by (Laver et al., 2003), the language of party manifesto is different from that used in political speeches and therefore it cannot be used as a reference language for making predictions in political debates. However, we hypotesize that the words used by politicians of various parties during Parliament debates differ to some extent since they should reflect the different stances of their party on specific issues and make use of words preferred by their political group. Therefore, the main aim of our second study is to determine to what extent it is possible to automatically predict the party of Parliament members from their speeches in the parliament chamber applying various language models built on their words and lemmas. Furthermore, we want to evaluate the performance of several NLP methods and algorithms on this task.

First, we extracted all the speeches uttered by members of the four parties whose Manifestos were analysed in the previous sections. Then, we removed the speeches which were produced by ministers and the Speaker in order to have a uniform corpus of speeches by ordinary Parliament members, since the speeches of ministers are generally longer while the Speaker only chairs the debates without participating actively in them. We also removed from the data the speeches which contained less than 7 words, getting a dataset of 15911 speeches and 3,145,226 tokens. The number of speeches and the number of tokens per party in the resulting datasets are in table 5. The experiments were run

Party	Number	Tokens
Danish People's Party	3864	785,785
Red-Green Alliance	3711	732,422
Social Democratic Party	4255	858,880
Liberal Party	4081	768,139

Table 5: Speeches and tokens per party

using the scikit-learn library in python. The transcriptions of the speeches were tokenized and lemmatized using the Centre for Language's tools available in the Danish infrastructure, CLARIN.DK. The data were transformed in csv-format so that every line contained a speech, the lemmas of the speech, and the party of the speaker. Punctuation marks were removed from the speeches. The module's algorithms which were tested are K-nearest Neighbors (KNN) multinomial Naive Bayes (NB), Multi-layer Perceptron classifier (MLP) with a lbgs solver, Support Vector Machine (SVM) with a rbf kernel, and Logistic Regression with the lbgs solver (LR). The dataset was randomly divided in a training set, 60% of the data, a testing set (20% of the data) and an evaluation set (the remaining 20% of the data). The baseline is provided by a majority classifier, and the results are reported in terms of precision (P), recall (R) and weighted F1-score (F1). Speeches of a politicians couls occur both in the training and test data. The algorithms were trained on the following datasets: a dataset consisting of bag-of-words (BOW), BOW of the speeches' lemmas (BOWL), the term frequency-inverse document frequency (tf*idf) extracted from the words (TFIDF) of the speeches and from their lemmas (TFIDFL). The tf*idf measure was developed in the field of Information Retrieval (Salton and McGill, 1986) in order to determine how central a word is to a document in a collection of documents and is also often used in NLP.

Stoplists consisting of the most frequent tokens (n>2500) and of the least frequent tokens (n<10) were applied when pre-processing the data. The removal of the least frequent tokens resulted in the deletion of most of the wrongly tokenised elements and numbers. The most frequently occurring lemmas on the other hand consisted of words like *tak* (thanks), *minister* (minister) and *lovforslag* (law bill) which often occur in the speeches from all parties, and therefore are not particularly characteristics of one of them. Table 6 shows the results of the baseline and of the three best performing algorithms, that is Naive Bayes , Support vector machine and Logistic Regression on the various language models. The results of all classifiers are significantly better than those obtained by the majority classifier or those

Algorithm	Data	P	R	F1
Majority		0.07	0.27	0.11
Multinom.	BOW	0.57	0.57	0.57
Naive	BOWL	0.52	0.52	0.51
Bayes	TFIDF	0.57	0.46	0.44
	TFIDFL	0.52	0.47	0.44
Support	BOW	0.52	0.52	0.52
Vector	BOWL	0.47	0.46	0.46
Machine	TFIDF	0.57	0.57	0.57
	TFIDFL	0.55	0.55	0.55
	BOW	0.52	0.52	0.52
Logistic	BOWL	0.49	0.49	0.49
Regression	TFIDF	0.57	0.56	0.56
	TFIDFL	0.53	0.53	0.53

Table 6: Results of predictions experiments

ter than those obtained by the majority classifier or those that can be obtained by chance (0.25). The best results, a weighted F1-score of 0.57, were obtained with the multinomial Naive Bayes trained on bag of words and the support vector classifier trained on tf*idf over words. The second best results were obtained by Logistic regression trained on the tf*idf over words (F1-score 0.56). The results are very promising since some of the speeches are short and the parliament members discuss the same law bills, and therefore they often use the same terminology. Moreover, speakers' individual characteristics in the form of e.g. number of disfluencies and self corrections were removed from the speeches. Therefore, the differences between the various speeches are not caused by these factors. Instead the differences in word use by different parties' members can be explained by party specific terminology and by party specific interests in various subjects . Both aspects should be investigated further in future studies.

Figure 1 is the normalized confusion matrix obtained with the support vector machine's tf*idf model. The diagonal of the confusion matrix shows the proportion of speeches which were correctly classified, while the other slots show the speeches which were wrongly attributed to another party. The confusion matrix shows that the model predicts

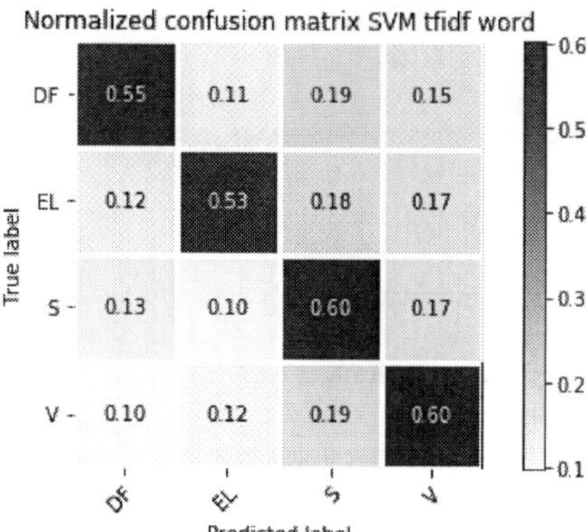

Figure 1: Confusion matrix

speeches from the four parties with F1-scores between 0.53 and 0.60, and the best scores were obtained on speeches by The Liberal Party's (V) and Social Democracy (S)'s members and the worse result was achieved in the identification of speeches by The Red-Green Alliance (EL). Not surprisingly, the best results regard the speeches of the two parties with the highest number of speeches. Similarly, the F1-score for The Red-Green Alliance's speeches is the lowest one since the speeches from the latter party are the least numerous. Moreover, the fact that the language model predicts in 0.19 of the cases that the speeches from The Danish People's Party are uttered by members of The Social Democratic Party confirms the qualitative analysis of the two parties' manifestos which indicated that The Danish People's Party and The Social Democratic Party use often the same terminology in a number of subjects (section 4.). The confusion matrix also shows that the speeches of the two parties which are less frequently confused are those from the most left- and most right-winged party. Furthermore, the matrix shows that the speeches of Social Democrats and Liberals are also often attributed to the other party (19% and 17% of the cases). Interestingly, the best performing algorithms give similar Precision and Recall scores (the same in our tables since we rounded the results up to two decimal digits). This shows that the false negatives and false positives are often the same, indicating again that the members of the Parliament talk about the same subjects and have some common terminology in approximately 40% of the cases even if they have different ideologies.

6. Conclusions and future work

In the paper, we described work act to a) present an analysis of the content of the manifestos of two left- and two right-winged Danish based on the most frequent and specific lemmas occurring in them, b) determine to what extent the words used in the parliament debates by members of the four parties can be used to train models that can distinguish the party of the speech producers c) test the performance of various features and classifiers on this task.

The analyses of the frequency of content lemmas in the manifestos indicate similarity and differences between the four parties ' programs, confirming that parties from both the left and right wing have similar positions on a number of subjects. The analyses also confirm previous research that successfully use word-based scores from party manifestos in order to distinguish the party's positions towards specific subjects (Laver et al., 2003; Slapin and Proksch, 2008). The results of our prediction experiments involving various language models based on NLP-technologies show that the best results are achieved by a support vector machine trained on a td*idf vector (F1-score= 0.57) obtained from the speeches' words and by the multinomial Naive Bayes trained on bag of words. These results are striking since the politicians discuss the same subjects in the Parliament Chamber. The confusion matrix for the best performing language model also confirms that the speeches of some parties (Social Democratic Party and Liberal Party as well as Social Democratic Party and Danish People Party) are more similar to each other than the speeches by members of other parties (Danish People's Party and Red-Green Alliance) with respect to lexical choice. In the future, we will include in the study the subjects of the speeches and other factors such as the age and gender of the parliament members. Moreover, the speeches of more parties and covering a longer period of time will be used in prediction experiments. Finally, our study could be extended to the Hansards of more parliaments and the words used by left-wings and right-wings politicians in different countries could be compared.

7. Acknowledgements

This work is done in CLARIN.DK.

8. Bibliographical References

Abercrombie, G. and Batista-Navarro, R. T. (2018). A sentiment-labelled corpus of hansard parliamentary debate speeches. In Darja Fiser, et al., editors, *Proceedings of the Eleventh International Conference on Language Resources and Evaluation (LREC 2018)*, Paris, France, may. European Language Resources Association (ELRA).

Ahrens, K. (2009). *Politics, Gender and Conceptual Metaphors*. PALGRAVE MACMILLAN.

Alexander, M. and Davies, M. (2015). Hansard corpus 1803-2005. Available online at http://www.hansard-corpus.org.

Björnsson, C.-H. (1968). *Läserbahed*. Liber, Stockholm.

Denny, M. J. and Spirling, A. (2018). Text preprocessing for unsupervised learning: Why it matters, when it misleads, and what to do about it. *Political Analysis*, 26(2):168–189.

Diermeier, D., Godbout, J.-F., Yu, B., and Kaufmann, S. (2012). Language and Ideology in Congress. *British Journal of Political Science*, 42(1):31–55.

Germann, U. (2001). Aligned hansards of the 36th parliament of canada. https://www.isi.edu/natural-language/download/hansard/.

Hansen, D. H., Navarretta, C., and Offersgaard, L. (2018). A Pilot Gender Study of the Danish Parliament Corpus. In Daria Fiser, et al., editors, *Proceedings of LREC 2018 Workshop ParlaCLARIN*.

Hansen, D. H., Navarretta, C., Offersgaard, L., and Wedekind, J. (2019). Towards the Automatic Classification of Speech Subjects in the Danish Parliament Corpus. In Costanza Navarretta, et al., editors, *DHN 2019 Digital Humanities in the Nordic Countries Proceedings*, volume 2364, pages 166–174.

Jongejan, B. and Damianis, H. (2009). Automatic training of lemmatization rules that handle morphological changes in pre-,in- and suffixes alike. In *Proceedings of the Joint Conference of the 47th AnnualMeeting of the ACL and the 4th International Joint Conference on Natural LanguageProcessing of the AFNLP*, pages 145–153, Singapore. ACL.

Landtsheer, C. D., (2009). *Collecting Political Meaning from the Count of Metaphor*, chapter 5, pages 59–78. Springer.

Laver, M., Benoit, K., and Garry, J. (2003). Extracting Policy Positions from Political Texts Using Words as Data. *American Political Science Review*, 97(2):311–331.

Merz, N., Regel, S., and Lewandowski, J. (2016). The Manifesto Corpus: A new resource for research on political parties and quantitative text analysis. *Research and Politics*, pages 1–8, April-June.

Onyimadu, O., Nakata, K., Wilson, T., Macken, D., and Liu, K. (2014). Towards Sentiment Analysis on Parliamentary Debates in Hansard. *Semantic Technology. JIST 2013. Lecture Notes in Computer Science*, 8388.

Pennebaker, J., Chung, C., Ireland, M., Gonzales, A., and Booth, R. (2007). *The development and psychometric properties of LIWC2007*. LIWC Inc, Austin Texas.

Rheault, L. and Cochrane, C. (2020). Word embeddings for the analysis of ideological placement in parliamentary corpora. *Political Analysis*, 28(1):112–133.

Salton, G. and McGill, M. (1986). *Introduction to modern information retrieval*. McGraw-Hill.

Schumacher, G., Hansen, D., van der Velden, M. A., and Kunst, S. (2019). A new dataset of Dutch and Danish party congress speeches. *Research and Politics*, 1-7.

Slapin, J. B. and Proksch, S.-O. (2008). A Scaling Model for Estimating Time-Series Party Positions from Texts. *American Journal of Political Science*, 52(3):705–722.

Zhou, S., Jeong, H., and Green, P. A. (2017). How consistent are the best-known readability equations in estimating the readability of design standards? *IEEE Transactions on Professional Communication*, 60(1):97–111.

Zirn, C., Glavas, G., Nanni, F., Eichorst, J., and Stuckenschmidt, H. (2016). Classifying topics and detecting topic shifts in political manifestos. In *Proceedings of the International Conference on the Advances in Computational Analy-sis of Political Text (PolText 2016)*, pages 88–93, Dubrovnik, Croatia, July.

Zirn, C. (2014). Analyzing Positions and Topics in Political Discussions of the German Bundestag. In *Proceedings of the ACL Student Research Workshop*, pages 26–33.

Proceedings of ParlaCLARIN II Workshop, pages 58–65
Language Resources and Evaluation Conference (LREC 2020), Marseille, 11–16 May 2020
© European Language Resources Association (ELRA), licensed under CC-BY-NC

Comparing Lexical Usage in Political Discourse across Diachronic Corpora

Klaus Hofmann[1], Anna Marakasova[2], Andreas Baumann[1], Julia Neidhardt[2], Tanja Wissik[3]

[1]University of Vienna, [2]TU Wien, [3]Austrian Academy of Sciences
Vienna, Austria
[1]{andreas.baumann, klaus.hofmann}@univie.ac.at,
[2]{anna.marakasova, julia.neidhardt}@tuwien.ac.at, [3]tanja.wissik@oeaw.ac.at

Abstract

Most diachronic studies on either lexico-semantic change or political language usage are based on individual or structurally similar corpora. In this paper, we explore ways of studying the stability (and changeability) of lexical usage in political discourse across two corpora which are substantially different in structure and size. We present a case study focusing on lexical items associated with political parties in two diachronic corpora of Austrian German, namely a diachronic media corpus (AMC) and a corpus of parliamentary records (ParlAT), and measure the cross-temporal stability of lexical usage over a period of 20 years. We conduct three sets of comparative analyses investigating a) the stability of sets of lexical items associated with the three major political parties over time, b) lexical similarity between parties, and c) the similarity between the lexical choices in parliamentary speeches by members of the parties vis-à-vis the media's reporting on the parties. We employ time series modeling using generalized additive models (GAMs) to compare the lexical similarities and differences between parties within and across corpora. The results show that changes observed in these measures can be meaningfully related to political events during that time.

Keywords: diachronic corpora, lexical stability, political discourse

1. Introduction

Lexical associations among words change over time. This is particularly evident for the lexical contexts associated with words denoting named entities, such as political parties in public discourse. Various approaches have been developed to make contextual (or semantic) drift quantitatively tangible (Kim et al., 2014; Hamilton et al., 2016a; Hilpert and Correia Saavedra, 2017). However, most of the research in this area has been limited to studies based on single diachronic corpora. The same is true of studies on political language usage, which either use single or structurally comparable corpora. In this paper we explore ways of comparing lexical contexts associated with named entities, viz. political parties, across two corpora with substantially different structures and text types, representing the language of the Austrian media and the Austrian parliament, respectively.

Our approach is motivated by a socio-linguistic interest in how different domains of text production (media vs. parliament) shape political discourse. An additional aim is to investigate to what extent discourse is sensitive to political events, such as elections, and the changing representational roles of political parties that elections entail. While much research on these topics is carried out by close reading of relevant primary texts (Fairclough, 1995a; Wodak, 2010), we demonstrate how such qualitative analyses can be guided and complemented by quantitative methods that are both transparent and relatively simple. To that end, we analyze two diachronic corpora of Austrian German, namely a diachronic media corpus (AMC) and a corpus of parliamentary records (ParlAT, Section 3.). We focus on the lexical contexts associated with political parties in both corpora and measure their cross-temporal stability. Since the two corpora show substantial differences with respect to their structure and size, one of the methodological challenges consists in extracting data from the datasets that allow for meaningful comparison.

In what follows, we discuss our data and the methods used to analyze them in more detail. We present the analytical results from the cross-corpus comparisons and interpret them in relation to Austria's political history over the past 20 years.

2. Related Work

Most diachronic studies on either lexico-semantic change or political language usage are based on individual or more or less comparable corpora. Many of the recent computer linguistic advances in the area of semantic change tracking and detection have been based on the large Google books corpus or a genre-controlled sub-sample from it (Hamilton et al., 2016b; Dubossarsky et al., 2017; Rosenfeld and Erk, 2018). While the great advantage of using this resource lies in its unmatched size, it is not a balanced linguistic corpus in the strict sense. For that reason, the *Corpus of Historical American English* (COHA) is also often used for studying semantic change (Hamilton et al., 2016a; Eger and Mehler, 2016). In either case, however, the internal structure(s) of the corpora have been of minor relevance for these studies, which are mostly interested in global linguistic mechanisms and trends regarding lexical semantic change and are therefore not primarily content-focused.

In contrast, content and internal structure are of critical importance for studies of political language usage. Studies approaching political discourse from a qualitative perspective often exploit one specific type of political texts, such as parliamentary records (Ilie, 2010; Sealey and Bates, 2016; Archer, 2018; Truan, 2019; Waddle et al., 2019). Qualitative analyses comparing parliamentary records to other resources are much rarer (Ilie, 2004; Archakis and Tsakona, 2010). Similarly, quantitative approaches to political language are usually confined to one source of politically relevant texts (Huang et al., 2019).

Systematic comparative research of political language usage across structurally different corpora, particularly employing quantitative methods, is still outstanding, not least because of the challenges that such an approach faces. The present contribution explores some avenues towards that goal.

3. Data

Parliamentary records are a prime source for studying political discourse. They are published periodically according to a stable procedure, which makes them particularly valuable for diachronic investigations, and even though they usually undergo some amount of editing, their almost verbatim character renders them closer to spoken discourse than related sources (Winters, 2017). A second type of texts that is also commonly used for studying both political discourse and language change is newspapers and media publications more broadly (Böhning, 2017; Gloning, 2017). Usually, these source types are used independently of each other. It is our aim to explore ways of studying them together.

3.1. Austrian Media Corpus

The Austrian Media Corpus (AMC) (Ransmayr et al., 2013) is a diachronic text corpus containing Austrian newspapers, magazines, press releases, transcribed television interviews, news stories from television etc. from the last 30 years. It was created as part of a public-private cooperation between the Austria Press Agency (APA) and the Austrian Centre for Digital Humanities (ACDH) at the Austrian Academy of Sciences (ÖAW). With over 44 million articles, it is one of the largest text corpora for German and definitely the largest for Austrian German. As it is a monitor corpus, new material is being processed and added continuously. The linguistic data has been tokenized, lemmatized and part-of-speech tagged. In all, it contains 10.5 billion tokens representing 40 million word forms and 33 million lemmas. Even though the AMC includes data from a longer time span, we only use data covering the years 1997 to 2016 in the present analysis, which coincides with the duration of six successive Austrian governments. We also restricted the data set to the newspaper sub-corpus which has 5.5 billion tokens.

3.2. Corpus of Austrian Parliamentary Records

The Corpus of Austrian Parliamentary Records (ParlAT) contains the parliamentary records of the National Chamber (*Nationalrat*) – one of two chambers of the Austrian parliament. At present, ParlAT covers the official transcripts (from shorthand) from the XXth to the XXVth legislative periods (1996–2017) (Wissik and Pirker, 2018). Besides being tokenized, part-of-speech tagged and lemmatized, ParlAT also contains special TEI markup in accordance with the Parla-CLARIN guidelines (Erjavec and Pančur, 2019). All speeches delivered by members of parliament (as well as unauthorized interjections by members) are marked up as utterances <u> and each speaker is identified and marked up, accordingly. Thus, every utterance can be linked to a specific speaker. Additional comments and notes supplied by the stenographers are also encoded (e.g. applause etc.). The corpus consists of approximately

75 million tokens representing over 600 000 word forms and 400 000 lemmas. Again, for the present study we only use the years 1997 to 2016.

3.3. Data preprocessing

Our basic aim is to compare the language used to talk about the parties in the media to the language used by party members themselves in parliament. This leads to a fundamental problem regarding the comparability of the data: one of the corpora (ParlAT) is made up of texts by individual speakers, whose party affiliations are relevant for our purposes, while the other (AMC) is made up of texts whose authorship is irrelevant. Thus, we had to preprocess our data in a specific way in order to make them amenable to comparative study. First it was necessary to determine which units of linguistic analysis were to represent political discourse. Based on the assumption that political topics and concepts are most emblematically represented by common nouns (such as *Arbeit* 'work, employment', *Marktwirtschaft* 'market economy' or *Nation* 'nation'), we limited our selection to this word class. It has been shown that nouns are most sensitive to semantic changes caused by cultural shifts (Hamilton et al., 2016a). We extracted all common nouns (by their lemmas) from the two corpora and applied stop words filtering. The list of stop words included numerals, the names of months and days of the week as well as the titles of officials (i.e. councillor, president, etc.), which were considered to be uninformative.

Next, we created subcorpora for each political party per year (from 1997 to 2016). The following political parties were included in the analysis: the Austrian People's Party (ÖVP), the Social Democratic Party of Austria (SPÖ) and the Freedom Party of Austria (FPÖ/BZÖ). The latter covers both the original Freedom Party as well as a splinter group – the Alliance for the Future of Austria – which formed in 2005 and took over the FPÖ's role in government. Because of personal and thematic continuities between the two, we decided not to separate them in the current study. Moreover, the Austrian Green Party (Die Grünen) were excluded due to potential confusion in the AMC with a German party of the same name.

Due to the different annotation structures in the two corpora and the fact that they represent markedly different types of texts in general, we had to define our notion of 'lexical contexts' in different ways. For ParlAT, it was the lexical items that politicians actually used in their speeches that we were primarily interested in, so 'lexical context' in this case denotes the set of common nouns that occurred in the party members' speeches. The process of linking speech to party was rather straightforward, since speaker IDs for every utterance can be linked to metadata including the speakers' party affiliations. Only speeches by elected representatives were included, whereas procedural utterances (e.g. by the chair) as well as interjections were omitted.

In order to obtain comparable subcorpora for the AMC, representing discourse *about* rather than *by* the respective parties, we extracted context windows around the party names (*SPÖ, ÖVP, FPÖ, BZÖ*) as they occurred in the text material. A window length of 20 words (10 nouns preceding and 10 nouns following a party name) was chosen, which is analogous to the median length (19 words) of the selected utterances in ParlAT. In sum, we compiled 120 subcorpora (one for each party in each year for each corpus), which we take to represent the lexical contexts of the parties across the 20-year investigation period.

4. Methods

The majority of studies on computational detection of diachronic change in word usage and meaning make use of a distributional semantics approach, and in particular, prediction-based word embedding models (Kutuzov et al., 2018; Tahmasebi et al., 2018). However, state-of-the-art word embedding models are rather sensitive to the amount of the data used for training. Apart from the fact that various subcorpora from our dataset are not sufficiently large to train a word embedding model, the specific ways in which we preprocessed our data, as determined by our comparative research interest, makes the application of word embedding models problematic. This is particularly so, since the already relatively small ParlAT corpus needs to be split into year-wise subcorpora in order to make diachronic comparisons possible.

Thus, we opted for a simpler but at the same time more accessible approach for investigating the lexical stability in the contexts of target words (in this case, party names) over time and across domains. Since it has been shown that semantic shifts can be usefully quantified by means of the Jaccard index (Jaccard, 1912) (i.e. the size of the intersection of two sets divided by the size of their union), we used it as a measure of similarity between two sets of words (Buntinx et al., 2017; Rodina et al., 2019) representing either different years, parties or corpora. Furthermore, we employed statistical modeling of time series to analyze the diachronic dynamics of the resulting Jaccard index values.

4.1. Word set statistics

In order to address the issue of the small sizes of the subcorpora for each party per year and their uneven distribution, we applied Jaccard distance to equally sized sets of words. Thus, for each year and political party under consideration we created a set of distinctive words, which we take to be characteristic of that party in that particular year. We examined several statistical measures (pointwise mutual information word co-occurrence matrix counts, logistic regression coefficients, cosine similarity of count-based word vectors, etc.) to obtain these characteristic word sets for each subcorpus. However, only two of these were found to be reliable and useful with regard to our research interest, namely word frequency and a χ^2-based keyword measure. All other measures under considerations yielded small intersections of word sets in diachronic comparisons, making similarity estimates unreliable.

The former statistic simply consists of the N most frequent words in a subcorpus. The χ^2-based keyword metric is calculated as follows: First, to measure distinctiveness of words in a subcorpus we ran a χ^2-test for all the word frequencies in the party subcorpus for the year X against the aggregated word frequencies for the remaining parties' subcorpora for the year X; then, we filtered the resulting statistics based on the p-value ($p < 0.05$) as well as on

positive/negative distinctiveness of the words, i.e. we only included words with a positive χ^2 statistic, representing words with a significantly higher occurrence likelihood for a given party compared to the other parties; and, finally, we sorted words by their χ^2 value and took N words with the highest value. Set size was chosen in such a way that noise is minimized. Sets of 200 words were found most informative and methodologically robust. Smaller sets were found to be overly sensitive to year-wise fluctuations, often producing values close to zero for any given year, while larger sets did not substantially alter the results. We conducted comparative analyses of Jaccard similarity in three different ways. First, in order to detect changes in the lexical sets for each party over time, we calculated the Jaccard similarity between the word set for any given year and the very first year to see to what extent the lexical sets had shifted. Second, for each year we computed pairwise similarity values between the word sets of the three parties to see to what extent their lexical usage overlapped. Third, for each party and year we examined the similarity between the word sets from the two corpora.

4.2. Time series modeling

Time series of similarity measures were modeled by means of generalized additive models (GAM) (Wood, 2017), in which time was implemented as a smooth predictor term. This allows a more fine-grained inspection of successive patterns of convergence and divergence between the word sets compared to standard linear regression models. In a graph representation of the model, the non-linear dependencies between variables become visible as curves. The number of knots in the smooth term (i.e. how flexible we allowed the curves to be) was optimized based on the model's Akaike Information Criterion (AIC), a measure of a model's goodness of fit that also considers complexity. This retains maximal informativity of the model while avoiding undue sensitivity to individiual data points. Autocorrelation in the time series was accounted for through autoregressive modeling (AR(1)) (Akaike, 1969). For computations, the R libraries `mgcv` (Wood, 2011) and `itsadug` (van Rij et al., 2017) were used.

5. Results

We conducted three sets of comparative analyses with the nominal word sets extracted from AMC and ParlAT (see Section 3.). The purpose was to establish a) how stable or changeable the noun vocabularies associated with the three major parties were in the two discourse domains during the 20 years under investigation, b) how similar the vocabularies linked to the individual parties were to one another, c) how much similarity there was between the vocabularies used by the parties in parliamentary speeches on the one hand and by the media in their reporting on the parties on the other. Additionally we asked whether any changes observed in these measures could be related to political events during that time.[1]

---

[1]All Jaccard indices can be found at https://drive.google.com/drive/folders/1m9Nuv1M6lac81aijiE-QXEPBJCj8J8T0?usp=sharing.

5.1. Lexical stability per party

First, we measured lexical stability both in the media's coverage of the three main political parties in Austria and in the parties' own language as used in parliament. The time series displayed in Figures 1 and 2 trace Jaccard indices (JI) of the χ^2-based keyword sets for each party, where the JI for any specific year represents the amount of lexical overlap between the set for that year and the set for the very first year of the investigated period (i.e. 1997). In essence, this measure gauges to what extent discourses by and about parties moved away from the point of departure.

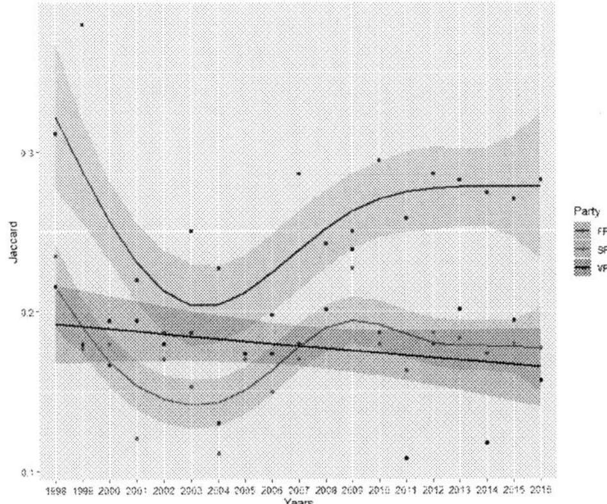

Figure 1: AMC, Jaccard index per party, 1997–2016, lexical similarity to first year, lexical sets based on χ^2-tests (n = 200 per party per year)

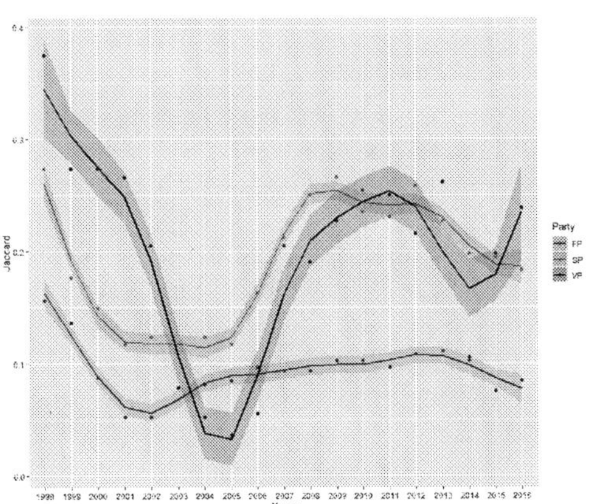

Figure 2: ParlAT, Jaccard index per party, 1997–2016, lexical similarity to first year, lexical sets based on χ^2-tests (n = 200 per party per year)

In the AMC, the keyword sets for the right-wing FPÖ/BZÖ and the centre-left SPÖ undergo significant changes in the first half of the period, represented by a significant drop in JI values. In the second half, the sets regain similarity with the keyword sets of the first year. The JIs for the two parties vary between 0.11 and 0.38, i.e. about 20% to 55% of the 200 keywords is shared between the years. For the centre-right ÖVP, no significant changes can be detected, the JIs

hovering around 0.18, i.e. roughly 30% overlap.

In ParlAT, similar patterns emerge for FPÖ/BZÖ and SPÖ, as both parties witness significant drops in lexical similarity to the first year, and again partly revert to the original keyword sets during the second half of the period. Here, the ÖVP also sees significant changes paralleling those of the other parties. JIs for all three parties oscillate between 0.04 and 0.38 (i.e. between 8% and 55% overlap). These findings indicate that the media discourse related to the ÖVP (as found in the AMC) is generally less variable compared to the other parties, even though all parties exhibit substantial variability in ParlAT. It is also worth noting that in the AMC the discourse surrounding the FPÖ/BZÖ remains relatively more faithful to its initial state compared to the other parties, while in ParlAT FPÖ/BZÖ generally exhibits lower values.

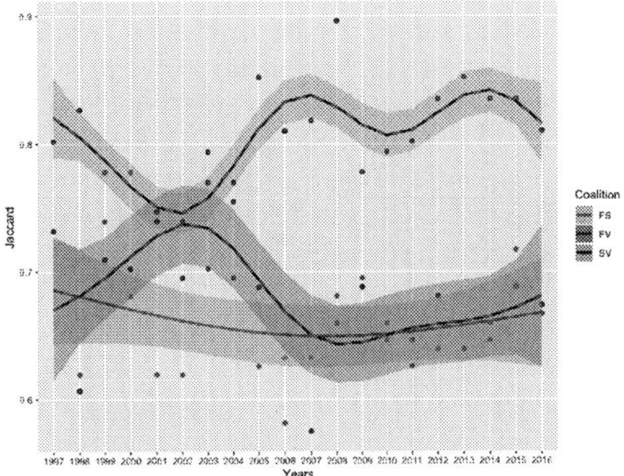

Figure 3: AMC, Jaccard index per party, 1997–2016, lexical similarity between parties, lexical sets based on frequency of occurrence (n = 200 per party per year)

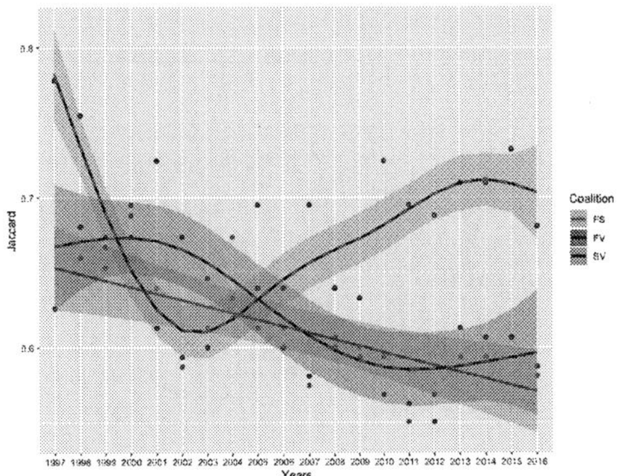

Figure 4: ParlAT, Jaccard index per party, 1997–2016, lexical similarity between parties, lexical sets based on frequency of occurrence (n = 200 per party per year)

5.2. Lexical similarity between parties

It is intriguing to relate the apparent slump in lexical stability during the first half of the investigated period to a major change in government: in 2000, the FPÖ (later BZÖ) entered into a coalition government with the ÖVP, which lasted (over two legislative periods) until 2007. To further explore this observation, we next investigated whether the political vocabularies associated with two political parties exhibit higher similarity metrics during years when the parties participated in a coalition government. For this analysis, we calculated between-party JIs from annual word sets consisting of the 200 most frequent common noun lemmas associated with each party in the two corpora. For this step, simple frequency-based sets were preferred over χ^2-based sets, since the latter by definition represent party-specific distinctive vocabularies, which would depress the JI measuring lexical overlap between parties. The results in Figures 3 and 4 bear out this expectation. In both the AMC and ParlAT the similarity metrics representing the shared noun vocabulary of the 'Grand Coalition' parties (SPÖ and ÖVP) are significantly reduced in the years of the ÖVP–FPÖ/BZÖ governments, while lexical similarity between the right and centre-right parties is elevated during that time. In contrast, lexical similarity between the parties never forming a coalition government (SPÖ and FPÖ/BZÖ) seems stable at a lower level throughout the 20 years. In addition, there seems to be more lexical overlap in the AMC between SPÖ and ÖVP even during years when they did not form a government compared to the remaining non-governing party combinations. This is indicated by higher JI values generally.

We further tested the correlation between lexical similarity and participation in government by constructing a simple linear model from the same data as above, with JI as the output variable, participation in government (GOV) as a two-valued categorical predictor variable (Gov, NoGov). The (hypothetical) coalitions (COAL) were also added as an interacting predictor variable (JI~GOV*COAL). Figure 5 and Tables 1 and 2 show that in both corpora lexical similarity between two parties is higher when they are in a coalition government together. Only in ParlAT the difference reaches statistical significance ($p < 0.001$), however, while in the AMC the difference is marginally significant ($p = 0.0582$). The models also confirm that there is a higher baseline similarity between the SPÖ and the ÖVP ($p < 0.001$) compared to other party combinations. In ParlAT, the identity of the parties does not add significantly to the predictiveness of the model.

Pred.	Levels	Est.	SE	Z	p
Intercept		.65	.02	30.02	<2e-16
GOV	NoGov	-.04	.02	-1.93	.06
COAL	FP/VP	.05	.03	1.92	.06
	SP/VP	.17	.02	9.57	2.64e-13
GOV× COAL	NoGov× FP/VP	.01	.03	.23	.82

Table 1: Table AMC model, Formula: (JI~GOV*COAL).

5.3. Lexical similarity across corpora

Up to this point, word sets from the two corpora have been analyzed separately, and any comparisons between them have rested on correlation tests with the corpus-specific JIs

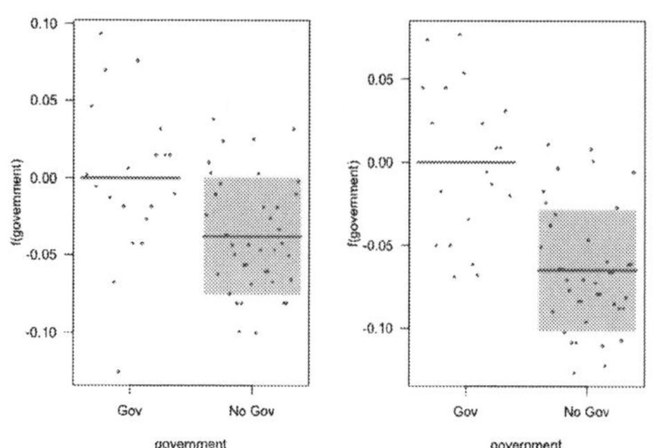

Figure 5: Linear regression models for AMC (left) and ParlAT (right), Formula: (JI~GOV*COAL).

Pred.	Levels	Est.	SE	Z	p
Intercept		.68	.02	32.56	<2e-16
GOV	NoGov	-.07	0.02	-3.48	.001
COAL	FP/VP	-.03	.03	-1.06	.29
	SP/VP	.02	0.02	1.38	0.17
GOV× COAL	NoGov× FP/VP	.02	.03	0.86	.40

Table 2: Table ParlAT model, Formula: (JI~GOV*COAL).

as input. In a third and final step, we addressed the question whether there is also a cross-corpus overlap between the word sets themselves and whether we could identify tendencies towards lexical convergence or divergence between the two discourse domains. For this analysis, we again relied on χ^2-based keyword sets. In this case, the JIs for each party in each each year represent the amount of lexical overlap between the keywords from the AMC contexts, representing media discourse about the parties, and the keywords extracted from ParlAT, representing the parties' own use of language.

As in the previous analyses, the results suggest a temporal split between the first and the second half of the investigation period, roughly corresponding to the changes in governing coalitions (Figure 6). Interestingly, two of the parties behave in an almost antithetical way: where the lexical sets from the two corpora tend towards greater convergence for the FPÖ/BZÖ, they diverge for the SPÖ, and vice versa ($r(18) = -0.86, p < 0.001$). The ÖVP takes an intermediate position: at first, its cross-corpus similarity metrics align more closely with those of the FPÖ/BZÖ, but after a peak during the early years of the the right/centre-right coalition government soon fall back to a trajectory that is counter-cyclical to that of the FPÖ/BZÖ and similar to that of the SPÖ (ÖVP vs. FPÖ/BZÖ: $r(18) = -0.45, p < 0.05$; ÖVP vs. SPÖ: $r(18) = 0.45, p < 0.05$). It should be noted that the JI measures in this analysis are generally smaller than those found for lexical stability per party within corpora (cf. Section 5.1.). JIs range between 0.02 and 0.21, which corresponds to between c. 4% and c. 35% shared nominal keyword vocabulary associated with the parties across the two domains.

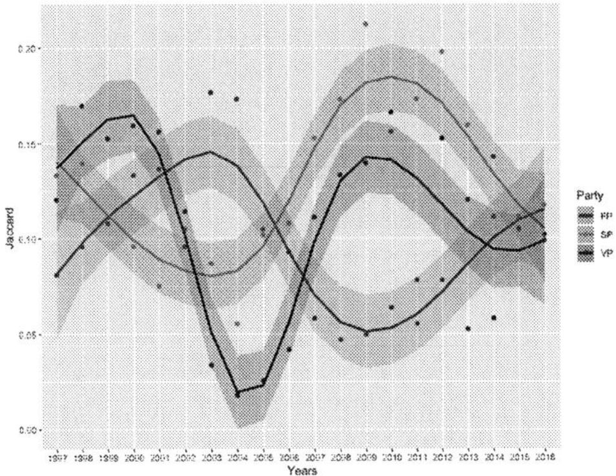

Figure 6: AMC, ParlAT, Jaccard index per party, 1997–2016, lexical similarity between corpora, lexical sets based on χ^2-tests (n = 200 per party per year)

6. Discussion

A common theme running through all the above analyses is that lexical usage in Austrian political discourse is sensitive to changes in political realities. More importantly for present purposes, the sensitivity of language to real-world events can be traced and explored comparatively with the help of the two corpus resources presented here, the AMC and ParlAT.

Thus, it emerges from the empirical analysis that changes in governing coalitions have a visible and robust impact both on the lexical inventory used by the media to report on the three major parties and on the vocabulary used by party representatives in parliament. This is evident in the way that lexical usage adapts to a party's democratic role during a legislative period (Section 5.1.), and also in the way that the parties' speech patterns converge when they join to form a government (Section 5.2.).

These findings are not altogether unexpected, considering that the change of a party's role within the structures of a representational democracy goes hand in hand with changes in executive responsibilities and procedural matters. At the same time, a closer inspection of the keyword sets for the individual parties also suggests that lexical differences between governing and opposition roles reflect different strategies of self-representation (Gruber, 2015). When in government, the SPÖ generally uses more positive and dynamic vocabulary, including *Arbeit* 'work, employment', *Lösung* 'solution', *Möglichkeit* 'opportunity', *Maßnahme* 'measure, action', *Projekt* 'project' and *Erfolg* 'success'. In opposition, the same party's vocabulary is more antagonistic and critical, including *Forderung* 'demand, request', *Kritik* 'criticism', *Problem* 'problem', as well as a wider range of unconcealed expressions of rebuke, such as *Chaos* 'chaos', *Desaster* 'disaster', *Doppelspiel* 'duplicity', or *Ellbogengesellschaft* 'elbow society', none of which features prominently in the party's speech when in government. Some of these tendencies seem to carry over to the

AMC, where *Lösung*, *Maßnahme* and *Möglichkeit* are also among the most prominent keywords associated with the SPÖ while in power. Findings such as these can serve to complement studies on how politicians defend their own record (Sealey and Bates, 2016) and negotiate differences (Harris, 2001; Archer, 2018; Waddle et al., 2019) within the confines of decorum and parliamentary rules.

Another finding worth commenting on highlights how the lexical effects of being in government may sometimes differ between parties. As seen in Section 5.3., the lexicon associated with the FPÖ/BZÖ during the right/centre-right government showed a much greater degree of convergence between parliamentary and media discourse relative to that of its coalition partner ÖVP. This could be interpreted as evidence that the FPÖ was generally more successful in having topics or its way of speaking picked up by the media. Without a closer reading of the source materials, it is not immediately clear if this was indeed the case. It is striking, however, that many of the most widely dispersed keywords linked to the FPÖ/BZÖ in both corpora during this time designate individuals, such as *Person* 'person', *Kollege* 'colleague', *Abgeordnete* 'representative, MP', *Freiheitliche* 'member of the freedom party' and *Mitglied* 'member'. This may be a reflection of internal conflicts within the FPÖ during this time, including a party coup in 2002 (known in Austria as 'Knittelfeld' after the venue of the coup) and the eventual break-up into two parties, FPÖ and BZÖ, in 2005. These tensions and their effect on parliamentary debate may well have had a more attractive media appeal than the ÖVP's contributions, a difference that integrates well with conceptions of contemporary politics that distinguish between 'frontstage' and 'backstage' politics (Wodak, 2010).

Equally intriguing are differences between the two corpora: For example, we found little evidence to suggest that the way that the only party in power throughout the 20-year period, the ÖVP, was represented in the media changed much at all (see Section 5.1.). At least based on the JIs measuring how much of the keyword vocabulary matches the first year's vocabulary, there was little movement over time. This differs starkly from the way that lexical items characterise the speech of the ÖVP in parliament, being subject to some of the strongest fluctuations of all parties. Continuity in government may level out media coverage, but the same may not necessarily hold true for the language in parliament. Findings such as these may prompt closer investigations of disparities between what a party does in parliament and what is said about the party in the wider public discourse (Wodak, 2010).

Finally, the results provide some basis to speculate about how a party's positioning in the media discourse may differ from its role in parliament. Thus, the findings in Section 4.2. imply that the so-called 'centrist' parties (i.e. SPÖ and ÖVP) display a significantly larger amount of lexical similarity in the media compared to how much keyword vocabulary either of them shares with the right-wing FPÖ/BZÖ. Importantly, this effect is independent of whether the centrist parties formed a coalition government or not. In contrast, no such elevated baseline of lexical overlap between the centrist parties could be observed in ParlAT: here joint participation in government turned out to be the only factor significantly influencing the amount of overlap between parties. Once again, this points to a potential disconnect between the two domains of political discourse.

Suggestive as these findings are, many of the points made above must await further study, either qualitatively by applying the analytical tools developed within the field of discourse analysis (Fairclough, 1995a; Fairclough, 1995b; Wodak and Meyer, 2001), or with a more sophisticated set of quantitative methods, including stylometric analysis of individuals or groups of speakers (Huang et al., 2019), computer-assisted content analysis and topic modeling for extracting political positions (Laver et al., 2003; Proksch and Slapin, 2010; Lauderdale and Herzog, 2016), or sentiment analysis (Taboada, 2016). Nonetheless, this study has demonstrated that a comparative analysis of two corpora with related contents but markedly different internal structures can succeed in yielding insightful and stimulating results, with great potential for the study of political discourse. Within the field of digital humanities, relatively simple and transparent methods such as the ones applied in this study can assist in identifying global trends in the compared data and point out areas of interest in the corpus data for closer scrutiny.

7. Conclusion

In this paper, we examined ways of comparing the stability and similarity of lexical usage across two corpora covering the same time period but otherwise exhibiting substantial differences in terms of annotation and content. We addressed these questions by means of a case study focusing on the lexical contexts associated with major Austrian political parties in two different diachronic corpora, i.e. AMC and ParlAT. We identified and discussed changes in the lexical contexts associated with political parties over time, between the parties and across the corpora. Furthermore, we were able to relate the results of the comparative analysis to real-world events.

8. Acknowledgements

The project *Diachronic Dynamics of Lexical Networks (DYLEN)* is funded by the ÖAW go!digital Next Generation grant (GDNG 2018-02).

9. Bibliographical References

Akaike, H. (1969). Fitting autoregressive models for prediction. *Annals of the Institute of Statistical Mathematics*, 21(1):243–247.

Archakis, A. and Tsakona, V. (2010). The wolf wakes up inside them, grows werewolf hair and reveals all their bullying': The representation of parliamentary discourse in greek newspapers. *Journal of Pragmatics*, 42:912–923.

Archer, D. (2018). Negotiating difference in political contexts: An exploration of Hansard. *Language Sciences*, 68:22–41.

Buntinx, V., Bornet, C., and Kaplan, F. (2017). Studying linguistic changes over 200 years of newspapers through resilient words analysis. *Frontiers in Digital Humanities*, 4:2.

Böhning, H. (2017). Zeitungen und Sprachentwicklung. Beobachtungen zu den ersten eineinhalb Jahrhunderten deutscher Zeitungen. In Oliver Pfefferkorn, et al., editors, *Die Zeitung als Medium in der neuen Sprachgeschichte. Korpora - Analyse - Wirkung*, pages 7–21. Walter de Gruyter, Berlin/Boston.

Dubossarsky, H., Grossman, E., and Weinshall, D. (2017). Outta control: Laws of semantic change and inherent biases in word representation models. In *Proceedings of the 2017 Conference on Empirical Methods in Natural Language Processing*, pages 1147–1156.

Eger, S. and Mehler, A. (2016). On the linearity of semantic change: Investigating meaning variation via dynamic graph models. In *Proceedings of the 54th Annual Meeting of the Association for Computational Linguistics,*, pages 52–58.

Erjavec, T. and Pančur, A. (2019). Parla-CLARIN: TEI guidelines for corpora of parliamentary proceedings. In *Book of abstracts of the TEI2019: What is text, really? TEI and beyond*. University of Graz.

Fairclough, N. (1995a). *Media discourse*. Arnold, London/New York.

Fairclough, N. (1995b). *Critical Discourse Analysis*. Longman, London.

Gloning, T. (2017). Alte Zeitungen und historische Lexikographie. Nutzungsperspektiven, Korpora, Forschungsinfrastrukturen. In Oliver Pfefferkorn, et al., editors, *Die Zeitung als Medium in der neuen Sprachgeschichte. Korpora - Analyse - Wirkung*, pages 121–147. Walter de Gruyter, Berlin/Boston.

Gruber, H. (2015). Policy-oriented argumentation or ironic evaluation: A study of verbal quoting and positioning in Austrian politicians' parliamentary debate contributions. *Discourse Studies*, 17(6):682–702.

Hamilton, W. L., Leskovec, J., and Jurafsky, D. (2016a). Cultural shift or linguistic drift? comparing two computational measures of semantic change. In *Proceedings of the Conference on Empirical Methods in Natural Language Processing. Conference on Empirical Methods in Natural Language Processing*, pages 2116–2121.

Hamilton, L. W., Leskovec, J., and Jurafsky, D. (2016b). Diachronic Word Embeddings Reveal Statistical Laws of Semantic Change. In *Proceedings of the 54th Annual Meeting of the Association for Computational Linguistics*. Association for Computational Linguistics.

Harris, S. (2001). Being politically impolite: Extending politeness theory to adversarial political discourse. *Discourse Society*, 12(4):451–472.

Hilpert, M. and Correia Saavedra, D. (2017). Using token-based semantic vector spaces for corpus-linguistic analyses: From practical applications to tests of theoretical claims. *Corpus Linguistics and Linguistic Theory*.

Huang, L., Perry, P. O., and Spirling, A. (2019). A general model of author 'style' with application to the UK House of Commons, 1935-2018. Working Paper, https://www.nyu.edu/projects/spirling/documents/VeryBoring.pdf.

Ilie, C. (2004). Interruption patterns in british parliamentary debates and drama dialogue. In *Dialogue Analysis*

IX: Dialogue in Literature and the Media, Part 1: Literature: Selected Papers from the 9th IADA Conference, pages 311–326.

Ilie, C. (2010). Strategic uses of parliamentary forms of address: The case of the u.k. parliament and the swedish riksdag. *Journal of Pragmatics*, 42:885–911.

Jaccard, P. (1912). The distribution of the flora in the alpine zone. *New Phytologist*, 11(2):37–50.

Kim, Y., Chiu, Y.-I., Hanaki, K., Hegde, D., and Petrov, S. (2014). Temporal analysis of language through neural language models. In *Proceedings of the ACL 2014 Workshop on Language Technologies and Computational Social Science*, pages 61–65.

Kutuzov, A., Øvrelid, L., Szymanski, T., and Velldal, E. (2018). Diachronic word embeddings and semantic shifts: A survey. In *Proceedings of the 27th International Conference on Computational Linguistics*, pages 1384–1397.

Lauderdale, B. and Herzog, A. (2016). Measuring political positions from legistlative speech. *Political Analysis*, 24(3):374–394.

Laver, M., Benoit, K., and Garry, J. (2003). Extracting policy positions from political texts using words as data. *American Political Science Review*, 97(2):311–313.

Proksch, S.-O. and Slapin, J. B. (2010). Position taking in european parliament speeches. *British Journal of Political Science*, 40(3):587–611.

Ransmayr, J., Mörth, K., and Ďurčo, M. (2013). Linguistic variation in the Austrian Media Corpus: Dealing with the challenges of large amounts of data. In *Procedia - Social and Behavioral Sciences 95. Proceedings of the 5th International Conference on Corpus Linguistics (CILC 2013)*, pages 111–115.

Rodina, J., Bakshandaeva, D., Fomin, V., Kutuzov, A., Touileb, S., and Velldal, E. (2019). Measuring diachronic evolution of evaluative adjectives with word embeddings: the case for English, Norwegian, and Russian. In *Proceedings of the 1st International Workshop on Computational Approaches to Historical Language Change*, pages 202–209.

Rosenfeld, A. and Erk, K. (2018). Deep neural models of semantic shift. In *Proceedings of the 2018 Conference of the North American Chapter of the Association for Computational Linguistics: Human Language Technologies*, page 474–484.

Sealey, A. and Bates, S. (2016). Prime ministerial self-reported actions in Prime Minister's Questions 1979-2010: A corpus-assisted analysis. *Journal of Pragmatics*, 104:18–31.

Taboada, M. (2016). Sentiment analysis: An overview from linguistics. *Annual Review of Linguistics*, 2:325–347.

Tahmasebi, N., Borin, L., and Jatowt, A. (2018). Survey of computational approaches to diachronic conceptual change. *CoRR*, abs/1811.06278.

Truan, N. (2019). Talking about, for, and to the people: Populism and representation in parliamentary debates on Europe. *Zeitschrift für Anglistik und Amerikanistik*, 67:307–337.

van Rij, J., Wieling, M., Baayen, R. H., and van Rijn, H. (2017). itsadug: Interpreting Time Series and Autocorrelated Data Using GAMMs. R package version 2.3.

Waddle, M., Bull, P., and Böhnke, J. R. (2019). 'He is just the nowhere man of British Politics': Personal attacks in Prime Minister's Questions. *Journal of Language and Social Psychology*, 38(1):61–84.

Winters, J. (2017). Tackling complexity in humanities big data: From parliamentary proceedings to the archived web. *Studies in Variation, Contacts and Change in English*, 19.

Wissik, T. and Pirker, H. (2018). ParlAT beta Corpus of Austrian Parliamentary Records. In *Proceedings of the LREC 2018 Workshop 'ParlaCLARIN: LREC2018 workshop on creating and using parliamentary corpora'*, pages 20–23.

Wodak, R. and Meyer, M. (2001). *Methods of Critical Discourse Analysis*. SAGE, London.

Wodak, R. (2010). *The discourse of politics in action: Politics as usual*. Palgrave Macmillan, Basingstoke.

Wood, S. N. (2011). Fast stable restricted maximum likelihood and marginal likelihood estimation of semiparametric generalized linear models. *Journal of the Royal Statistical Society (B)*, 73(1):3–36.

Wood, S. (2017). *Generalized Additive Models: An Introduction with R*. Chapman and Hall/CRC, 2 edition.

Proceedings of ParlaCLARIN II Workshop, pages 66–74
Language Resources and Evaluation Conference (LREC 2020), Marseille, 11–16 May 2020

The Europeanization of Parliamentary Debates on Migration in Austria, France, Germany, and the Netherlands

Andreas Blätte, Simon Gehlhar, Christoph Leonhardt
University of Duisburg-Essen, University of Duisburg-Essen, University of Duisburg-Essen
andreas.blaette@uni-due.de, simon.gehlhar@uni-due.de, christoph.leonhardt@uni-due.de

Abstract

Corpora of plenary debates in national parliaments are available for many European states. For comparative research on political discourse, a persisting problem is that the periods covered by corpora differ and that a lack of standardization of data formats inhibits the integration of corpora into a single analytical framework. The solution we pursue is a 'Framework for Parsing Plenary Protocols' (frappp), which has been used to prepare corpora of the Assemblée Nationale ("ParisParl"), the German Bundestag ("GermaParl"), the Tweede Kamer of the Netherlands ("TweedeTwee"), and the Austrian Nationalrat ("AustroParl") for the first two decades of the 21st century (2000-2019). To demonstrate the usefulness of the data gained, we investigate the Europeanization of migration debates in these Western European countries of immigration, i.e. references to a European dimension of policy-making in speeches on migration and integration. Based on a segmentation of the corpora into speeches, the method we use is topic modeling, and the analysis of joint occurrences of topics indicating migration and European affairs, respectively. A major finding is that after 2015, we see an increasing Europeanization of migration debates in the small EU member states in our sample (Austria and the Netherlands), and a regression of respective Europeanization in France and – more notably – in Germany.

Keywords: corpus creation, parliamentary debates, topic modeling, Europeanization, migration

1. Introduction: Migration and Europeanization

European politics have been challenged profoundly by the large inflow of refugees in 2015 and successive years.[1] Migration has moved to the top of the political agenda of Europe and has become a highly controversial issue – with a huge impact on electoral politics, coalition formation and parliamentary proceedings. For instance, in the Netherlands, a dispute over basic care for rejected asylum seekers in 2015 almost provoked the premature end of the governing coalition. In Germany, the governing coalition of Christian Democrats (CDU), the Christian Social Union (CSU) and the Social Democratic Party (SPD) has been on the verge of collapse due to migration disputes between the coalition parties in 2018. In France, the Asylum and Immigration Act passed in July 2018 triggered a fierce parliamentary dispute. In Austria, Sebastian Kurz from the Austrian People's Party (ÖVP) won the Federal Chancellery in October 2017, having moved the party to a more restrictive stance towards immigration.

Migration has become one of the most challenging issues for the future of the European Union (EU). In the 2019 campaign for the elections for the European Parliament, migration affairs were center stage. However, it is important to gain a comprehensive understanding, whether a European perspective is systematic or episodic in policy debates. A common ground and a common view of key challenges in the European political landscape is deemed to be necessary for European policy-making. Yet if the prospect of European politics depends on the commonality of perceptions, the question arises, whether issues are generally contextual-

ized in a European manner or whether perceptions remain being defined exclusively from the national context. This is why the Europeanization of migration debates in the national parliaments of EU countries is relevant for the outlook of European politics.

Of course, debates on migration and integration are not at all limited to parliamentary debates. Discursive hotspots will often be located somewhere else, in the digital realm amongst others. However, the parliamentary arena has a central role for the agenda of the political-administrative system. Also, one advantage is that plenary debates provide comparative data. Still, comparing parliamentary debates is not an easy road. Whereas pdf documents are almost universally accessible and in the public domain, standardized and machine-readable versions of parliamentary debates covering the same period under investigation remain a goal yet to be reached when working towards the aim of safeguarding a "data-rich" future for social science research (King, 2011).

For this purpose, we develop a "Framework for Parsing Plenary Protocols", or "frappp" in short. This framework defines a generic workflow for preparing corpora of plenary protocols, limiting the marginal cost for preparing a corpus for an additional parliament to defining regular expressions and the development of supplementary data to consolidate the corpus.

Previously, the *frappp*-approach has been used to prepare corpora of all German regional parliaments and of the UN General Assembly. To explore and demonstrate the advances that may result from an improved data preparation workflow, we started to apply the procedure to a limited number of parliaments across Europe. Based on the theoretical consideration that Western European states have experienced a comparable political development, including a similar history of immigration (Messina, 2007), this study focuses on Germany, France, the Netherlands and Austria. The corpora prepared for the German

---

[1]We gratefully acknowledge funding of the Stiftung Mercator for the Mercator Forum Migration and Democracy (MIDEM) that has been instrumental for this research. MIDEM is a research center of the Technische Universität Dresden in cooperation with the University of Duisburg-Essen, funded by Stiftung Mercator.

Bundestag, the French Assemblée Nationale, the Tweede Kamer of the Netherlands and the Austrian Nationalrat are called "GermaParl", "ParisParl", "TweedeTwee" and "AustroParl".

The data covers two decades (1999-2019). From a technical point of view, our investigation begins at a time when parliaments started to offer "born digital" versions of parliamentary proceedings. Furthermore, our timeframe is defined by important events regarding migration policy in Europe. The Tampere Summit of October 1999 was an important milestone for the closer cooperation of European countries on migration policy, including far-reaching steps towards the harmonization of European asylum law (Trauner, 2016). The May 2019 European elections were dominated by the migration issue and can be seen as a preliminary endpoint of a long period with a high salience for the issue. Methodologically, we use topic modeling (Blei et al., 2003) as a technique to detect the thematic focal points of debates and the co-occurrence of migration-related topics and topics indicating a European perspective. Our paper demonstrates that using computer-assisted text analysis in combination with large-scale textual data is a highly efficient approach to gain findings about the degree of Europeanization of debates on migration in national parliaments. These findings would be utterly tedious to obtain otherwise. But before we turn to data, methodology and results in more detail, we develop the theoretical vanguard more precisely.

2. Theory: Europeanization as a Matter of Attention

Do policies become more similar across the European countries? The assumption of an increasing convergence of policies among EU countries is deeply embedded in the European integration project. In the social sciences, convergence was initially understood as a legislative harmonization process among countries. Researchers have identified various factors leading to convergence. At a systemic level, increasing interdependencies of nation states and the continuous expansion of international organizations (e.g. the EU), were expected to bring about convergence. Interdependence results in legal and normative obligations that should, at least theoretically, lead to legislative convergence of EU countries (Holzinger et al., 2007).

A large number of policy areas can be the subject of convergence processes, including migration policy. Indeed, the ability of EU countries to regulate migration has been shaped profoundly by European integration. The establishment of the European Single Market and the free movement of EU citizens has imposed a set of important restrictions on EU countries to regulate migration at the national level. In addition, some issues have shifted to the European level. The EU has gained relevance for asylum policy as well as security and border control (Trauner, 2016). Thus, the comparative analysis of the convergence of the policy output in migration policy-making is a well-justified and interesting research perspective.

Indeed, convergence studies have a strong focus on policy output (Nordbeck, 2013). In this context, convergence is defined as "any increase in the similarity between one or more characteristics of a certain policy (e. g. policy objectives, policy instruments, policy settings) across a given set of political jurisdictions (supranational institutions, states, regions, local authorities) over a given period of time" (Knill, 2005).

But convergence can be understood more broadly. Kerr (1983) defines convergence as a "tendency of societies to grow more alike, to develop similarities in structures, processes and performances". Accordingly, convergence does not necessarily mean a congruent or identical reaction to a certain problem, but rather it refers to a gradual approximation, for example in the choice of policies (Scholz, 2012). Theories of convergence entail the empirical necessity to measure similarities across political systems. Accordingly, the focus on specific policies or political outcomes is just one option. A focus on the discursive and communicative patterns of parliaments is a viable alternative. With regard to the question of a common European perception and contextualization of specific problems, we draw on the literature on Europeanization and on the emergence of a European public sphere.

Studies on the European public sphere argue that the EU depends on a common frame of reference shared by citizens of EU countries (Trenz, 2015; Lingenberg, 2010). A common approach taken by these studies is to identify a European public sphere based on the salience of issues in national media systems (Trenz, 2015). The public sphere is defined "as a site where public discourses and popular identities are framed" (Trenz, 2015). At the heart of this approach is the conviction that the mass media constitute the public sphere. In this research, Europeanisation is measured by the "general level of attention the media pays to political news from the EU" (Trenz, 2015). The visibility of European events, actors and issues is the empirical hallmark of this approach.

With regard to our research, the parliamentary arena is no less important to understand Europeanization and convergence, similar to media system analysis. A focus on the frame of reference of parliamentary attention has important methodological consequences. Our interest in the larger trends concerning migration and European affairs implies that an in-depth analysis of the speeches is not necessary. Distant reading rather than close reading is required (Moretti, 2013). Statements about parliamentary attention at a higher level of abstraction make parliamentary discourse comparable and indicate using text mining techniques. The focus on attention structures is furthermore supported by the methodology of the Comparative Agendas Project (CAP).

The CAP monitors policy processes by tracking government activity in response to the challenges they face. These activities can take a variety of forms, including holding hearings or giving speeches (Baumgartner et al., 2019). Bevan (2019) argues that measuring attention is important because every policy change assumes that the "policy is first attended to". The project has established a comprehensive database recording the "date as well as a minimum of additional information about each issue" (Baumgartner et al., 2019). Baumgartner el al. (2019) argue: "If the key issue is how much attention is being directed at an issue, and if the attention reflects enthusiasm or criticism, then traditional 'deep reading' of the text was not needed".

The CAP methodology justifies why an abstract measurement of attention in parliamentary discourse may provide important insights. This is the starting point of our research: Speeches can be classified with the help of computer-based procedures (topic models). The aim is to identify attention for two relevant issues in speeches: First, speeches with a migration policy reference and second, speeches with a European policy reference. When we know which speeches address migration policy, and which speeches refer to the European level of policy-making, we can obtain statements on the overlap of categories. It is assumed that the appearance of both categories in one speech is an indicator that the migration issue was discussed in the European context, in the sense that a Europeanization of the topic is taking place.

3. Data

3.1. A Framework for Parsing Plenary Protocols

In line with our research interest, we prepared and augmented four corpora of parliamentary debates, from Austria's Nationalrat ("AustroParl"), the French Assemblée Nationale ("ParisParl"), Germany's Bundestag ("GermaParl") and the Dutch Tweede Kamer ("TweedeTwee").[2] The raw data for building the corpora was obtained from the parliaments' websites. While most of the necessary data is provided as pdf documents,[3] this format is not apt for technically advanced analyses. A toolchain of several R packages developed in the context of the PolMine Project was used to transform the raw data into a more format suitable for corpus analysis: The first of those, `trickypdf`, processes pdf files with challenging layouts, providing a convenient workflow to extract text from pdf documents with more complex layouts featuring two columns as well as text on the margins.[4]

In the next step, the plain text output of `trickypdf` needs to be scanned for structural information and annotated accordingly. To ensure replicability and sustainability, plenary data should be prepared in a way which satisfies the principles of FAIR (Wilkinson, 2016). At the same time, barriers of data preparation should be minimized. With these goals in mind, instead of resorting to individual solutions for each parliament, the R package `frappp` was developed which strives "[t]o reduce necessities to re-invent the wheel in new corpus preparation projects, [and] uses techniques of object-oriented programming and offers a framework that runs the user through the corpus preparation workflow" (Blätte and Leonhardt, 2019).

To transform plain text to XML, regular expressions are used to extract relevant meta-information and to store it in the structured data format of the XML output document. Thus, corpora contain information on the legislative period and the date of a speech. They report the parliamentary group membership of a speaker as well as the role of the speaker. Interjections are also annotated. This structural annotation of the original text permits to create complex and multi-layered sub-corpora, which are the prerequisite for comparative analyses. Undoubtedly, a coherent standardization of plenary data is required. One of the most valid solutions is provided by the guidelines of the Text Encoding Initiative (TEI).[5] While being merely TEI-inspired, the XML output of `frappp` is a preliminary simplified approximation that may be an initial step towards standardization.

TEI/XML is useful for standardization and as a data exchange format. However, it is not necessarily appropriate for analysis. Changing the format is only a first step. After this stage of "XMLification", the speeches were tokenized and annotated linguistically.[6] All words were lemmatized and assigned to a part of speech. Stanford CoreNLP was used for tokenization and Part-of-speech-tagging (as well as Named Entity Recognition for the Austrian corpus) (Manning et al., 2014). The TreeTagger was used for lemmatization (Schmid, 1995). The general preparation process of the TEI files is described more in-depth for the GermaParl corpus which served as a model and prototype for the further corpora that have been prepared (Blätte and Blessing, 2018).

In a last step, the data was imported into the IMS Open Corpus Workbench (Evert and Hardie, 2011). This was done with the R package cwbtools. Thus, a data release will entail offering the TEI/XML data as well as the CWB indexed corpus. For reproducing results, the latter is the relevant basis.[7]

Only a part of the corpus we use in this analysis for the Dutch case is prepared as described above. Data before 15 September 2015 is taken from the ParlSpeech corpus by Rauh et al. (2017b) and then merged with a newly prepared corpus of Dutch protocols.

3.2. Structural annotation

Structural annotation is the key to obtain relevant research findings inside the corpora. As previously mentioned, while XML is ideal for long-term storage and interoperability, the indexed corpus version is the relevant resource for concrete research and publication projects. In the jargon of the Corpus Workbench (CWB), annotation layers are called "structural attributes". Table 1 provides an overview about available attributes, their description, possible values and the corpora they are available for.

---

[2]These corpora were developed experimentally at the time of writing. They shall be released in 2020.

[3]The German Bundestag switched to a thoroughly annotated XML format starting with the 19th legislative period (beginning in September 2017).

[4]The package is available at GitHub, see: `https://github.com/PolMine/trickypdf`.

[5]The Parla-CLARIN standard (Erjavec and Pančur, 2019) discussed at the 2019 ParlaFormat Workshop is the reference suggestion at this stage.

[6]The Dutch corpus was tokenized using the openNLP interface for R (Hornik, 2016) with its Dutch language model (Hornik, 2015).

[7]In the case of GermaParl, which serves as a model for future releases of the other corpora, the XML data is available via a GitHub repository (see `https://github.com/PolMine/GermaParlTEI`). The indexed corpus is deposited at Zenodo (Blaette, 2020), to be deposited at a CLARIN repository at a later stage.

Structural Attribute	Description	Possible Values	Availability
date	date of utterance	YYYY-MM-DD	AT, FR, GER, NL
year	year of utterance	YYYY	AT, FR, GER, NL
speaker	speaker of utterance	full name of speaker	AT, FR, GER, NL
party	party affiliation of speaker	party of speaker	AT, FR, GER, NL
session	number of session, the utterance was held in	numeric	AT, FR, GER, NL
interjection	whether utterance is interjection or not	logical, TRUE or FALSE	AT, FR, GER, NL
role	role of the speaker	presidency / mp / government	AT, FR, GER
lp	legislative period	numeric	AT, FR, GER
agenda_item	agenda item	number of the agenda item	AT, FR, GER[†]
agenda_item_type	type of agenda item	debate / question_time / government_declaration	AT, GER[†]
id	continuous number of processed plenary protocols	numeric, starting from 1	AT, FR
parliamentary_group	parliamentary group of party	parliamentary group of speaker	FR, GER

[†] Applies to the released version of the GermaParl corpus, not the update used in the following analysis.

Table 1: Structural Attributes of Corpora

Structural attributes are named in an intuitive way. Yet the distinction between party and parliamentary group needs to be explained: The attribute *party* denotes the party affiliation of a speaker. This may be different from the parliamentary group of the speaker, as indicated by the attribute *parliamentary_group*. This distinction is particularly decisive. For instance, government actors are often members of a party, but do not necessarily adhere to a parliamentary group. It also happens that politicians from different parties or with no party affiliation join a common parliamentary group.

The annotation of interjections is another particular feature: Interjections are not part of a speech itself but are "infused'" by other participants of the debate. For example, applause during a speech would be annotated as an interjection (AustroParl: "Allgemeiner Beifall", ParisParl: "Applaudissements sur divers bancs", GermaParl: "Beifall bei der CDU/CSU und der SPD", TweedeTwee: "Applaus"), as would be laughter (AustroParl: "Allgemeine Heiterkeit", ParisParl: "Rires"), interjections by individual speakers (GermaParl: "Speaker [Parliamentary Group]: Das ist ja unglaublich!") and context information such as the closing of the session (TweedeTwee: "Sluiting 22.22 uur").

Finally, *agenda_item* and *agenda_item_type* describe the agenda item of a debate as identified in the protocol. Whereas *agenda_item* provides a running number of agenda items by protocol, *agenda_item_type* provides a categorization of the agenda item call.

At this stage, not all structural attributes are available for all corpora. TweedeTwee is sparsely annotated by comparison. This is due to the fact that we use the Dutch ParlSpeech corpus as a basis and adopt the annotation provided there (Rauh et al., 2017a). In addition, as Rauh et al. (2017a) explain, the attribute for session is not available before January 2011 and is thus identical with the date for Dutch data. Explicit information about interjections are also only available in TweedeTwee after September 2015. Furthermore, the parliamentary group is only annotated in the GermaParl and the ParisParl corpus. Yet due to the dynamics of the French party system (at least when it comes to party names), this attribute is annotated less reliably in the French corpus than in its German counterpart.

Finally, the difficulty to achieve a reliable annotation agenda items is substantial. For instance, small variations in the language used by a parliament's presidency when calling a new agenda item may cause regular expressions to fail. These limitations need to be kept in mind when working with large and diverse data that has been prepared in an automated process. Given the workflow we used, Austrian and German protocols are rather similar and easier to process than the French and Dutch data. For both AustroParl and GermaParl, documents were available digitally born for the entire period of interest. Both interjections and speakers could be detected in a reliable fashion in the text. For TweedeTwee, we addressed issues of the limited data availability (in a format we wanted to work with at least) by using data previously prepared by Rauh et al. (2017a). ParisParl presented particular challenges: Interjections were presented as very short speeches. Speakers were annotated with a variation of patterns that chal-

lenged the approach of `frappp` that is based on regular
expressions. This was addressed by adjusting the extraction pipeline to include further text formatting information to identify speaker calls and by employing a rather
large collection of external data (parliamentary data from
Wikipedia, see Blätte and Blessing (2018)) to check for
speaker mismatches. To conclude: We do acknowledge
that every new corpus preparation project has its own in-
tricacies. Still, while some data specific adjustments to
the pipeline are still required, the framework `frappp` enhanced the efficiency of the data preparation process substantially and was a prerequisite to obtain a congruent
dataset for the four countries under investigation.

3.3. Descriptive Statistics

The following descriptive statistics present essential information on the subsets of the corpora that have been used.
The period of investigation we defined covers the period between the Tampere summit in October 1999 to the elections
to the European Parliament in May 2019 (always including
the full month). The corpora cover a broader time span, yet
with variations, making the temporal standardization necessary. Once the consistency of coverage is ensured, AustroParl comprises about 62 million tokens. ParisParl has a
size of about 203 million tokens. The subset of GermaParl
examined here is 97 million tokens. Finally, TweedeTwee
comprises of about 135 million tokens. To supplement this
initial overview over the data, figure 1 reports the number
of tokens in the four corpora per year.

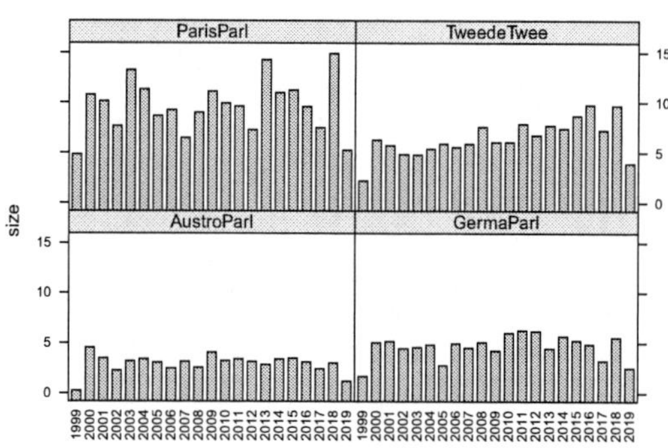

Figure 1: Corpus size per year

As presented in figure 1, there are substantial differences
among parliaments in terms of plenary productivity. This
observation is particularly true when shifting our attention
from a blunt token count to a more substantial identification of speeches. Indeed, parliamentary proceedings have
a specific logic. The notion of *speeches* in our data set is
derived from a technical definition. A "speech" is defined
as a coherent set of utterances of an individual speaker on a
single day. Since it is reasonable to assume that a speaker
can present more than one speech per day, the following
heuristic is used: If two utterances of the same speaker on
the same day are interrupted by more than 500 tokens of another speaker, these two utterances are assumed to be two
separate speeches. If they are interrupted by less than 500
tokens, they are assumed to be one speech merely inter-

rupted by interjections or organizational interventions. As
Rauh et al. (2017a) noted, the number of speeches differs
between countries due to different parliamentary settings
and understandings. This also applies to the annotation of
interjections – which differs as well (Rauh et al., 2017a).
We can confirm this statement beyond the corpora examined by Rauh.
The procedure to identify speeches results in an initial distinction of speeches that does not assume a minimum required length for considering an utterance a speech. As
illustrated by 2, a histogram of the lengths of (unfiltered)
speeches for four parliamentary corpora, there is a substantial variation of the lengths of speeches.

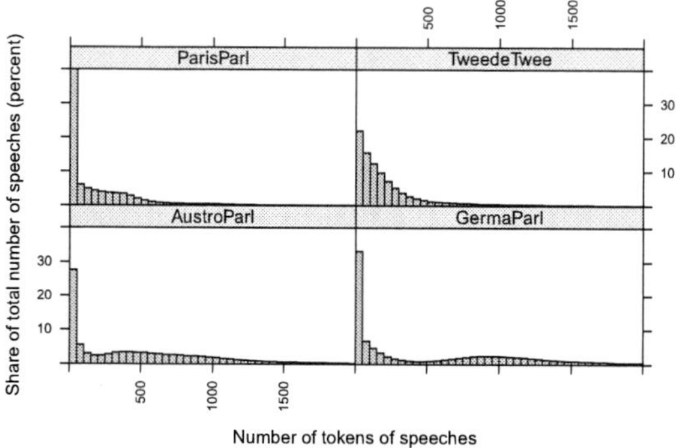

Figure 2: Length of speeches - histogram

An interesting insight conveyed by the histograms is that
the distribution of the length of speeches is very different
between Germany and Austria on the one side, and the
Netherlands and France on the other side. Differences in
parliamentary culture may explain this variation.[8] The histograms also indicate that the computational heuristic to detect speeches results in many very short contributions to
parliamentary debates. These stumps are very unlikely to
be speeches in a substantial sense. For our analysis, we
assumed that contributions of a speaker need to surmount
100 tokens to qualify as a speech. This kind of threshold
is also an appropriate requirement that the topic modeling
technique will work well.
Assuming that at least 100 words are required to make a
speech, figure 3 conveys the number of speeches given in
the Assemblée Nationale, the Tweede Kamer, the Nationalrat and the Bundestag per year. The plot conveys that
speeches are not evenly distributed across time. There is
a notable fluctuation between the years that is easily explained for the fringe years: The period of investigation
starts with the Tampere summit (October 1999) and ends
with the May 2019 European election. The number of
speeches in the initial and trailing year is unsurprisingly
curtailed. Furthermore, parliaments are subject to cyclical
fluctuations. There is a decline of the number of speeches
during election years. Notably, this is much clearer in Germany, Austria and France than in the Dutch parliament.

---

[8]Exploring these differences between the corpora is beyond
the scope this paper, but deserves further investigation.

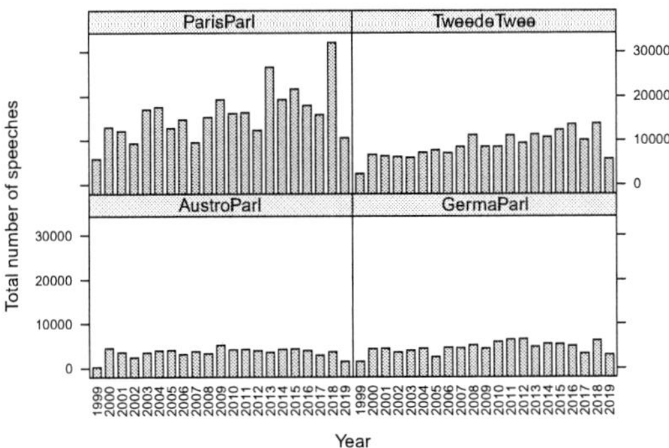

Figure 3: Number of speeches per year

To sum up core findings on speeches in the four corpora, table 2 presents the total number of speeches computationally detected, the number of speeches with at least 100 tokens and the share of speeches that are stumps (less than 100 tokens). Excluding stumps from the analysis has a mitigating effect on the number of speeches analyzed, but there is a remaining substantial variation of the extent of plenary speech-making to be considered. Speeches technically detected that are not stumps (more than 100 words) were that basis for the topic modeling described in the next section.

corpus	speeches (all)	speeches (min. 100)	stumps (per cent)
GermaParl	158 537	95 537	39.7
ParisParl	785 707	334 627	57.4
TweedeTwee	296 184	185 912	37.2
AustroParl	110 198	73 794	33.0

Table 2: Summary of core features of the corpora

4. Methodology: Measuring Europeanization Using Topic Models

We are interested in shifts in the combined attention targeting both migration and European affairs. To process a very substantive amount of data, a method classifying data in an efficient and reproducible way is needed: The parliamentary discourse during this period comprises millions of words and several hundred thousand speeches. The data-driven method of topic modeling is a useful solution. Topic models are methods for determining thematic structures in large unstructured text collections (Bock et al., 2016) which have been applied successfully to corpora of parliamentary speech in previous studies (Greene and Cross, 2017). Latent Dirichlet Allocation (LDA) is a classic procedure in topic modeling (Blei et al., 2003) and is still considered to be a state-of-the-art solution for probabilistic topic models (Rahimi et al., 2016).

The LDA makes two assumptions: First, documents consist of several topics with different weights and second, the text corpus is composed of a certain number of topics (Bock et al., 2016). An LDA model describes the probability distribution of topics over the complete corpus and indicates the share of each topic in the respective documents or speeches.

It also describes the probability that specific words belong to a specific topic. In the LDA context, the term "topic" should not be equated prematurely with what is understood as a topic or issue in a social science context. Topics, within the context of topic modeling, are latent constructs that are indicated by a collection of words that are related. The thematic definition of specific topics is performed by the researcher by giving an interpretation to the most probable words contained in a topic by assigning a label to it (Wiedemann and Niekler, 2016). In research practice, some topics are unspecific and difficult to interpret, while other topics are much clearer and easier to classify. To achieve a valid classification, a close reading of texts will usually be desirable.

Knowing which mixture of topics is present in a speech, we can make statements about the joint occurrence of migration and European affairs in a speech, and on the Europeanization of migration debates. To implement this idea, an LDA model was calculated for each corpus, which was then interpreted by the members of the MIDEM research project. The coding instructions were simple and straightforward. A reference to migration issues or to European affairs was determined based on the 50 most relevant terms of the topic. The joint interpretation of the models by the team of researchers was sought to establish intersubjectivity. A number of examples shall illustrate the topics which have been selected.

- For *GermaParl*, three topics were identified as indicative for migration (152, 181 and 210). For example, the top words for topic 152 are "Deutschland" (Germany), "Flüchtlinge" (refugees), "Menschen" (people), "Asylbewerber" (asylum seekers) and "Asyl" (asylum). Three topics were selected as indicative for a European reference (54, 71 and 179). Topic 54 is characterized by the words "Europa" (Europe), "Union" (union), "Europäischen" (European), "europäischen" (European) and "Europäische" (European).

- In the analysis of *ParisParl*, two topics indicate a reference to migration (66 and 135). The top words for topic 66 are "asile" (asylum), "immigration" (immigration), "pays" (country), "droit" ("law") and "étrangers" (foreigners). Three topics were seen to convey a reference to Europe (61, 162 and 195). Topic 61 is characterized by the words "européenne" (European), "directive" (directive), "européen" (European), "Commission" (commission) and "Union" (union).

- For *TweedeTwee*, three topics were selected for migration (187, 206 and 243). Topic 187 is described by "asielzoekers" (asylum seekers), "Nederland" (the Netherlands), "mensen" (people), "land" (country), "IND" (probably the Dutch Immigration and Naturalisation Service). Three topics entail European references (1, 24 and 160). Top words for topic 1 are "Europese" (European), "Europa" (Europe), "Unie" (union), "lidstaten" (member states) and "Europees" (European).

- Three migration topics were identified in *AustroParl* (41, 64 and 152). The top words for topic 41 are "Österreich" (Austria), "Asylbewerber" (asylum seeker), "Asyl" (asylum), "Verfahren" (procedure) and "Asylverfahren" (asylum procedure). Three topics (57, 212 and 215) indicate European references. For topic 57, top words are "Union" (union), "Europäischen" (European), "Europa" (Europe), "Europäische" (European) and "europäischen" (European).

An extensive documentation of the topics identified to pertain either to migration or European affairs is included in the Technical Annex for this paper that is available online.[9]

5. Analysis: The Europeanization of Migration Debates

The empirical strategy we pursue is to analyze co-occurrences of migration and European issues in speeches based on topic models. These co-occurrences were determined based on the five most probable topics per speech. The number of top topics considered may be chosen based on various criteria. Based on several tests, opting for the first five topics per speech was considered a suitable choice. This way we identified speeches with a migration reference (mig), speeches with a European reference (eu), and speeches with both references (mig+eu).

To generate results that are neither too rough nor too fine-grained, we aggregated the investigation period into roughly five-year periods. There is a set of reasons to be considered. First, there is the cyclical fluctuations already mentioned, i.e. the slumps of plenary activity in election years. Second, aggregation is necessary to achieve significant numbers.

For the GermaParl corpus a total of 4341 speeches with reference to migration and 6632 speeches with reference to European issues have been found. 324 of those overlap. See table 3 for a breakdown per period of interest.

mig+eu	mig	eu	rel	chi	period
63	596	1793	10.57	24.43	1999-2004
39	572	1480	6.82	1.50	2005-2009
94	1144	1910	8.22	19.49	2010-2014
128	2029	1449	6.31	5.62	2015-2019

Table 3: Topic Cooccurrences in the GermaParl corpus

While the absolute number of speeches referencing migration increases, the number of speeches referencing both migration and Europe increases less rapidly in absolute terms. Their relative share compared to all migration related speeches all in all decreases.

As can be seen in table 4 In the ParisParl corpus, there were significantly more speeches with both migration and European references. A total of 10751 speeches with reference to migration could be found compared to 20070 speeches with reference to European issues. 1123 of those overlap. Table 4 illustrates the breakdown by period of interest.

[9] https://polmine.github.io/ParlaCLARIN2020/TechnicalAnnex.html.

mig+eu	mig	eu	rel	chi	period
151	1583	4758	9.54	87.86	1999-2004
164	1829	4030	8.97	81.38	2005-2009
343	2770	5496	12.38	329.44	2010-2014
465	4569	5786	10.18	294.12	2015-2019

Table 4: Topic Cooccurrences in the ParisParl corpus

Similar to GermaParl, the absolute number of speeches concerning migration increases in ParisParl. The number of speeches referring to Europe remains relatively stable. The same applies to the relative share of speeches which are both referencing migration and Europe which, after a slight peak in the period of 2010 to 2014 almost returns to its initial value.

In the Netherlands, shown in table 5, both the migration issue and the European issue also received a considerable amount of attention. Although significantly smaller than the French or German parliaments, a total of 9162 speeches were given on migration policy. In comparison, 14789 speeches were delivered on European policy issues. The overlap between the two topics was 870. See table 5 for the description period by period. A look at the relative share shows a moderate increase from 7.50 percent in the first period under study to 12.88 percent in the fourth period.

mig+eu	mig	eu	rel	chi	period
148	1974	3025	7.50	5.48	1999-2004
161	2168	3439	7.43	3.72	2005-2009
181	2070	4034	8.74	19.31	2010-2014
380	2950	4291	12.88	206.23	2015-2019

Table 5: Topic Cooccurrences in TweedeTwee corpus

In the Dutch corpus, the number of speeches about both migration and Europe increases while the relative share of migration speeches also referencing Europe sees an uptick in the final period of investigation.

mig+eu	mig	eu	rel	chi	period
36	480	1282	7.50	6.47	1999-2004
69	770	1582	8.96	6.64	2005-2009
72	682	1488	10.56	24.92	2010-2014
303	1505	1245	20.13	508.39	2015-2019

Table 6: Topic Cooccurrences in the AustroParl corpus

The number of speeches on migration policy issues in Austria increased strongly during the period under study, while the number of speeches on European policy first increased and then decreased again. A total of 3437 migration policy and 5597 European policy speeches were found. Table 6 provides an overview over the development by period.

Resulting from a rise in the number of migration speeches and a slight decrease in the number of European policy speeches, a substantial increase of the relative frequency of Europeanized migration speeches was observed.

The development of the relative share of the number of

speeches concerned with migration which also refer to European topics compared to all migration related speeches is comparable to the TweedeTwee corpus. It is increasing steadily.

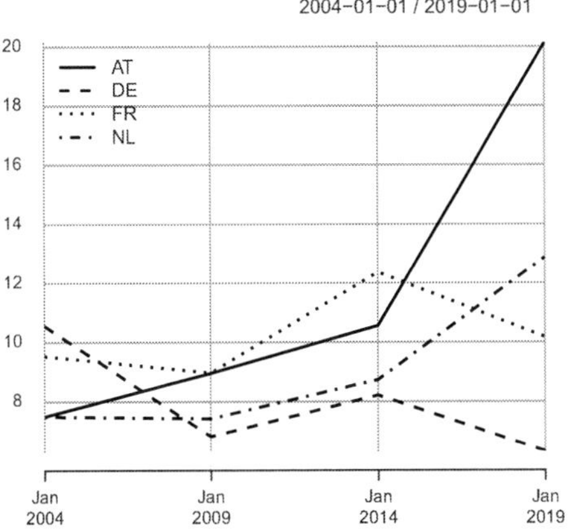

Figure 4: Shares of Europeanized Migration Speeches

The final plot 4 combines the data on the share of migration speeches that include a co-occurrence with a European reference obtained for the individual parliaments. The operationalization of Europeanization as the presence of a European reference in speeches on migration affairs shows a noteworthy trend: The four parliaments examined have witnessed a considerable absolute increase of speeches that address migration affairs. But there is a difference between debates in the national parliaments of the large and smaller EU countries. In France and Germany, the share of speeches on migration that entailed a European dimension decreased, indicating a more nation-centric and inward-looking perspective rather than a perspective that is Europeanized and takes Europe into account. The shared trend notwithstanding, France and Germany are still different: The level of Europeanization is significantly higher in France during the periods examined; the disappearance of the European point of reference is a much more a specifically German phenomenon. In juxtaposition to that, parliamentary debates in Austria and the Netherlands – two smaller EU countries – gain a stronger European orientation and get more Europeanized, as the challenges they face make the European point of view more relevant when the stakes are high.

6. Conclusion and Outlook

It is a well-founded suspicion rather than a consolidated research finding that an increasing salience of migration spurs very different trends with respect to Europeanization in small EU countries as compared to large EU countries. A next step is to validate the observed patterns and the explanatory thrust with a close reading of the speeches that have been classified as addressing migration and European affairs. Indeed, there are many ensuing questions that can be asked to understand and to give interpretative substance to our descriptive finding on the mixed trends of Europeanization of migration debates in the four parliaments

investigated. This limitation notwithstanding, we are confident that our data and our methodology yield a result that is robust at the descriptive level.

The purpose of this paper is to demonstrate that the data basis for making statements about changing attention patterns and Europeanization can be obtained with reasonable effort, and that we do have the methodology to make statements about speech-making in the longue durée. It would be very difficult to obtain the kind of results we present without large-scale corpora and efficient techniques of corpus preparation and text analysis. The preparation of corpora of parliamentary debates is a precondition for this kind of comparative research. Using enhanced procedures for preparing corpora with limited marginal costs, such as the frappp, the "Framework for Parsing Plenary Protocols", may help to bring the vast potential of text analysis to fruition.

7. Bibliographical References

Baumgartner, F. R., Breunig, C., and Grossman, E. (2019). The Comparative Agendas Project. Intellectual Roots and Current Developments. In *Comparative Policy Agendas*, pages 3–16. Oxford University Press.

Bevan, S. (2019). Gone Fishing. The Creation of the Comparative Agendas Project Master Codebook. In *Comparative Policy Agendas*, pages 17–34. Oxford University Press.

Blaette, A. (2020). Germaparl. linguistically annotated and indexed corpus of plenary protocols of the german bundestag. CWB corpus version 1.0.6.

Blätte, A. and Blessing, A. (2018). The GermaParl Corpus of Parliamentary Protocols. In Nicoletta Calzolari (Conference chair), et al., editors, *Proceedings of the Eleventh International Conference on Language Resources and Evaluation (LREC 2018)*, Miyazaki, Japan, May 7-12, 2018. European Language Resources Association (ELRA).

Blätte, A. and Leonhardt, C. (2019). The Framework For Parsing Plenary Protocols (frappp). Why parlaTEI matters. Slides presented at the ParlaFormat Workshop May 2019.

Blei, D. M., Ng, A. Y., and Jordan, M. I. (2003). Latent Dirichlet Allocation. *J. Mach. Learn. Res.*, 3:993–1022.

Bock, S., Du, K., Huber, M., Pernes, S., and Pielström, S. (2016). Der Einsatz quantitativer Textanalyse in den Geisteswissenschaften. *DARIAH-DE Working Papers*, 18, 01.

Erjavec, T. and Pančur, A. (2019). Parla-clarin: Tei guidelines for corpora of parliamentary proceedings.

Evert, S. and Hardie, A. (2011). Twenty-first century Corpus Workbench: Updating a query architecture for the new millennium.

Greene, D. and Cross, J. P. (2017). Exploring the Political Agenda of the European Parliament Using a Dynamic Topic Modeling Approach. *Political Analysis*, 25(1):77–94.

Holzinger, K., Jörgens, H., and Knill, C., (2007). *Transfer, Diffusion und Konvergenz: Konzepte und Kausalmechanismen*, pages 11–35. VS Verlag für Sozialwissenschaften, Wiesbaden.

Hornik, K., (2015). *openNLPmodels.nl: Apache OpenNLP Models for Dutch*. R package version 1.5-2.

Hornik, K., (2016). *openNLP: Apache OpenNLP Tools Interface*. R package version 0.2-6.

Kerr, C. (1983). *The Future of Industrial Societies: Convergence or Continuing Diversity?* Harvard University Press, Cambridge, Mass., 2nd edition.

King, G. (2011). Ensuring the data rich future of the social sciences. *Science*, 331(11):719–721, 2011.

Knill, C. (2005). Introduction: Cross-national policy convergence: concepts, approaches and explanatory factors. *Journal of European Public Policy*, 12(5):764–774.

Lingenberg, S., (2010). *Einleitung*, pages 13–22. VS Verlag für Sozialwissenschaften, Wiesbaden.

Manning, C. D., Surdeanu, M., Bauer, J., Finkel, J., Bethard, S. J., and McClosky, D. (2014). The Stanford CoreNLP Natural Language Processing Toolkit. In *Association for Computational Linguistics (ACL) System Demonstrations*, pages 55–60.

Messina, A. M. (2007). *The Logics and Politics of Post-WWII Migration to Western Europe*. Cambridge University Press.

Moretti, F. (2013). *Distant Reading*. Verso, London.

Nordbeck, R., (2013). *Nationale Umweltpolitik in einem internationalisierten Kontext*. Springer Fachmedien Wiesbaden, Wiesbaden.

Rahimi, M., Zahedi, M., and Mashayekhi, H. (2016). A two level probabilistic topic model. In *2016 24th Iranian Conference on Electrical Engineering (ICEE)*, pages 108–112.

Rauh, C., De Wilde, P., and Schwalbach, J. (2017a). Release note. In *The ParlSpeech data set: Annotated full-text vectors of 3.9 million plenary speeches in the key legislative chambers of seven European states*. Harvard Dataverse.

Rauh, C., De Wilde, P., and Schwalbach, J. (2017b). The ParlSpeech Data Set. Annotated Full-Text Vectors of 3.9 Million Plenary Speeches in the Key Legislative Chambers of Seven European States.

Schmid, H. (1995). Improvements in Part-of-Speech Tagging with an Application to German. In *Proceedings of the ACL SIGDAT-Workshop*.

Scholz, A., (2012). *Einleitung*. VS Verlag für Sozialwissenschaften, Wiesbaden.

Trauner, F. (2016). Wie sollen Flüchtlinge in Europa verteilt werden? Der Streit um einen Paradigmenwechsel in der EU-Asylpolitik. *integration*, 39(2):93–106.

Trenz, H.-J., (2015). *Europeanising the Public Sphere – Meaning, Mechanisms, Effects*, pages 233–251. Springer Fachmedien Wiesbaden, Wiesbaden.

Wiedemann, G. and Niekler, A. (2016). Analyse qualitativer Daten mit dem Leipzig Corpus Miner.

Wilkinson, M. D. (2016). The FAIR Guiding Principles for scientific data management and stewardship. *Scientific Data*, 3(1).

Proceedings of ParlaCLARIN II Workshop, pages 75–79
Language Resources and Evaluation Conference (LREC 2020), Marseille, 11–16 May 2020
© European Language Resources Association (ELRA), licensed under CC-BY-NC

Querying a Large Annotated Corpus of Parliamentary Debates

Sascha Diwersy, Giancarlo Luxardo
Praxiling UMR 5267 (Univ Paul Valéry Montpellier 3, CNRS)
sascha.diwersy@univ-montp3.fr, giancarlo.luxardo@univ-montp3.fr

Abstract

The TAPS corpus makes it possible to share a large volume of French parliamentary data. The TEI-compliant approach behind its design choices facilitates the publishing and the interoperability of data, but also the implementation of exploratory data analysis techniques in order to process institutional or political discourse. We demonstrate its application to the debates occurred in the context of a specific legislative process, which generated a strong opposition.

Keywords: political discourse, parliamentary corpora, metadata, cooccurrences.

1. Introduction

The present paper describes the current version of a family of parliamentary corpora called *Transcription and Annotation of Parliamentary Speech* (TAPS). A previous publication introduced the methodology adopted to set up the corpora and the basic software components (Diwersy *et al.*, 2018). After a reminder of the corpus structure and of the technologies implemented, we focus on an example of application, the debates about a proposed legislation, involving both text retrieval functionalities and the processing of the extracted lexicons through two data analysis techniques: correspondence analysis and specificity analysis.

2. Text segmentation and linguistic annotation

TAPS-fr is a corpus (or more precisely a family of corpora) allowing the access to the complete transcription of the French parliamentary debates in plenary sitting. It is compiled making use of the XML-based open data published on the Web site of the *Assemblée Nationale*, transformed through multiple steps.

The TAPS format is a compromise stemming from the use of several formats:

- the metadata extracted from the source open data (based on an undocumented model),
- the TEI guidelines for the transcription of oral corpora,
- the components of the IMS Open Corpus Workbench (CWB), and in particular the Corpus Query Processor (CQP) (cf. Evert & Hardie, 2011).

A CWB corpus is stored according to a tabular format (token-based), which encapsulates an XML mark-up. CQP tools allow to produce frequency counts coded within data tables. These tables can be processed using statistical procedures (usually in the R environment). The integration of common open source software (CWB, R) facilitates the data interchange and the experimentation with various tools. Among other tools integrating the aforementioned technologies, the TXM textometry software, developed in the French communities of digital humanities and discourse analysis, was used to process the TAPS-fr corpus. In addition, TXM provides functionalities for a Web-based publication (TEI-compliant) of the corpus, which makes possible the online access of the TAPS-fr corpus[1].

The XML encoding used for TAPS is basically the one described by the TEI <u> (utterance) element included in the module: *Transcription of speech*. In our context, the segment applied in the scope of <u> is not a single utterance, but the text portion determined by the change of speaker (the speaker's turn). A number of attributes are added to the <u> element, describing the speaker (name, party, role in the debate, etc…). The repetition of this metadata for every single speech leads to some redundancy but allows a fast text retrieval. The identification of the sitting and its date are instead found at the top level of the tree or in the TEI header (multiple sittings may occur in the same day). TEI also allows to describe paralinguistic events (incidents associated to a speech, such as noise or interruptions).

The CQP environment distinguishes two annotation levels related to the units generated by the compilation process:

- the structural units are those provided by the text tokenization (and in our case derived from the TEI encoding), they describe both the text semantics and some formatting characteristics,
- the lexical units represent the linguistic annotation and are added to each token in the text.

Two optional annotation modes have been experimented with TAPS for the linguistic annotation:

- morphosyntactic tagging and lemmatization by means of TreeTagger (lemma + part-of-speech), *cf.* (Schmid, 1994),
- syntactic analysis, with additional features, in particular related to dependency relations (the Bonsai pipeline was experimented), *cf.* (Candito *et al.* 2010a, 2010b).

In the remainder of this paper, we concentrate on the description of procedures, which can be basically implemented within the CWB and R environments, independently of higher-level tools. The TreeTagger option was chosen.

3. Use scenario

We now demonstrate some analysis techniques that can be performed on TAPS, taking as an example the debates held

---

[1] https://textometrie.univ-montp3.fr/

in the course of the review of the law named « loi Travail » or « loi El Khomri », adopted on the 8th of August 2016. The presentation of this law, which aimed to simplify the French Labor Code in order to reduce unemployment, provoked numerous popular protests in the country and the discussions in parliament, started in February 2016, entailed a split in the majority previously supporting the government. These protests, including spontaneous demonstrations (such as those known as *Nuit debout*) or strikes initiated by trade unions or student organizations, were supported by part of the left: left parties not participating in the government, but also by members (also known as *frondeurs*) of the Socialist Party, the leading majority party, as well as some ecologists (while their party, *Europe Écologie – Les Verts*, was still in the majority).

It is then interesting to question the vocabularies used by the different political parties during the related sittings. More specifically, questions relevant for a political analysis are about the cohesion of the discourses within the majority parties (socialists, radicals, ecologists) represented in the government and the possibility to find out unexpected proximities with other parties.

4.   Collocational analysis based on TAPS-fr-2

The analysis is performed against the corpus named TAPS-fr-2, covering the period April 2012 – February 2017 and totaling about 28 million occurrences of tokens. Although functionalities are available to extract a subcorpus of a smaller size (faster to process), the search is here performed over the full corpus: the resulting frequency distributions then include the occurrences of other periods of debates. The following approach is taken:

-   starting from a CQP query, a lexical table comprised of the collocates (represented as lemmas) appearing within the same utterance in the left and right co-text of the node "loi travail" or "loi El Khomry" (including possible variants)[2] is built: the list is restricted primarily to nouns, proper nouns, adjectives, adverbs and verbs;
-   various thresholds for the minimum co-frequency of the collocates are tested;
-   various statistical tests are applied to measure the significance level of each collocate with each political group (Fisher's exact test being the first choice);
-   another table "cross-tabulating" these collocates and the political groups of the speakers related to the utterances is generated (seven political groups are identified, including non-attached members), filtering

the rows according to either the test score or the minimum threshold;
-   a correspondence analysis is performed on the cross-tabulation;
-   for each party, the most characteristic collocates are provided by means of a specificity analysis.

5.   Results

The following political groups are considered:
-   Écolo: Groupe écologiste
-   GDR: Gauche démocrate et républicaine
-   NI : Non inscrits
-   RRDP :   Radical,   républicain,   démocrate   et progressiste
-   SRC_SER :   Socialiste, républicain et citoyen / Socialiste, écologistes et républicain
-   UDI : Union des démocrates et indépendants
-   UMP_LR : Union pour un Mouvement Populaire / Les Républicains[3]

The table cross-tabulating groups and lemmas is produced using a minimum threshold of 10 for the co-frequency count. It contains 5313 rows.

The application of a correspondence analysis (CA) produces results displayed by Figure-1[4], which illustrates the distance between the parties.

According to the contributions generated by the CA, the first axis shows an opposition mainly between SRC_SER (socialists) and Écolo (ecologists). On the second axis, the opposition is between GDR and Écolo.

The graphic represented by Figure-2 also shows the most contributive lemmas.

The most characteristic lemmas of each group can be highlighted by the study of the results of the CA, but also by means of the computation of frequency specificities[5]. This technique, based on the hypergeometric distribution, is described by (Lafon, 1980). The three bar plots displayed by Figure-3 show the contrasts between the various parties of the TAPS corpus based on the 10 most characteristic lemmas of the three mostly contributing groups to the CA.

The interpretation of the presence of the items associated to each political group requires some caution. Verifications of the related co-text (e.g. with a concordance function) are necessary, sometimes revealing collocations that result from recurrent formulaic expressions. The following comments may be attempted:

1.   The socialists (SRC_SER) focus on several details of the content of the law (*formation, compétence, assurance, permis[6]*) as well as the legislative procedure (*amendement, validation[7]*).

---

[2] The CQP query expression we used to identify the node is as follows (with frlemma and frpos representing the (positional) attributes lemma and PoS): [frlemma="loi" %cd] [frpos="PUN.*" %cd]? [frlemma="travail" %cd] | [frlemma="loi" %cd] []? [frlemma="relatif|relative|sur" %cd] [] [frlemma="travail" %cd] | [frlemma="loi" %cd] []? [word="el" %cd] []? [word="k.*o.*" %cd]

[3] SRC and UMP groups have changed their name during the legislature.
[4] We used the R packages *FactoMineR* (Lê et al., 2008) to compute the CA, and *explor* (Barnier, 2017) to generate the plots shown in Figures 1 and 2.
[5] We computed the specificity scores by means of the R package *textometry* (Heiden, 2010).
[6] English: training, competency, insurance (the English *assurance* would be unlikely here), permit
[7] as in English

2. The discourse of the ecologists appears related to the *Nuit debout* movement, in connection with the adoption of the law: *mouvement, contestation, précarité, démocratie, manifester, mobilisation*[8]. The presence of the word *urgence* suggests an interference with the situation of state of emergency (*état d'urgence*) declared in France after the attacks of November 2015.

3. The characteristic items of the left-wing opposition (GDR) are instead related to the social aspect of the law and its expected consequences: *temps, partiel, pauvreté, salaire*[9]. Other words are related to arguments assuming a relationship with the European treaties: *plan, traité*.

The position of the École group opposed to SRC_SER is an unexpected result, which deserves a thorough examination of the related contexts. It appears that the retrieved speakers' turns for the ecologists are only seven, related to four members of the parliament (in four different sittings), all of them critical of the law or the process to adopt it. It must also be noted that the relatively small volume of contributions associated to the ecologists is explained by the fact that the group was dissolved in May 2016, as six members decided to join the socialist group.

The results of our analysis do not highlight a specific critical trend within the socialists with respect to the government, which can be explained by the smaller number of contributions of the most critical members of the group (four of them leaving the group during the legislature). However, more detailed observations at the level of individual members of the parliament should be performed.

6. Conclusion

In this paper, we have described an application scenario of the TAPS-fr corpus involving a large volume of parliamentary data. We consider that within the analytical framework of textometry and with the common tools of the corpus linguistics area it is possible to make an effective use of the resource. Similar approaches can be adopted on different use scenarios, including those based on other variables (e.g. time or speaker status), in addition to party affiliation. While the presented scenario has the advantage to make use of a meaningful participation, in terms of volume of data and contrasted positions, it would be interesting to consider other types of scenarios, more technical and possibly more challenging for the methods here demonstrated.

While the resource is already published and openly accessible, efforts need to be undertaken in order to improve its dissemination and long-term preservation. Future developments also include new features allowing a continuous expansion of the corpus, with the latest sessions of the assembly, and possibly as well extensions to additional institutions.

7. Bibliographical References

Barnier, J. (2017). *explor: Interactive Interfaces for Results Exploration* (Version 0.3.3). Retrieved from https://CRAN.R-project.org/package=explor

Diwersy, S., Frontini, F., Luxardo, G. (2018). The Parliamentary Debates as a Resource for the Textometric Study of the French Political Discourse, in *Proceedings of ParlaCLARIN workshop, 11th edition of the Language Resources and Evaluation Conference (LREC2018)*.

Candito, M., Crabbé, B., and Denis, P. (2010a). Statistical French dependency parsing: treebank conversion and first results. In *Seventh International Conference on Language Resources and Evaluation - LREC 2010*, pages 1840–1847, La Valletta, Malta, May. European Language Resources Association (ELRA).

Candito, M., Nivre, J., Denis, P., and Henestroza Anguiano, E. (2010b). Benchmarking of Statistical Dependency Parsers for French. In *23rd International Conference on Computational Linguistics - COLING 2010*, pages 108–116, Beijing, China, August. Coling 2010 Organizing Committee.

Evert, S. and Hardie, A. (2011). Twenty-first century Corpus Workbench: Updating a query architecture for the new millennium. In *Proceedings of the Corpus Linguistics 2011 Conference*, Birmingham, Birmingham, UK.

Evert, S. (2019). *CQP Query Language Tutorial*, CWB Version 3.4.16. http://cwb.sourceforge.net/

Heiden, S. (2010). The TXM Platform: Building Open-Source Textual Analysis Software Compatible with the TEI Encoding Scheme. In K. I. Ryo Otoguro (Ed.): *24th Pacific Asia Conference on Language, Information and Computation - PACLIC24* (p. 389-398). Institute for Digital Enhancement of Cognitive Development, Waseda University, Sendai, Japan.

Lafon, P. (1980). Sur la variabilité de la fréquence des formes dans un corpus. *Mots. Les langages du politique*, 1(1):127–165.

Lavrentiev, A., Heiden, S., Decorde, M. (2013). Analyzing TEI encoded texts with the TXM platform. *The Linked TEI: Text Encoding in the Web. TEI Conference and Members Meeting 2013*, Oct 2013, Rome, Italy. halshs-01118120

Lê, S., Josse, J., & Husson, F. (2008). FactoMineR: An R Package for Multivariate Analysis. *Journal of Statistical Software*, 25(1), 1–18.

Schmid, H. (1994). Probabilistic part-of-speech tagging using decision trees. In *Proceedings of International Conference on New Methods in Language Processing*, Manchester, UK.

---

[8] English: movement, contestation, precarity, democracy, protest, rallying

[9] part, time, poverty, salary

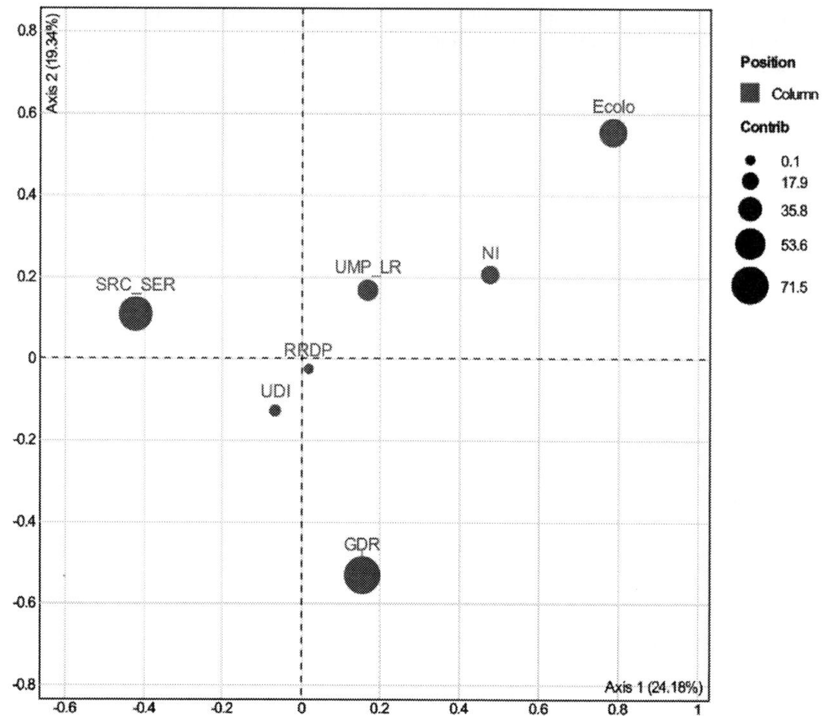

Figure 2- CA (rows hidden)

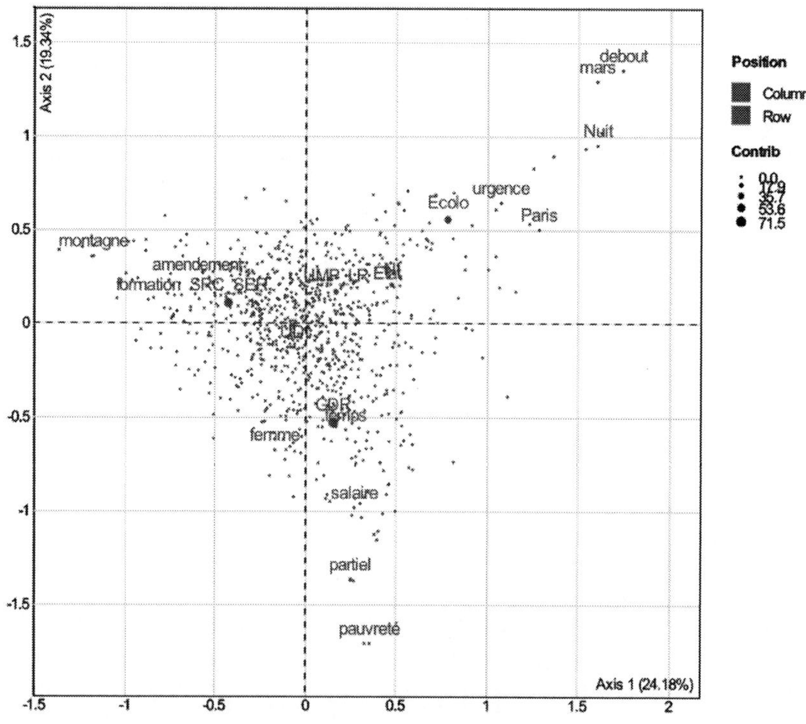

Figure 1 - CA (displaying most contributive rows)

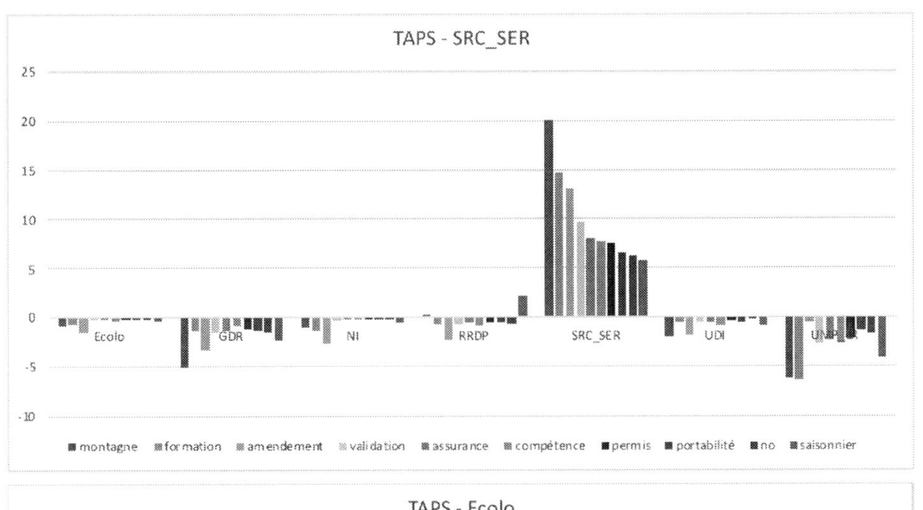

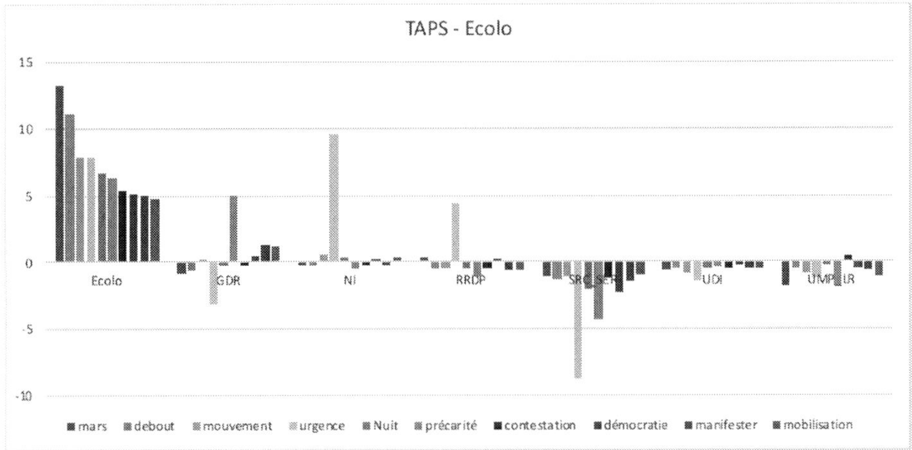

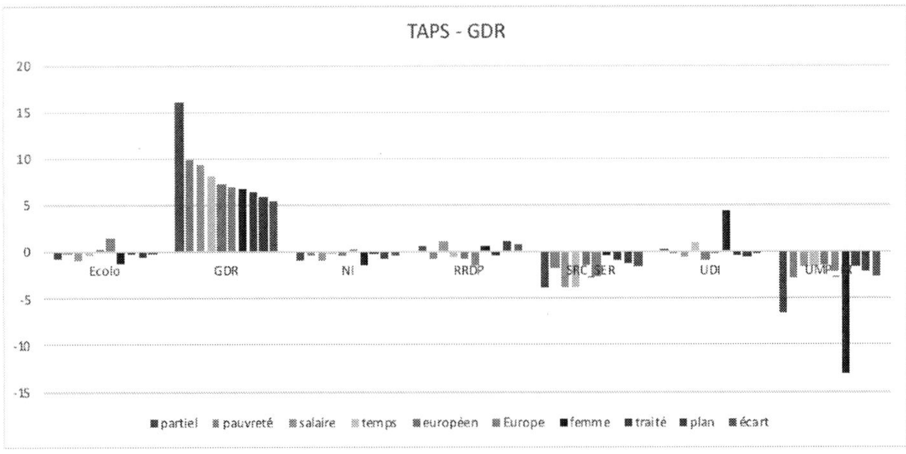

Figure 3 - Specificity analysis for three groups